THE CAMBRIDGE COMPANIC
ALFRED HITCHCOCK

Alfred Hitchcock was, despite his English origins and early career, an American master. Arriving on U.S. shores in 1939, over the next three decades he created a series of masterpieces that redefined the nature and possibilities of cinema itself: *Rebecca, Notorious, Strangers on a Train, Rear Window, Vertigo*, and *Psycho*, to name just a few. In this *Companion*, leading film scholars and critics of American culture and imagination trace Hitchcock's interplay with the Hollywood studio system, the Cold War, and new forms of sexuality, gender, and desire through his American career. This *Companion* explores the way in which Hitchcock was transformed by the country where he made his home and did much of his greatest work. This book is invaluable as a guide for fans and students of Hitchcock and twentieth-century American culture, providing a set of new perspectives on a much-loved and hugely influential director.

Jonathan Freedman is Marvin Felheim Collegiate Professor of English, American, and Jewish Studies at the University of Michigan. His monographs include *Professions of Taste: Henry James, British Aestheticism, and Commodity Culture*; *The Temple of Culture: Assimilation and Anti-Semitism in Literary Anglo-America*; and *Klezmer America: Jewishness, Ethnicity, Modernity*. Freedman has also coedited, with Richard Millington, *Hitchcock's America* as well as anthologies of criticism on Henry James and Oscar Wilde. He has held fellowships from the Guggenheim Foundation and the National Humanities Center.

THE CAMBRIDGE
COMPANION TO

AMERICAN STUDIES

This series of Companions to key figures in American history and culture is aimed at students of American studies, history, and literature. Each volume features newly commissioned essays by experts in the field, with a chronology and guide to further reading.

VOLUMES PUBLISHED

The Cambridge Companion to Frederick Douglass edited by Maurice Lee
The Cambridge Companion to Bob Dylan edited by Kevin Dettmar
The Cambridge Companion to W. E. B. Du Bois edited by Shamoon Zamir
The Cambridge Companion to Benjamin Franklin edited by Carla Mulford
The Cambridge Companion to Thomas Jefferson edited by Frank Shuffelton
The Cambridge Companion to Malcolm X edited by Robert Terrill
The Cambridge Companion to Abraham Lincoln edited by Shirley Samuels
The Cambridge Companion to John F. Kennedy edited by Andrew Hoberek

THE CAMBRIDGE
COMPANION TO

ALFRED
HITCHCOCK

EDITED BY
JONATHAN FREEDMAN
University of Michigan

CAMBRIDGE
UNIVERSITY PRESS

CAMBRIDGE
UNIVERSITY PRESS

32 Avenue of the Americas, New York, NY 10013-2473, USA

Cambridge University Press is part of the University of Cambridge.

It furthers the University's mission by disseminating knowledge in the pursuit of
education, learning, and research at the highest international levels of excellence.

www.cambridge.org
Information on this title: www.cambridge.org/9781107514881

First published 2015

Printed in the United States of America

A catalog record for this publication is available from the British Library.

Library of Congress Cataloging in Publication Data
The Cambridge companion to Alfred Hitchcock / [Edited by] Jonathan Freedman,
University of Michigan.
pages   cm. – (Cambridge companions to American studies)
Includes bibliographical references.
ISBN 978-1-107-10757-1 (hbk.) – ISBN 978-1-107-51488-1 (pbk.)
1. Hitchcock, Alfred, 1899–1980 – Criticism and interpretation.
I. Freedman, Jonathan, 1954– editor.
PN1998.3.H58C35   2015
791.4302′33092–dc23   2014047365

ISBN 978-1-107-10757-1 Hardback
ISBN 978-1-107-51488-1 Paperback

CONTENTS

ILLUSTRATIONS

NOTES ON CONTRIBUTORS

SARA BLAIR is Professor of English at the University of Michigan, where she teaches modernist literature and visual cultures. She is the author of *Henry James and the Writing of Race and Nation* (Cambridge University Press, 1995); *Harlem Crossroads: Black Writers and the Photograph in the Twentieth Century* (Princeton University Press, 2007); and, with Eric Rosenberg, *Trauma and Documentary: Photography and the FSA* (University of California Press, 2012).

CARL FREEDMAN is the Russell B. Long Professor of English and a Distinguished Research Master at Louisiana State University. He has published many books and articles, most recently *The Age of Nixon* (Zero Books, 2012); *Versions of Hollywood Crime Cinema: Studies in Ford, Wilder, Coppola, Scorsese, and Others* (Intellect, 2013); and *Art and Idea in the Novels of China Miéville* (Gylphi, 2015).

JONATHAN FREEDMAN is the Marvin Felheim Professor of English, American, and Jewish Studies at the University of Michigan. He has written *Professions of Taste: Henry James, British Aestheticism and Commodity Culture* (Stanford University Press, 1991); *The Temple of Culture: Assimilation, Aggression and the Literary Anglo-America* (Oxford University Press, 1998); and *Klezmer America: Ethnicity, Identity, Modernity* (Columbia University Press, 2008). He also coedited, with Richard Millington, *Hitchcock's America* (Oxford University Press, 1999).

MARK GOBLE is Associate Professor of English at the University of California, Berkeley. He is the author of *Beautiful Circuits: Modernism and the Mediated Life* (Columbia University Press, 2010) and has published essays in such journals as *American Literature*, *Modern Fiction Studies*, *ELH*, *MLQ*, and *ELN*, as well as in collections on Alfred Hitchcock, Henry James, and global modernism.

DAVID GREVEN is Professor of English at the University of South Carolina. Greven specializes in both nineteenth-century American literature and Hollywood film. His books include *Gender Protest and Same-Sex Desire in Antebellum*

American Literature (Ashgate, 2014); *Psycho-Sexual: Male Desire in Hitchcock, De Palma, Scorsese, and Friedkin* (The University of Texas Press, 2013); *The Fragility of Manhood: Hawthorne, Freud, and the Politics of Gender* (The Ohio State University Press, 2012); *Representations of Femininity in American Genre Cinema: The Woman's Film, Film Noir, and Modern Horror* (Palgrave Macmillan, 2011); *Manhood in Hollywood from Bush to Bush* (The University of Texas Press, 2009); and *Men Beyond Desire: Manhood, Sex, and Violation in American Literature* (Palgrave Macmillan, 2005).

ALAN NADEL is the William T. Bryan Professor at the University of Kentucky. He has authored four books: *Television in Black-and-White America: Race and National Identity* (University Press of Kansas, 2005); *Flatlining on the Field of Dreams: Cultural Narratives in the Films of President Reagan's America* (Rutgers University Press, 1997); *Containment Culture: American Narrative, Postmodernism, and the Atomic Age* (Duke University Press, 1995); and *Invisible Criticism: Ralph Ellison and the American Canon* (University of Iowa Press, 1988). He is the editor of three books: *The Men Who Knew Too Much: Alfred Hitchcock and Henry James*, coedited with Susan Griffin (Oxford University Press, 2011); *August Wilson: Completing the Twentieth-Century Cycle* (University of Iowa Press, 2010); and *May All Your Fences Have Gates: Essays on the Drama of August Wilson* (University of Iowa Press, 1994).

HOMER B. PETTEY is Associate Professor of Literature and Film at the University of Arizona. Along with R. Barton Palmer, he has coedited *Film Noir* and *International Noir* for Edinburgh University Press. Currently, he is coediting *Hitchcock and Moral Philosophy* for SUNY Press. He is also coediting two other volumes, *Classical French Literature on Screen* and *Biopics and British National Identity*.

BRIGITTE PEUCKER is the Elias Leavenworth Professor of German and Professor of Film Studies at Yale University. She is the author of *Arcadia to Elysium* (Bouvier, 1980); *Lyric Descent in the German Romantic Tradition* (Yale University Press, 1987); *Incorporating Images: Film and the Rival Arts* (Princeton University Press, 1985); and *The Material Image; Art and the Real in Film* (Stanford University Press, 2007). She is also the editor of the *Blackwell's Companion to Rainer Werner Fassbinder* (Wiley-Blackwell, 2012).

MURRAY POMERANCE is Professor in the Department of Sociology and Director of the Media Studies Working Group at Ryerson University. He is the author of *Marnie* (BFI, 2014); *The Economist* (Oberon, 2014); *The Eyes Have It: Cinema and the Reality Effect* (Rutgers University Press, 2013); *Alfred Hitchcock's America* (Polity, 2013); *Tomorrow* (Oberon, 2012); *Michelangelo Red Antonioni Blue: Eight Reflections on Cinema* (University of California Press, 2011); *Edith Valmaine* (Oberon, 2010); *The Horse Who Drank the Sky: Film Experience Beyond Narrative and Theory* (Rutgers University Press, 2008); *Johnny Depp Starts Here*

(Rutgers University Press, 2005); *An Eye for Hitchcock* (Rutgers University Press, 2004); *Savage Time* (Oberon 2005); and *Magia D'Amore* (Sun and Moon, 1999).

THOMAS SCHATZ is Professor in the Department of Radio-Film-Television in the School of Communications at the University of Texas, Austin. His books include *Hollywood Genres: Formulas, Filmmaking, and the Studio System* (McGraw-Hill, 1981); *The Genius of the System: Hollywood Filmmaking in the Studio Era* (Pantheon, 1989); and *Boom and Bust: American Cinema in the 1990s* (University of California Press, 1999).

JANET STAIGER is the William P. Hobby Centennial Professor of Communication and Professor of Women's and Gender Studies at the University of Texas, Austin. She is the author of numerous books and articles on film and media, including *Media Reception Studies* (New York University Press, 2005); *Perverse Spectators: The Practices of Film Reception* (New York University Press, 2000); *Bad Women: Regulating Sexuality in Early American Cinema* (University of Minnesota Press, 1995); *Interpreting Films: Studies in the Historical Reception of American Cinema* (Princeton University Press, 1992); and, coauthored with David Bordwell and Kristin Thompson, *The Classical Hollywood Cinema: Film Style and Mode of Production to 1960* (Routledge & Kegan Paul/Columbia University Press, 1985).

STEPHEN TIFFT is Professor of English at Williams College, where he teaches modernist literature, film, and a variety of courses examining the intersection of aesthetic and political theory. He has written on Jarry, Eisenstein, Joyce, Synge, Renoir, Lubitsch, and others.

SUSAN WHITE is Professor of Film and Comparative Literature in the English Department at the University of Arizona. She has also taught at the University of Michigan and the Sorbonne. She is the author of numerous articles on film and *The Cinema of Max Ophüls: Magisterial Vision and the Figure of Woman* (Columbia University Press, 1995).

ACKNOWLEDGMENTS

I would like to thank Ray Ryan, for proposing this *Companion*; Caitlin Gallagher, for patiently shepherding it through the pre-production process; and Aran Ruth, for working long and hard to help produce the manuscript in manageable form. Thanks are due too to the amazing Sara Blair, for aid, comfort, and support, and to Ben and Miriam Freedman, for making it worthwhile and keeping it real.

CHRONOLOGY

For a complete list of Hitchcock's American films, plus availability on DVD and Blu-ray, see the Filmography.

1899 Born, just outside of London, to William and Emma Hitchcock, a prosperous greengrocer's family; Roman Catholic in Anglican England.

1920–1925 After working for Henley Telegraph and Cable by day and taking art courses by night, Hitchcock moves to the advertising department and then lands a job with Famous Players-Lasky (Paramount), designing titles. He rapidly learns the new craft of moviemaking. Lasky bought by Gainsborough Films, and Hitchcock continues his process of self-education there.

1921 Becomes engaged to Alma Reville, a film editor. They marry in 1926.

1925 Hitchcock loaned to the UFA studio in Berlin, where he sees firsthand the techniques of German expressionist filmmaking.

1926 Having directed two inconsequential films, *The Pleasure Garden* (1926) and *The Mountain Eagle* (1927), Hitchcock teams with star Ivor Novello to make *The Lodger*, which premieres to great acclaim the following year.

1927–1934 Hitchcock works in a number of different genres, including an adaptation of Sean O'Casey's *Juno and the Paycock* (1930), followed by a turn back to the thriller/mystery/suspense film with *The Man Who Knew Too Much* (1934).

1935–1938 Hitchcock masters this form with *The 39 Steps* (1935), followed in rapid succession by a number of others – *Secret*

Agent (1936), *Sabotage* (1936), *Young and Innocent* (1937), and climaxing with *The Lady Vanishes* (1938).

1939   The Hitchcocks move to the United States; Alfred works with David O. Selznick on *Rebecca*.

1940   *Rebecca* released; wins an Academy Award for Best Film of 1940. Hitchcock nominated for an Oscar as Best Director but does not win.

1940–1946   Working largely but not exclusively with Selznick, Hitchcock turns largely to the thriller genre – *Foreign Correspondent* (1940), *Suspicion* (1941), *Saboteur* (1942), *Spellbound* (1945), and, most gloriously, *Notorious* (1946).

1948–1953   After completing his last film for Selznick, *The Paradine Case* (1947), Hitchcock works with friend Sidney Bernstein in an independent production company, emerging with *Rope* (1948) and *Under Capricorn* (1949). Neither is a box office success. He moves to Warner Brothers, for whom he makes one of his most memorable American films, *Strangers on a Train* (1951), as well as *I Confess* (1952) and *Dial M for Murder* (1954).

1954–1960   Working variously at Universal, Paramount, and Warner Brothers, and almost always serving as his own producer, Hitchcock enters his major phase of undeniable masterpieces: *Rear Window* (1954), *Vertigo* (1958), *North by Northwest* (1959), and *Psycho* (1960). *Psycho* had to be produced by Hitchcock's own production company, Shamley Productions, because Paramount refused to be associated directly with such shocking material, although it distributed the film. There are a number of lesser-valued but still estimable films from this period as well: *To Catch a Thief* (1955), *The Trouble with Harry* (1955), the remake of *The Man Who Knew Too Much* (1956), and *The Wrong Man* (1956).

1955–1965   Hosts *Alfred Hitchcock Presents* on television; directs 20 (out of roughly 360) episodes.

1963–1969   At Universal. *The Birds* (1963) and *Marnie* (1964) – quirky and troubling investigations of themes of arbitrary terror and mental extremity – date to this period. Followed by *Torn Curtain* (1966) and *Topaz* (1969), generally considered to be among Hitchcock's weakest films (although some critics have made a case for each).

1968   Hitchcock is awarded the Irving Thalberg Award by the Academy of Motion Picture Arts and Sciences – still never to win an Oscar as Best Director.

1972   Hitchcock returns to England to shoot *Frenzy*.

1976   *Family Plot*, his last film.

1980   After receiving the last rites, Hitchcock dies on April 29. He is survived by Alma, who dies two years later, and his daughter Patricia, an actress (who appeared in three of his films, most memorably *Strangers on a Train*).

GUIDE TO FURTHER READING

Included here are many of the major critical responses to, and accounts of, Hitchcock's Hollywood films, his engagement with America, and other aspects of the forty-odd years he spent in the United States. Several of the DVDs included in the filmography contain excellent critical commentary and contextualization as well. These are marked with an *.

Biography

Hitchcock, Pat, and Laurent Bouzereau. *Alma Hitchcock: The Woman Behind the Man*. New York: Berkley Books, 2003.

McGilligan, Patrick. *Alfred Hitchcock: A Life in Darkness and Light*. New York: Regan Books/HarperCollins, 2003.

Spoto, Donald. *The Dark Side of Genius: The Life of Alfred Hitchcock*. Boston: Little, Brown and Company, 1983.

Critical Studies

Allen, Richard. *Hitchcock's Romantic Irony*. New York: Columbia University Press, 2007.

Allen, Richard and Ishii-González, Sam. *Alfred Hitchcock: Centenary Essays*. London: British Film Institute, 1999.

Hitchcock: Past and Future. New York: Routledge, 2004.

Aulier, Dan. Vertigo: *The Making of a Hitchcock Classic*. New York: St. Martin's Press, 1998.

Belton, John. *Alfred Hitchcock's* Rear Window. Cambridge: Cambridge University Press, 2000.

Borden, Diane. "Travelogue as Traumalogue: Space, Place and Memory in Vertigo. In Cunningham, *The San Francisco of Hitchcock's Vertigo"*: *Place, Pilgrimage, and Commemoration*. Lanham, Md: The Scarecrow Press, 2011, 153–176.

Boyd, David and R. Burton Palmer. *After Hitchcock: Influence, Imitation, Intertextuality*. Austin: University of Texas Press, 2006.

Brand, Dana. "Rear-View Mirror: Hitchcock, Poe, and the Flaneur in America." In Jonathan Freedman and Richard Millington, eds., *Hitchcock's America*. Oxford and New York: Oxford University Press, 1999, 123–134.

Brill, Lesley. *The Hitchcock Romance: Love and Irony in Hitchcock's Films.* Princeton, NJ: Princeton University Press, 1991.

Cavell, Stanley. "*North by Northwest,*" *Critical Inquiry* 7:4 (Summer 1981), 761–776.

Cunningham, Doug, ed. *The San Francisco of Hitchcock's* Vertigo: *Place, Pilgramage, and Commemoration.* Lanham, Md: The Scarecrow Press, 2011.

Curtis, Scott. "The Making of *Rear Window.*" In John Belton, ed., *Alfred Hitchcock's Rear Window.* New York: Cambridge University Press, 1999, 21–56.

DeRosa, Stephen L. *Writing with Hitchcock: The Collaboration of Alfred Hitchcock and John Michael Hayes.* New York: Faber and Faber, 2001.

Deutelbaum, Marshall and Leland Poague. *A Hitchcock Reader.* London: Wiley-Blackwell, 2009.

Doane, Mary Ann. "Female Spectatorship and the Machines of Projection: *Caught* and *Rebecca.*" In Doane, *The Desire to Desire: The Woman's Film of the 1940s.* Bloomington: Indiana University Press, 1987.

Durgnat, Raymond. *A Long Hard Look At* 'Psycho'. London: BFI, 2002.

    The Strange Case of Alfred Hitchcock, or the Plain Man's Hitchcock. Cambridge, MA: MIT Press, 1974.

Edelman, Lee. "*Rear Window*'s Glasshole." In Ellis Hanson, ed., *Out Takes: Essays on Queer Theory and Film.* Durham, NC: Duke University Press, 1999, 72–96.

Fawell, John. *Hitchcock's* Rear Window: *The Well-Made Film.* Carbondale: Southern Illinois University Press, 2001.

Foery, Raymond. *Alfred Hitchcock's* Frenzy – *The Last Masterpiece.* Lanham, MD: Scarecrow Press, 2012.

Freedman, Jonathan, "From *Spellbound* to *Vertigo*: Alfred Hitchcock and Therapeutic Culture in America." In Jonathan Freedman and Richard Millington, eds., *Hitchcock's America.* Oxford and New York: Oxford University Press, 1999. 77–98.

    eds. *Hitchcock's America.* Oxford and New York: Oxford University Press, 1999.

Freeman, David and Alfred Hitchcock. *The Last Days of Alfred Hitchcock: A Memoir Featuring the Screenplay of "Alfred Hitchcock's* The short night." Woodstock, NY: Overlook Press, 1999.

GoGwilt, Christopher Lloyd. *The Fiction of Geopolitics: Afterimages of Culture: From Wilkie Collins to Alfred Hitchcock.* Stanford, CA: Stanford University Press, 2000.

Gordon, Paul. *Dial "M" for Mother: A Freudian Hitchcock.* Madison, NJ: Fairleigh Dickinson University Press, 2008.

    Framing Hitchcock: Selected Essays From the Hitchcock Annual. Detroit, MI: Wayne State University Press, 2002.

Gordon, Paul, Susan Griffin, and Alan Nadel. *The Men Who Knew Too Much: Henry James and Alfred Hitchcock.* Oxford and New York: Oxford University Press, 2012.

Jacobowitz, Florence. "Hitchcock and Feminist Theory from *Rebecca* to *Marnie.*" In Thomas Leitch and Leland Poague, eds., *A Companion to Alfred Hitchcock.* Malden: Wiley-Blackwell, 2011, 452–471.

Jameson, Fredric. "Allegorizing Hitchcock." In *Signatures of the Visible.* New York: Routledge, 1993, 99–127.

"Spatial Systems in *North by Northwest*." In Slavoj Žižek, ed., *Everything You Always Wanted to Know About Lacan (But Were Afraid to Ask Hitchcock)*. London: Verso, 2010, 47–72.

Kapsis, Robert. *Hitchcock: The Making of a Reputation*. Chicago: University of Chicago Press, 1992.

Kolker, Robert Phillip. *Alfred Hitchcock's* Psycho: *A Casebook*. New York: Oxford University Press, 2004.

Leff, Leonard. *Hitchcock & Selznick: The Rich and Strange Collaboration of Alfred Hitchcock and David O. Selznick in Hollywood*. New York: Weidenfeld & Nicolson, 1987.

Leigh, Janet and Christopher Nickens. Psycho: *Behind the Scenes of the Classic Thriller*. New York: Crown, 1995.

Leitch, Thomas. *Find the Director and Other Hitchcock Games*. Athens: University of Georgia Press, 1991.

Leitch, Thomas and Leland Poague, eds. *A Companion to Alfred Hitchcock*. Malden, MA: Wiley-Blackwell, 2011.

Miller, D. A. "Anal *Rope*"(1990). In Diana Fuss, ed., *Inside/Out: Lesbian Theories, Gay Theories*. New York: Routledge, 1991.

"Hitchcock's Hidden Pictures." *Critical Inquiry* 37.1 (Autumn 2010), 106–130.

Modleski, Tania. *The Women Who Knew Too Much: Hitchcock and Feminist Theory*. New York: Routledge, 1988, 2005.

Moral, Tony Lee. *Hitchcock and the Making of* Marnie. Revised edition. Lanham, MD: Scarecrow Press, 2013.

The Making of Hitchcock's The Birds. Harpenden, UK: Oldcastle Books, 2013.

Mulvey, Laura. "Alfred Hitchcock's *Psycho* (1960)." *Death 24x a Second: Stillness and the Moving Image*. London: Reaktion Books, 2006, 84–103.

"Visual Pleasure and Narrative Cinema." In Mulvey, *Visual and Other Pleasures*. Bloomington: Indiana University Press, 1989, 14–30.

Orr, John. *Hitchcock and Twentieth-Century Cinema*. London: Wallflower, 2005.

Païni, Dominique. *Hitchcock and Art: Fatal Coincidences*. Montreal: The Montreal Museum of Fine Arts, 2000.

Pomerance, Murray. *Alfred Hitchcock's America*. London: Polity Press, 2013.

An Eye for Hitchcock. New Brunswick, NJ: Rutgers University Press, 2004.

Marnie. BFI Film Classics. London: British Film Institute, 2014.

Rebello, Stephen. *Alfred Hitchcock and the Making of "Psycho."* New York: St Martin' s Press, 1998.

Rohmer, Eric and Claude Chabrol. *Hitchcock: The First Forty-four Films*. Trans. Stanley Hochman. New York: Frederick Ungar, 1979.

Rothman, William. *Hitchcock: The Murderous Gaze*. Second ed. Albany: SUNY Press, 2012.

Must We Kill the Thing We Love? Emersonian Perfectionism and the Films of Alfred Hitchcock. New York: Columbia University Press, 2014.

"Scottie's Dream, Judy's Plan, Madeleine's Revenge." In Katalin Makkai, ed. *Vertigo (Philosophers on Film)*. New York: Routledge, 2013, 45–70.

Sarris, Andrew. *The American Cinema: Directors and Directions, 1929–1968*. New York: DaCapo, 1996.

Silverman, Kaja. *The Acoustic Mirror: The Female Voice in Psychoanalysis and Cinema*. Bloomington: Indiana University Press, 1988.

Smith, Joseph W. *The* Psycho *File: A Comprehensive Guide to Hitchcock's Classic Shocker*. Jefferson, NC: McFarland & Co., 2009.

Spoto, Donald. *The Art of Alfred Hitchcock: Fifty Years of His Motion Pictures*. New York: Anchor, 1991.

Spellbound By Beauty: Alfred Hitchcock and His Leading Ladies. New York: Three Rivers Press, 2009.

Strauss, Marc. *Hitchcock Nonetheless: The Master's Touch in His Least-Celebrated Films*. Jefferson, NC: McFarland & Co., 2007.

Thomson, David. *The Moment of Psycho: How Alfred Hitchcock Taught America to Love Murder*. New York: Basic Books, 2009.

Walker, Michael. *Hitchcock's Motifs*. Amsterdam: Amsterdam University Press, 2005.

White, Patricia. "Hitchcock and Hom(m)osexuality." In Richard Allen and Sam Ishii-Gonzalès, *Hitchcock: Past and Future*. New York: Routledge, 2004, 211–228.

Williams, Linda. "Discipline and Fun: *Psycho* and Postmodern Cinema." In Robert Phillip Kolker, ed. Alfred Hitchcock's Psycho: *A Casebook*. Oxford and New York: Oxford University Press, 2004, 164–204.

Wood, Robin. *Hitchcock's Films Revisited*. Rev. ed. New York: Columbia University Press, 2002.

Žižek, Slavoj, ed. *Everything You Always Wanted to Know About Lacan (But Were Afraid to Ask Hitchcock)*. London: Verso, 2010.

Interviews, Conversations

Alfred Hitchcock interview. BBC, 1956. https://www.youtube.com/watch?v=7dRcRUNfxPM. Consulted July 15, 2014.

Alfred Hitchcock – Masters of Cinema. 1972. https://www.youtube.com/watch?v=umfiwI-7IoM. Consulted July 15, 2014.

Bogdanovich, Peter. Peter Bogdanovich Interviews Alfred Hitchcock, 1963. http://zakka.dk/euroscreenwriters/interviews/alfred_hitchcock.htm. Consulted July 15, 2014.

Gottlieb, Sidney. *Alfred Hitchcock: Interviews*. Jackson: University Press of Mississippi, 2003.

Hitchcock Interviewed by Robert Robinson. Picture Parade, BBC. 1960. https://www.youtube.com/watch?v=FDmpJq912fI. Consulted July 15, 2014.

Truffaut, François and Helen G. Scott. *Hitchcock*. New York: Simon and Schuster, 1985.

Rebecca. 1940. Selznick International Pictures. Producer: David O. Selznick. Starring: Joan Fontaine, Laurence Olivier, George Sanders. Screenplay: Robert Sherwood and Joan Harrison, from the novel by Daphne Du Maurier. Nominated for eleven Academy Awards; won for Best Picture (Hitchcock's only such award). DVD: MGM Home Entertainment, 2008; also in MGM, Alfred Hitchcock Premiere Collection;* Blu-ray: MGM Home Entertainment, 2012.

Foreign Correspondent. 1940. Walter Wanger Productions. Producer: Walter Wanger. Starring: Joel McCrae, Laraine Day, Herbert Marshall. Screenplay: Charles Bennett and Joan Harrison. Dialogue by James Hilton and Robert Benchley. Nominated for six Academy Awards, including Best Picture. Blu-ray/DVD: Criterion, 2014.*

Mr. and Mrs. Smith. 1941. RKO/Radio Pictures. Producer: Harry Edington. Starring: Carole Lombard, Robert Montgomery. Screenplay: Norman Krasna. DVD: Warner Home Video, 2004.

Suspicion. 1941. RKO/Radio Pictures. Producer: Harry Edington. Starring: Cary Grant, Joan Fontaine, Cedric Hardwicke, Nigel Bruce, Dame Edith Whittey. Screenplay: Samuel Raphaelson, Joan Harrison, and Alma Reville. Nominated for four Academy Awards; Joan Fontaine won for Best Actress. DVD: Warner Home Video, 2004.

Saboteur. 1942. Universal Pictures/Frank Lloyd Productions. Producer: Frank Lloyd. Starring: Robert Cummings, Priscilla Lane, Otto Kruger. Screenplay: Peter Viertel, Dorothy Parker, and Alfred Hitchcock. DVD: Universal, 2006. Blu-ray: Universal, 2012.

Shadow of a Doubt. 1943. Universal Pictures/Skirball Productions. Producer: Jack Skirball. Starring: Joseph Cotton, Teresa Wright. Original Story: Gordon McDonnell. Screenplay: Thornton Wilder, Sally Benson, and

Alma Reville. Nominated for one Academy Award. DVD: Universal, 2005. Blu-ray: Universal, 2012, in *Alfred Hitchcock: The Masterpiece Collection.**

Lifeboat. 1944. 20th Century Fox. Producer: Kenneth Macgowan. Starring: Tallulah Bankhead, William Bendix, Walter Slezak, Mary Anderson. Story by John Steinbeck. Screenplay: Jo Swerling. Nominated for three Academy Awards, including Best Picture. DVD: MGM: *Alfred Hitchcock Premiere Collection,** 2008.

Spellbound. 1945. Selznick International Pictures/Vanguard Pictures. Producer: David O. Selznick. Starring: Ingrid Bergman, Gregory Peck, Leo G. Carroll. Screenplay: Ben Hecht, from *The House of Dr. Edwardes* by "Francis Breeding" (John Palmer and Hilary St. George Saunders). Dream sequence designed by Salvador Dali. Special consultant on matters psychoanalytic: May Romm. Nominated for eight Academy Awards. DVD: MGM Home Entertainment (stand-alone and in *Premiere Collection*), 2008.* Blu-ray: MGM Home Entertainment, 2012.*

Notorious. 1946. RKO/Vanguard Pictures. Producers: David Selznick, Alfred Hitchcock. Starring: Cary Grant, Ingrid Bergman, Claude Rains, Leopoldine Konstantin. Screenplay: Ben Hecht and Alfred Hitchcock. Nominated for two Academy Awards. DVD: MGM Home Entertainment (stand-alone and in *Premiere Collection*), 2008;* Blu-ray: MGM, 2012.*

The Paradine Case. 1947. Selznick International/Vanguard Pictures. Producer: David O. Selznick. Starring: Gregory Peck, Anne Todd, Charles Laughton, Ethel Barrymore. Screenplay: James Bridie, Ben Hecht, and Alma Reville. DVD: MGM *Premiere Collection, 2008.**

Rope. 1948. Warner Brothers Films/Transatlantic Pictures. Producer: Alfred Hitchcock. Starring: James Stewart, John Dahl, Farley Granger. Screenplay: Hume Cronyn and Arthur Laurents. DVD: Warner Brothers, 2006. Blu-ray: Universal, *Alfred Hitchcock, the Masterpiece Collection*, 2012.

Under Capricorn. 1949. Transatlantic Pictures/Warner Brothers. Starring Michael Wilding, Ingrid Bergman, Joseph Cotten. Screenplay: James Bridie, from the novel by Helen deGuerrie Simpson. DVD: Stand-alone not available; in *The Ultimate Hitchcock Collection.*

Stage Fright.** 1950. Producer: Alfred Hitchcock. Starring Jane Wyman, Richard Todd, Marlene Dietrich, Alastair Sim. Screenplay: Whitfield Cook, Ranald MacDougal, and Alma Reville, from a story by Selwyn Johnson. DVD: Warner Brothers, 2004 (n/a); in *Alfred Hitchcock: The Signature Collection.*

Strangers on a Train. 1951. Warner Brothers. Producer: Alfred Hitchcock. Starring: Farley Granger, Robert Walker, Ruth Roman, Leo G. Carroll.

Screenplay: Raymond Chandler, Whitfield Cook, Czenzi Ormonde, and Ben Hecht, from the novel by Patricia Highsmith. One Academy Award nomination (Best Cinematography). DVD: Warner Brothers 2004. Blu-ray: Warner Brothers, 2012.

I Confess. 1953. Warner Brothers. Producer: Alfred Hitchcock. Starring: Montgomery Clift, Karl Malden, Anne Baxter. Screenplay: George Tabori and William Archibald from a play by Paul Anthelme. DVD: Warner Home Video, 2004.

Dial M For Murder. 1954. Warner Brothers. Producer: Alfred Hitchcock. Starring: Grace Kelly, Ray Milland, Robert Cummings. Screenplay: Frederick Knott, from his own play. DVD: Warner Brothers, 2004. Blu-Ray: Warner Brothers, 2012.

Rear Window. 1954. Paramount. Producer: Alfred Hithcock. Starring: James Stewart, Grace Kelly, Raymond Burr, Thelma Ritter. Screenplay: John Michael Hayes, from a story by Cornell Woolrich. Nominated for three Academy Awards. DVD/Blu-ray: Universal, 2012.

To Catch a Thief. 1955. Paramount. Producer: Alfred Hitchcock. Starring Cary Grant, Grace Kelly, and the South of France. Screenplay: John Michael Hayes, from a novel by David Dodge. Academy Award, Best Cinematography. DVD/Blue-ray: Warner Brothers, 2007.

The Trouble with Harry. 1955. Paramount. Producer: Alfred Hitchcock. Starring John Forsythe, Shirley MacLaine, Edmund Gwenn. Screenplay: John Michael Hayes, from a novel by Jack Trevor Story. DVD: Universal, 2002. Blu-ray: Universal, 2013.

The Man Who Knew Too Much. 1956. Paramount. Producer: Alfred Hitchcock. Starring: James Stewart, Doris Day. Screenplay: John Michael Hayes, from the 1934 film of the same title. Academy Award, Best Original Song. DVD: Universal, 2007. Blu-Ray: Universal, 2013.

The Wrong Man. 1956. Warner Brothers. Producer: Alfred Hitchcock. Starring: Henry Fonda, Vera Miles, Anthony Quayle. Screenplay: Angus MacPhail, from a novel by Maxwell Anderson. DVD: Warner Brothers, 2004.

Vertigo. 1958. Paramount. Producer: Alfred Hitchcock. Starring: James Stewart, Kim Novak, Barbara Bel-Geddes. Screenplay: Alec Coppel and Samuel Taylor, from a novel by Boileu-Narcajac (Pierre Boileu and Pierre Ayraud). Nominated for two Academy Awards. DVD/Blu-ray: Universal, 2014.

North by Northwest. 1959. MGM. Producer: Alfred Hitchcock. Starring: Cary Grant, Eva Marie Saint, James Mason, Martin Landau. Screenplay:

Ernest Lehman. Nominated for three Academy Awards. DVD/Blu-ray: Warner Brothers, 2010.

Psycho. 1960. Shamley Productions (Hitchcock's own unit: distributed by Paramount). Producer: Alfred Hitchcock. Starring: Anthony Perkins, Janet Leigh, Vera Miles, Martin Balsam. Screenplay: Joseph Stefano, from the novel by Robert Bloch. Nominated for four Academy Awards. DVD/Blu-ray: Paramount, 2010.

The Birds. 1963. Universal. Producer: Alfred Hitchcock. Starring: Tippi Hedren, Rod Taylor, Suzanne Pleshette. Screenplay: Evan Hunter, from a story by Daphne DuMaurier. One Academy Award nomination. DVD/Blu-ray: Universal, 2014.

Marnie. 1964. Universal. Producer: Alfred Hitchcock. Starring: Tippi Hedren, Sean Connery. Screenplay: J. Presson Allen, from the novel by Winston Graham. DVD: Universal, 2006. Blu-ray: Universal, 2012, in *Alfred Hitchcock: The Masterpiece Collection*.

Torn Curtain. 1966. Universal. Producer: Alfred Hitchcock. Starring: Paul Newman, Julie Andrews. Screenplay: Brian Moore. DVD: Universal, 2006. Blu-ray: Universal, 2012, in *Alfred Hitchcock: The Masterpiece Collection*.

Topaz. 1969. Universal. Producer: Alfred Hitchcock. Starring: Frederick Stafford, John Forsythe, Dani Robin, Michel Piccoli, Phillipe Noiret. Screenplay: Samuel A. Taylor, from the novel by Leon Uris. DVD: Universal, 2006.

Frenzy.** 1972. Universal. Producer: Alfred Hitchcock. Starring: Jon Finch, Alec McGowan, Barry Foster, Billie Whitelaw, Anna Massey. Screenplay: Anthony Shaffer, from a novel by Arthur LaBern. DVD: Universal, 2006. Blu-ray: Universal, 2012.

Family Plot. 1976. Universal. Producer: Alfred Hitchcock. Starring: Karen Black, Bruce Dern, Barbara Harris, William Devane. Screenplay: Ernest Lehman. DVD: Universal, 2006. Blu-ray: Universal, 2012.

NOTES

* Particularly recommended commentary, critical apparatus on DVD or Blu-ray.
** Shot in England with British crew, but American financing, distribution.
  N.B: Alma Reville is credited on the screenplay or story of six of these films, but she had a hand in virtually all of them.

JONATHAN FREEDMAN

Introduction

Alfred Hitchcock (1899–1980) is, of course, one of the most renowned as well as one of the most commercially successful filmmakers the world has ever known. Although he began his career in Great Britain, and learned much of his craft in Berlin, arguably Hitchcock's greatest and certainly his most acclaimed films were made in the United States. It is there that such masterpieces as *Notorious*, *Strangers on a Train*, *Vertigo*, *North by Northwest*, *Psycho*, and *The Birds* were scripted, shot, and distributed; there too that a number of only slightly lesser accomplishments, such as *Rope*, *Shadow of a Doubt*, *Spellbound*, and a host of others, were conceived, birthed, and sent out into the world.

Fifteen years ago, Richard Millington and I edited a volume devoted to the claim that Hitchcock's work is essential to the understanding of American life in the twentieth century, and vice versa. With respect to the central features of American life in this period – such matters as the rise of the national-security state, anonymity and voyeurism in urban life, and the increasing consciousness of the farther shores of psychic organization – we and our contributors argued that Hitchcock's films are as site-specific as his frequent allusions to such national monuments as the Statue of Liberty, the United Nations building, and Mount Rushmore.[1] The contributors to this volume would agree, and go further, suggesting that Hitchcock's American films are of such substance and such importance, so vitally engaged with as well as so fully energized by the national situation in which they were conceived, produced, and consumed, that he is entitled to be included in a series devoted to American icons. This volume surveys the whole of Hitchcock's career but focuses with particular intensity on his American films because these seem the most compelling to us – for Hitchcock's time, and for our own.

But, as I read over the essays, and watch and think about Hitchcock's films, it seems to me that one may want to push further still. For with respect to such charged issues as sexuality and identity, freedom and surveillance, madness and sanity, Hitchcock's films continue to provoke and challenge our normative ideals as much as they did those of the audiences of his own time. Working within the framework of his time and place, his art continues to speak to our imaginations – and our imaginings of disaster – in ways that unsettle. He is not just an American master but a maker of modernity at large – at least if one is to define modernity, as I do, not by the master-works of high modernism or, *pace* Fredric Jameson, the cultural logic of high capitalism, but rather as the process of undermining complacencies of all sorts: about knowledge and the self, about one's place in the world, about the stability of that world. That his films frequently do so with a mor-dant wit only adds to their unsettling effect.

By way of introduction, I want to flesh out these points in the context of Hitchcock's career, before and after his move to America. Hitchcock, I suggest, transformed central topoi of his own times and places – the late nineteenth century just after which he was born and in whose cultures he was steeped; that period's surprisingly subversive understanding of sexual-ity, which he made his own; and the America he moved to and moved in – in ways that startle and subvert across the twentieth century, and beyond. Critically reflecting upon and redirecting the culture industries by which he was shaped, commenting on and augmenting the imaginative structures of the country in which he spent most of his career, his cinema works in such a way as to extend and even call into question their raisons d'être – and prepares us to question our own.

Hitchcock and the Fin de Siècle

It is important to remember, as Sara Blair reminds us in this volume (Chapter 3), that Hitchcock was born in 1899, when Queen Victoria still sat on the British throne. This was the same year in which Freud was put-ting the final touches on his first masterpiece: *The Interpretation of Dreams*. Each of these historical markers is important for understanding Hitchcock's conjunction with a transforming United States.

The fin de siècle just after which Hitchcock emerged is often thought of as one of cultural decline and imperial overreach – the moment when the sun began to set on the British Empire – but it was also a time of extraordinary cultural ferment and experimentation.[2] On the level of high culture, aesthet-icism and decadence moved to the head of the queue. Oscar Wilde's *Picture of Dorian Gray* (1890) – a novel that Hitchcock knew and admired – put into currency the figure of the aristocratic dandy and the pursuit of art for art (both with an undertone of sexual perversity); their sensational appeal was barely dissipated – it was, if anything, augmented – by Wilde's trial and imprisonment in 1895. The best-selling status of that novel reminds us that the period also witnessed the rise of a mass print culture, facilitated by changes in technologies, the availability of cheap pulp paper, and the rising literacy rate, including popular books and magazines and sensational newspapers such as the *News of the World*, which made its reputation via narratives of serial killers and other sensational crimes. Stage performances, too, boomed, with music halls and spectacular melodramas challenging the bourgeois West End theater for popularity, and a host of other mass entertainments – pantomimes, puppet shows, fairs – were supplemented with new ones: dioramas, magic-lantern shows, and primitive motion picture devices such as the zoopraxiscope. Through the efforts of Eadweard Muybridge, whose studies of horses and (nude) men and women began cinema in the contemporary understanding of the word, and those of (among many others) Thomas Edison in America, G. A. Smith and Robert Paul in England, and the Lumière brothers and George Méliès's in France, a new medium seemed suddenly to appear, as if by magic: cinema.

Hitchcock entered the historical stage, in other words, at a moment of media revolution. He brought all of the forms gestating in the years before his birth and in his youth to bear on his work. Wilde's dandy, as David Greven notes in Chapter 7, informs such characters as Uncle Charlie in *Shadow of a Doubt* (1943) and Bruno in *Strangers on a Train* (1951). So does the figure of the double, which, as Carl Freedman suggests in Chapter 5, originates in Hitchcock's encounters with such texts as *Dorian Gray* and Robert Louis Stevenson's *Dr. Jekyll and Mr. Hyde* (1886) and works itself out throughout his oeuvre, for my money most memorably in *Strangers on a Train*, where it is thematized as the logic of "criss-cross," and *North by Northwest* (1959), where Roger Thornhill is haunted by a nonexistent entity for whom he is mistaken and whom he arguably becomes. The legitimate stage enters into the mise-en-scène of *Murder!* (1930), as well as becoming the subject of Hitchcock's 1950 Hollywood-meets-England extravaganza, *Stage Fright*; it's alluded to at the opening of *Rear Window* (1954), whose credits appear over bamboo shades that open like a theater curtain and whose set is indebted to the physical architecture of the theater in many ways. Radio makes an early appearance in Hitchcock's films – news of "the Avenger"'s murders on the streets of London is broadcast on that medium in *The Lodger* (1927), five years after the first news program on the BBC. So, more prominently, do the wider array of popular entertainments that flourished in Hitchcock's youth including the chorus girls who open Hitchcock's first film, *The Pleasure Garden* (1926); the fashion-cum-girlie-show in *The Lodger*; the circus in *Murder!*; and, memorably, the music hall in *The 39 Steps* (1935). The Edwardian popular press's serial-killer obsession is explicitly referenced in *The Lodger,* and Hitchcock appears in a cameo role in the newsroom. That obsession remains in place, as Mark Goble reminds us in Chapter 12, throughout Hitchcock's career, reaching its ugliest formulation in *Frenzy* (1972).

Most compelling of all the new media forms of the era is the emerging film industry itself. It is striking to see how much early films anticipate later Hitchcock, and not just because they already realize, in prototype form, his ideal of "pure cinema."[3] The British filmmaker G. A. Smith was, in the years immediately before and after Hitchcock's birth, making movies that antici- pated the latter's interest in technologies of visuality and its links to the psy- chic derangements of voyeurism. In Smith's *As Seen Through a Telescope,* shot in 1900, for example, a gleeful gentleman witnesses a young man sur- reptitiously patting his girlfriend's ankle through that device, then finds him- self cuffed on the head as punishment – a move Hitchcock himself makes at the end of *Rear Window,* when Jeff's voyeuristic camerawork, no matter how accurate, earns him a second broken leg.

Hitchcock cited Smith to Truffaut, in their book of interviews, as essen- tially inventing, along with the American filmmaker Edwin Porter, the technique of montage, or cutting.[4] That founding cinematic technique was later perfected by Eisenstein, Pudovkin, and (especially, Hitchcock felt) Lev Kuleshov – whose famous experiment showing that audiences ascribed quite different emotions to a screen actor after witnessing shots of him gazing intercut with differing point-of-view shots of what he is gazing at, proved crucial to his own cinematic practice. Hitchcock's other great influ- ence was German film, which he viewed extensively alongside avant-garde Soviet cinema at the London Film Society but which he also, more signif- icantly, witnessed when his British employer, Gainsborough Films, sent him to intern at the finest, most advanced film studio in the world, UFA (Universum Film-Aktien Gesellschaft), in Berlin. There he encountered both technical and narrative forms that marked his mise-en-scène for the rest of his career. Hitchcock absorbed the lessons of expressionist styles prominent in UFA films – distorted camera angles, aggressive use of light and shadow, and a host of other devices frequently deployed in the service of depicting extreme states of emotion, distress, or madness. And he had the chance to work with the best, most advanced directors of his moment, most promi- nently F. W. Murnau, whose filming of *The Last Laugh* (1924) Hitchcock directly observed, and whose use of a mobile camera he adapted to his own purposes.[5] UFA's films, too, provided a thematic as well as a stylistic bridge to Hitchcock. The tracing of the thin line between sanity and mad- ness that is on display in such films as the expressionist classic *The Cabinet of Dr. Caligari* (1920) or Fritz Lang's brilliant *The Testament of Dr. Mabuse*

(1933), and the shifting of audience sympathy from police to criminal that is magnificently instantiated in Lang's *M* (1931) (even if already present in *The Lodger*), provide structural patterns that either anticipate or mirror Hitchcock's plot devices and index his persistent obsessions.

What Hitchcock can be said uniquely to do, then, is bundle together media cultures forming in the early years of the twentieth century and make them broadly available for the new modes of cinematic storytelling emerging at midcentury. He does the same with respect to that period's theorizing of the unconscious and its relation to sexualities – commonplaces for a contemporary audience, but in their moment, controversial ways of thinking about the human psyche and its pulsings and compulsions. Again, a long tradition of thought stands behind Hitchcock. The idea of an unconscious force within human beings, dictating their actions beyond their knowledge, is one that originates with the Greek idea of the daimon; it was articulated most fully in the nineteenth century by the German philosopher Arthur Schopenhauer, whose notion of an all-determining "will" was transformed by his student Eduard Hartmann into the notion of an "unconscious," which, with contributions from French medical practitioners such as Jean-Martin Charcot, became the basis of Freud's paradigm-reshaping writings. I mention this history because it suggests just how common, powerful, and shared this idea was before Freud put it into cultural play, and how fully Hitchcock, like Freud himself, was shaped by a general habit of European thought as he reshaped it in his films. Indeed, the sinister alienist in *The Lady Vanishes* (1938) rings with many fin de siècle echoes, as does the weird hypnotic episode in *The Man Who Knew Too Much* (1934 version). Hitchcock's interest in unconscious motivation came to the fore in his American films in ways that do not simply illustrate but move well, and sometimes creepily, beyond Freud – as the subject of *Spellbound* (1945), as the basic ground of *Vertigo* (1958), and, as Stephen Tifft shows in Chapter 8, as an object of vibrant contestation and dialogue as late as *Psycho* (1960).

The relation of psychic life to sexualities is perhaps Hitchcock's most fertile engagement with this broad theorizing of a darker or hidden aspect of the normative psyche. The crucial text here is Viennese psychiatrist Richard von Krafft-Ebing's *Psychopathia Sexualis* (1886), a book that anatomizes a whole range of deflections from the sexual norm. Krafft-Ebing's work emerged in the 1880s and gave currency in the decades that followed to the ideas of sadism and masochism (already put in cultural play by the figures after whom they were named); to these he added a wide variety of so-called perversions, including pedophilia, nymphomania, and fetishism, as well as homosexuality and lesbianism, all described in extensive case studies combined with classifications offered in an authoritative-sounding nomenclature from which, it might be noted, we have yet to recover. Here, too, what is important about Hitchcock is the way he encapsulated these relatively new formulations and repackaged them for a mainstream audience. His films may be thought of as a cinematic equivalent of *Psychopathia Sexualis*, running through just about every standard "perversion" and adding his own Hitchcockian touches to them, ranging from cross-dressing in *Murder!*, erotic handcuff play (anticipated in *The Lodger* [1927]) in *The 39 Steps*, extending to *Rebecca* (1940), with its sadomasochistic, lesbian-inflected relationship (complete with the fondling of underwear) between the nameless second Mrs. DeWinter and Mrs. Danvers, to *Rear Window* (1954) (scopophilia), to *Vertigo* (1958) (fetishism combined with a species of necrophilia), and to *Psycho* (which invokes all of the above). And there is a career-long fascination with the erotic psychology of sadism and masochism, never better anatomized than in *Notorious* (1946), in which a relationship begins with a knockout punch delivered by secret agent Devlin (Cary Grant), and where the more rigidly and judgmentally he acts toward the recipient of his attentions, Alicia Huberman (Ingrid Bergman), the more deeply she falls in love with him, and *Vertigo*, in which Judy's decision not to flee but rather to stay and make Scottie fall in love with her leads to her subordination to his obsession and, ultimately, her death.

This investigation of sadism and masochism, and its connection to a self-destructiveness so great that it might be thought of as a death impulse, is one of the most profound themes in Hitchcock, leading him to his subtlest and most sublimely tragic representational engagements. Of equal importance, perhaps, is his interest in queer desire – especially, but not exclusively, male homosexuality. (Aside from the dynamics between Mrs. DeWinter II and Mrs. Danvers, direct references to lesbianism are few and far between in Hitchcock – as an example, I can think only of a classically butch patron at the diner in *The Birds* [1963].) The late nineteenth century, many critics have argued, was the era in which "homosexuality" was identified, named, and defined, and a host of literary and paraliterary texts as well as Wilde's example constructed the modern notion of homosexual desire: Proust's *Sodom et Gomorre* (1921–1922) and Gide's *Les Faux-monnayeurs* (1925), for instance. If the works of these and a host of other writers in the twentieth century taught people, in David Halperin's words, "how to be gay" (or, more precisely, how to be gay men), so did Hitchcock's films, especially *Rope* (1948) and *Strangers on a Train* (1951), in which flamboyantly homosexual men defined the lineaments of the type.[6] And even though in both cases – in *Strangers* in particular – the gay man is represented as a kind of psychopath, Hitchcock works, as he does throughout his films, to break down the barriers between straight and queer, normal and deviant.

It is, after all, the hyper-straight guy, appropriately named Guy (played, with a Hitchcockian touch, by an openly bisexual actor, Farley Granger), who brushes his leg against the ostentatiously queer Bruno (played, in an equally mordant piece of counter-typecasting, by the thoroughly straight Robert Walker), initiating the contact between the two of them. There is, in Hitchcock, no untroubled sexuality of any sort; it is all – that is to say, fundamentally – queer, none more so, perhaps, than the normative variety as represented by the likes of Guy, much less the scopophile L. B. Jeffries or the impotent fetishist Scottie. Of the major American films, only Roger Thornhill can be said to be a straight straight man, but, come to think of it, about that thing he has for his mother....

Hitchcock the American

Just as Hitchcock instructed an American audience in the hidden byways of the human, so too his American films both reflected and articulated the rapid transformations of state and society that marked the United States' emergence as a world power. It is all here: World War II (*Lifeboat* [1944]); postwar national-security hysterics (*Strangers on a Train*, *North by Northwest*); imperial tourism and worldwide adventurism (*The Man Who Knew Too Much* [1956]); even impending ecological catastrophe (*The Birds* [1963]). In his American films, he gives us a remarkable response to the changing conditions of American life, which frequently merge seamlessly with his own thematic and stylistic preoccupations.

Shadow of a Doubt is a classic example. Playing off the familiar small town–big city dichotomy emerging from such contemporaries as Frank Capra in the 1930s and 1940s (think of the contrast between Bedford Falls and Pottersville in *It's a Wonderful Life* [1946]), *Shadow* deconstructs that opposition, suggesting as it sends Uncle Charlie (Joseph Cotten) from a seedy urban rooming house to the idyllic locus of Santa Rosa, California – where he meets relatives who discuss magazine descriptions of murder scenarios with relish, and a niece with whom he shares an intimate relation not untouched with incestuous overtones – that the small town is itself a fit locus for the sexual and murderous fantasies that are realized in the big city.[7] (This small town, it should be noted, also contains a dive bar as sinister as anything one could imagine in an urban setting.) Hitchcock's ambitions to lay siege to the small-town ideal are suggested not only by his much-publicized (and not-so-consequential) employment of Thornton Wilder as a scriptwriter for the film but by his hiring of Sally Benson, who had just published a collection of stories full of nostalgia for a small town hovering on the verge of modernity, *Meet Me in St. Louis* (1944), which was

Figure I.1. Young Charlie at the threshold of dark knowledge in her own home. *Shadow of a Doubt* (1943).

made into a movie by another great director, Vincente Minnelli, the year after *Shadow* premiered.

Hitchcock's style here goes a considerable way toward enacting this process. Following for the most part Young Charlie's unfolding awareness of her uncle's guilt and her recognition of the kinky nature of his relation to her – at one point he gives her a ring he has taken from a woman he has seduced and murdered – the film becomes literally darker, a film noir before the term had been coined. Exterior shots of her house, initially sunlit, become dappled with shade; more of the film comes to take place at night (not only Charlie's walk to the library to learn of her uncle's perfidy but also her confrontation scene with him at the bar); interiors, too, become full of shadows (Figure I.1), climaxing with a remarkable shot of Young Charlie, having read the newspaper item describing the crime that he has tried to hide from her, standing in the public library casting an enormous shadow that enacts her haunted consciousness (Figure I.2).

This device is taken straight from German expressionism; so too are the odd, contorted camera angles that define Uncle Charlie as well as Young Charlie (Figure I.3).

It is as if Hitchcock enacts the undoing of the all-American small-town ideal by representing it with a European-born technique, a tactic Orson

Figure I.2. Shadow of a certainty: Young Charlie faces Uncle Charlie's guilt.
Shadow of a Doubt.

Figure I.3. UFA angles in a California bungalow.
Shadow of a Doubt.

Wells adopts in his most commercially successful film, *The Stranger* (1946) – a film that rings with echoes of *Shadow of a Doubt.*

If the myth of the small town is on Hitchcock's American radar, so is the critical examination of the big city and its moral and behavioral effects

Figure I.4. Urban sunbathing ...
Rear Window (1954).

on its inhabitants, effects that line up neatly with film itself. Consider, for example, that hymn to urban voyeurism *Rear Window*. Early on, Jeff is staring out his window when two young women climb up to the roof, toss their clothes on the railing, and prepare to sunbathe. Although their bodies (in bikinis?) are hidden from Jeff – and from us – a helicopter hovers over-head, getting the glimpse of female figures that is denied us and Jeff alike. Hitchcock critics might want to concentrate on the ways in which our own desire to look is both implicated and frustrated by the helicopter's ability to spy on what is hidden from us (Figures I.4, I.5, I.6).

But equally important is the way this episode implicates an entire cultural formation in the acts of voyeurism. "We've become a race of Peeping Toms," Stella, the attending nurse, exclaims; even if this is true, that propensity is a product as much of environment as of genes. Everything in *Rear Window* is designed to suggest that it is the lineaments of urban modernity – the design of apartment houses, the lives of the culture workers who populate the building (no working-class folk would have the leisure time Jeff, the composer, the artist, and Miss Torso do to contemplate or perform for one another) – that create new possibilities of visual consumption and display. This most self-conscious of all films shows itself to be a part of that ensemble, a commentary on but also a component of the voyeuristic/exhibitionistic sphere of urban modernity.

Similarly, the opening-credit sequence of *North by Northwest* firmly plants Roger Thornhill in a space of urban modernity – a city of sleek, mir-roring glass windows and jostling crowds through which Roger maneuvers

Figure I.5. attracts ...
Rear Window.

Figure I.6. a traffic helicopter.
Rear Window.

with transparent cynicism: he steals a cab, claiming that he made the person he stole it from feel happy for the sacrifice. Roger's own cynical attitudes and the world of urban anonymity are as one. It makes perfect sense in an environment composed of anonymous offices, streets, and hotel rooms that he could be mistaken for George Kaplan, setting in motion the movie's plot: such a substitution would be impossible in Bodega Bay, or Santa Rosa, California. Last, to complete this triptych of urban scene-setting, are the opening shots of *Psycho*, in which a new Sun Belt metropolis, Phoenix, Arizona, appears in all its sun-baked mediocrity, framed in gritty black and white, as the camera reverses the movements of *Rear Window* by probing inside a seedy hotel room where Marion and her lover are lingering after engaging in a bout of adulterous sex. The anonymity of the city provides both the occasion and the cover for their lunchtime liaison – an anonymity that is broken when, later in the day, Marion is spied on by a leering client whose money she has embezzled.

These opening shots – and one could cite more as well, such as the panorama of urban blight that begins *Shadow of a Doubt*, as Sara Blair argues in Chapter 3 – define Hitchcock as a poet of urban life. His is the cinema, Dana Brand has suggested, of Walter Benjamin's flaneur, the nineteenth-century character who wanders through the city streets, part aesthete, part voyeur, part detective.[8] Yet in his cinema the city itself is also a locus of malevolent, masculine power. Consider *Vertigo*. Hitchcock planned the film around San Francisco's landmarks, which he displays with no less picturesque flair than he brings to his representation of the South of France in *To Catch a Thief* (1955) – half suspense film, half travelogue. This sense is particularly strong in those scenes where Scottie follows "Madeleine" – really the shopgirl Judy, trained by Scottie's friend Gavin Elster to impersonate his wife, who is acting (the role-playing itself becomes vertiginous) as if she is possessed by the spirit of a nineteenth-century San Franciscan, Carlotta Valdes.

San Francisco proves more than a place of beautiful sites, however; it's also a place of unexpected dangers. Hitchcock's film is, in Diane Borden's lovely term, as much traumalogue as travelogue.[9] We may see a beautiful cityscape with roofs glinting in the sun from Scottie's friend Midge's windows in a gorgeous apartment overlooking North Beach, but other rooftops, not far away, have just been revealed to us as the site of tragedy and trauma. It is on top of one of them that Scottie was afflicted with newly discovered vertigo, lost his grip on a fellow policeman's wrist, and let him drop to his death. Even the Golden Gate Bridge and Coit Tower turn out to be backdrops for deceit and sexual obsession. Judy as "Madeleine" fakes a suicide with the bridge as backdrop to draw Scottie further into the plot, and later wakes up undressed in a bed in his apartment under the phallic Coit Tower – consciously chosen, Hitchcock told an interviewer, for precisely that quality.

The symbolic role played by the city goes even further to connect the urban locus with malevolent male power. The near-mythic world of old San Francisco woven into the Carlotta plot is invoked by Gavin Elster, Scottie's friend and the author of the plot against him; it was, he tells Scottie, a place where men "had the freedom, they had the power" – and in some sense

Scottie recognizes just how powerfully Elster seeks to recreate that world when he realizes the nature of the plot. Scottie echoes these words ironically in talking about Elster to Judy – even "with all of his wife's money and all that freedom and power, he ditched you," he reminds her. But there is a sense that even after Elster decamps, a form of power radiates through new as well as old San Francisco, trapping Judy and the unmanned Scottie in a logic that is as inexorable as Elster's plot. It's the city streets, with their relentless flow of daytime crowds, that bring the at-loose-ends Scottie face to face with Judy (and us – she is framed by the camera in a brilliant one-shot as Scottie sees her in front of a flower store) in a chance meeting well after he thinks Madeleine is dead. Indeed, the entire plot of the last third of the movie is made possible by a set of uniquely urban institutions. Judy works in one department store – I. Magnin's – and it is in another that Scottie, with the help of the staff, transforms Judy into Madeleine. Judy lives in the Empire Hotel – its name another signifier of power – where she, transformed back into the form of "Madeleine," and Scottie consummate their relationship in his room lit by the neon sign, that urban icon becoming the source of a green-shaded romantic haze. They then plan a dinner at the place they first met, "Ernie's" – dressing up for which Judy thoughtlessly puts on "Carlotta's" jewels, and hence unwittingly reveals her role-playing as Madeleine to Scottie.[10] Although they travel down the coast to meet their fate in a tower, where one is left dead and the other paralyzed with guilt and madness, it is the city, with its strange mixture of anonymity and intimacy, its opportunities for disguised identities and chance encounters, its distinctive institutions (department stores, flower shops, hotels, restaurants), that brings Scottie and Judy together after the real Madeleine's death has separated them, and impels them toward their tragic end.

Between small town and big city, and for that matter through and beyond open spaces, there is one more topos to be mentioned in Hitchcock's spatial encounter with the United States: that of movement. Travel, to be sure, is a hallmark of his British films as well – to Scotland and back to London in *The 39 Steps*; all around central Europe in *The Lady Vanishes* – but it becomes a centerpiece of numerous American films, from *Saboteur* (1942) through *Strangers on a Train* and *North by Northwest* (where the train itself becomes an object of erotic humor, with its famous closing shot of an engine thrusting into a tunnel). The road qua road takes over in films such as *Psycho* and *Marnie* (1964) – as Murray Pomerance has recently reminded us, Mark Rutland and Marnie stop at a Howard Johnson's on one of America's new superhighways (I-95, to be specific) en route from Philadelphia to a rendezvous with Marnie's mother and the uncovering of her childhood trauma in Baltimore.[11] This trope carries through all the way to *The Birds*, which involves a journey in a sports car up the California coast to Bodega Bay and ends with a return journey by boat to escape the avian plague. (Hitchcock's proposed final shot involved a mass of birds greeting Mitch and his crew on their arrival at the Golden Gate Bridge.) The extraordinary physical mobility of American life is both persistently evoked and resolutely deconstructed by Hitchcock's American films, where it is shown to be a resource – an escape, a locus of desire, a way out of the morass, moral or otherwise, of the big city – yet at the same time a place of potential assault, unexpected terror, and, always, transformation. After all, it is the road in the most extended sense that leads Bruno to Guy (or is it the other way around?), Roger to a cornfield where he is strafed by a cropduster, and Marion to her death in a motel. The mobility of identity that the road evokes structures these films, allowing characters to shape and reshape their destinies and identities over the course of their journeys. Kane, the protagonist of *Saboteur,* Guy from *Strangers*; Roger Thornhill, Marnie, Melanie – they are none of them the same as when they undertake and certainly not when they finish their experiences on the road, for better and for worse. Just as the émigré Hitchcock remade himself in Hollywood by playing the stereotypical Englishman he was not, so all identities in his films are subject to fluid reanimation. The questioning and ultimately the reformulation of those identities are undertaken in whatever locus he finds – big city, small town, or the roads that pass through spaces in between.

Hitchcock, Our Contemporary

For these reasons and many others, Hitchcock is profitably to be thought of not only as a representative American artist but as one who passes through the specific sites (and sights) he locates in this country to a broader interrogation of identities, new and old, made, fabricated, and authenticated, across the board. With respect to the dynamics of modernity at its most crucial – in terms of sexuality, identity, and the destabilizing of a stable sense of place, to wrap these up in one tidy bundle – Hitchcock is as much an Emersonian "representative man" as Emerson himself was of transcendentalism, as Frederick Douglass was of race and the struggle for black self-identification, as Bob Dylan was of the 1960s and the vast transformations that era initiated. But as I have suggested, what is truly remarkable about Hitchcock is the way in which he not only focuses the issues of his own moment but also strikingly anticipates our experience, both as Americans and as subjects of a complex and challenging modernity.

For example, consider one moment in *The Birds*. Several years ago, I was teaching that film and focusing on the amazing cut from the devastation

Figure I.7. Bird's-eye view of havoc.
The Birds (1963).

being wrought in Bodega Bay – exploding gas tanks, screaming people – to an uncanny bird's-eye view, as the malevolent avian air force prepares to return to the fray (Figure I.7).

The turn from the mini-narratives on the ground, however horrific (a driver dropping a match, oblivious of the bird-caused fuel leak; Melanie and the townspeople trying vainly to warn him), to the impersonal freedom of the skies was, I realized in the middle of a lecture, uncannily parallel to the shots just then released by WikiLeaks of deadly drone attacks on journalists and wedding parties. The same uncanny silence, the same assumption of the superior point of view, the same distance between the spectator's vision of the act and its effect (the birds hover overhead; the drones deliver their pictures to a base in Tampa, Florida) was palpable in both cases, shocking in its impersonality. This uncanny moment in Hitchcock becomes even more uncanny, in other words, as it comes to anticipate – or in Richard Grusin's useful term, "premediate"[12] – the very possibilities of drone attacks and the spectatorial stances that accompany them, which make the split between witnessing and act that drone warfare instantiates possible in the first place.

There are other uncanny moments in Hitchcock that seem to anticipate the postmodern and what has been called the posthuman. I am thinking here of a chilling sequence of point-of-view shots in the infamous shower scene in *Psycho*, the first from Marion's perspective as she looks up at the shower before Norman murders her (Figure I.8), the second the repetition of the same point-of-view shot after her death, a point-of-view shot from the perspective of no one, located nowhere (as William Rothman has observed),[13]

Figure I.8. The shower, from Marion's point of view.
Psycho (1960).

Figure I.9. The shower, from the point of view of no one.
Psycho.

except from the perspective of death itself (Figure I.9). That is a version of posthumanism with a vengeance – and it is becoming second nature to us, whatever our nature is becoming.

In testing the boundaries of identification and point of view in these respects and more, Hitchcock's oeuvre, unlike those of many of his great contemporaries such as Jean Renoir and Akira Kurosawa, projects a thoroughly dystopian understanding of the world. Hitchcock's is ultimately a grim and empty universe: a place of sudden, shocking death delivered from the skies; random spasms of malevolence erupting from nowhere, even (especially) in the most pastoral and benign of settings; ubiquitous surveillance; and an almost surreal deployment of the power of the entertainment industry to shape perceptions, affects, and desires. His dystopian world is closest, if anything, to that of the most postmodern of modernists, Samuel Beckett, or to that of the director who comes closest in spirit and technique to him, and one who traded both technical and thematic places with Hitchcock over both of their long careers: Fritz Lang. That Hitchcock's oeuvre is leavened with humor, self-referential jokes, and frequently a tone of wry distancing only adds to the postmodern affect; given the extraordinary influence Hitchcock has had in the media at large even after his career concluded, it would seem that these elements contributed to the construction of that very cultural mode. Hitchcock's films, in short, offer not simply a portrait of his own times but also an astonishingly prescient account of ours. It is why we turn again and again to his films, to learn not only about where we have come from, or even where we are now, but how to confront with grimness, asperity, and humor where we may be going.

This volume is addressed to a wide variety of readers, and its contributors represent a wide variety of critical positions and traditions. Our primary goal, however, is to connect with readers who are not necessarily acquainted with the ins and outs of Hitchcock criticism or film theory, but who are curious about exploring his work further. Indeed, I can't think of any director whose films have at once been so popular and received so much critical attention. From 1926–27, when he found his footing with *The Lodger*, to his last movie, his films were enormously popular with the viewing public (even the much-maligned *Family Plot* [1976] did good business), and, beginning at least in the 1960s, among intellectuals as well, first in France, then in England and America. Moreover, as film criticism developed within and outside the academy, Hitchcock became identified as a test case for its various assertions. He was, for example, Exhibit A for the French critics, such as François Truffaut and Eric Rohmer, writing for the influential *Cahiers du cinéma*, of the auteur theory – the idea that a film is authored by a director in the same way a book is by its writer. More importantly, they identified Hitchcock's work as the essence of pure cinema, a cinema that eschewed "pictures of people talking"[14] in favor of the representation of action with as few words as possible. Similarly, when Laura Mulvey and other feminist film critics wanted to define the essence of male spectatorship, they turned to readings of Hitchcock. So too with psychoanalytic critics, especially those following in the post-Lacanian footsteps of Slavoj Žižek. And so too with so-called apparatus theory, uniting formal and ideological critique, as practiced by French critics of the 1970s such as Jean-Louis Comolli; film history, as practiced by our contributor Thomas Schatz, which focuses on accounts of the studio system as a way of historicizing the medium; and reception studies, which look at audience reactions and the critical commentary generated in and around a film as critical parts of its social meaning and effect. Recently, as critics have moved in the direction of cultural criticism and then new visual studies, Hitchcock remains central to their meditations on modes of mediation and on visuality as a social practice.

But it is not only film critics who have turned to Hitchcock. As Sara Blair observes in her essay (Chapter 3), surely it is no coincidence that one of America's greatest contemporary philosophers, Stanley Cavell, and one of its greatest theorists of postmodernism, Fredric Jameson, both wrote brilliant essays on *North by Northwest*, instantiating their own approaches while offering transformative readings of that great film. Meanwhile, what Janet Staiger identifies here as the "Hitchcock brand" – self-consciously crafted in his English salad days, extended in his American ones by countless droll interviews and his appearances in his own films – has been carried forward well after his death. In 2012, an HBO film dramatized his notoriously turbulent relations with Tippi Hedren; the next year, a feature film emerged centering on his relations with his wife, Alma, and the making of *Psycho*. And as I try to show in my essay, directors in the past forty years, many well after Hitchcock's death in 1980, have not only recycled his techniques but engaged in serious and substantive dialogue with his central themes and preoccupations in a wide variety of genres.

No single volume can speak to all the dimensions of Hitchcock's influence, nor do more than gesture at all the approaches that have been taken to his films over the past thirty years of extensive criticism. The essays included only represent the tip of the iceberg of the work done by scholars and critics who have engaged with it, and especially with Hitchcock's American films; readers will, I hope, be inspired to look at the selected bibliography and start to read more. Roughly half of these essays are drawn from the discipline of film studies. Thomas Schatz examines Hitchcock's complex interplay with the studio system, from his arrival here courtesy of David O. Selznick (he repaid the favor by making the exterior of the insane asylum in *Spellbound* look suspiciously like that of Selznick Films International) to his happy years of autonomy with Paramount and his less-successful final stint at Universal. Janet Staiger assesses the collaboration between the press and Hitchcock that created the "Hitchcock brand." Brigitte Peucker focuses on the meanings generated by form – in this case, those that grow out of the use of the color red in Hitchcock's color films (and even one of his black-and-white ones, *Spellbound*, which ends with a dash of color when its villain, Dr. Murchison, turns a gun on himself and shoots). Susan White assesses the extrafeminist origins of a feminist film theory that focuses closely on Hitchcock to see what it might offer for our readings of Hitchcock and of cinema itself even as we move to a so-called third wave, encompassing queer and other desires. David Greven exemplifies that wave by surveying its practitioners so as to offer brilliant queer readings of the films. Homer Pettey uses genre theory to trace, via Hitchcock's relation to film noir, his engagement with the dynamics of class, reflected even in such relatively understudied films as *I Confess* (1953) and *The Wrong Man* (1956). Class is also on the mind of Murray Pomerance, a sociologist of U.S. culture as well as a writer on film, who looks at differing intonations of plot, speech, and character in the English and American versions of *The Man Who Knew Too Much* (1934, 1956).

Many are drawn to Hitchcock from fields or forms of inquiry outside film studies per se, and roughly half of us, like Hitchcock himself, think of ourselves as émigrés of one sort or another. Stephen Tifft engages psychoanalytic theory to read *Psycho* – and vice versa, despite (or in some ways because of) what is usually taken to be the film's dismissive treatment of psychoanalysis in a doctor's pat summary of Norman's "case" in the film's final reel. Carl Freedman uses *Shadow of a Doubt* to locate Hitchcock, newly arrived on American shores, in a long-standing American literary tradition of writing and thinking about evil, including Hawthorne and Poe in its ranks. Alan Nadel places Hitchcock's *North by Northwest* in a different tradition – that of Cold War America – highlighting Hitchcock's skeptical attitude toward two of its central institutions, the United Nations and the CIA. Cultural and visual studies scholars Sara Blair and Mark Goble view Hitchcock's films through a broader lens. Blair finds him ringing multiple changes on the idea and ideology of this self-monumentalizing country, America, its sacred spaces (the Statue of Liberty, Mount Rushmore), and its stars, such as the possibly Jewish-born Englishman Archibald Leach, a.k.a. Cary Grant. And Goble concludes our survey of Hitchcock's career by considering what we can learn about Hitchcock's work as a whole from the idea that in the 1970s, as his inhibitions were released by age, security, and the changing mores of the time, he gave in to his desire, present from the very first shot of *The Lodger*, to represent the bodies of dead women. I try to show that, while engaging with Hitchcock's characteristic themes (freedom and its relation to constraint; voyeurism, pleasure, and control) led some directors, such as Brian De Palma, to out-Hitchcock Hitchcock, others – Jonathan Demme, Atom Egoyan, Florian Henckel von Donnersmarck – pushed in a different direction, one that sees possibilities for artistic or human transcendence of the dire necessities that Hitchcock delineated with such grim power.

Formal or cultural, literary or cinematic, historical or feminist, interpretive or fact-focused, or many and perhaps at times all of the above, these essays, taken together, evidence the range and depth of the critical responses Hitchcock has elicited. We hope, collectively, that as you read them, you will be provoked to turn and return to Hitchcock's American films, which at their best have much to teach us about the nature of cinema, psyche, culture, and America in a passionately memorable way. This is a companion to Hitchcock, yes, but it invites you to make Hitchcock himself your companion as you explore such issues in tandem with his amazing, half-century-long, pathbreaking art.

NOTES

1 Jonathan Freedman and Richard Millington, eds., *Hitchcock's America* (Oxford and New York: Oxford University Press, 1999).
2 For a similar argument, with a different spin, see Richard Allen, *Hitchcock's Romantic Irony* (New York: Columbia University Press, 2007), pp. 117 and ff.
3 The most accessible version of the famous 1963 interview of Hitchcock by Peter Bogdanovich, which covers this idea, can be found online: http://zakka.dk/euro-screenwriters/interviews/alfred_hitchcock.htm. Accessed July 15, 2014.
4 François Truffaut and Helen G. Scott, *Hitchcock* (New York: Simon and Schuster, 1985), p. 57.
5 So, too, Thomas Leitch has suggested, "from Murnau Hitchcock took not only the Expressionist cast of his British films and the fascination with the moving camera ... but more generally the idea of the director as a visual impresario, a showman whose camera-eye upstaged the performers and their material as the real star of the film." Leitch, *Find the Director and Other Hitchcockian Games* (Athens: University of Georgia Press, 1991), p. 45. For a more detailed account of Murnau's influence on Hitchcock, see Chapter 4 of this volume.
6 David Halperin, *How to Be Gay* (Cambridge, MA: Belknap Press, 2012).
7 Here I am following in the footsteps of Robin Wood's classic essay, "Ideology, Genre, Auteur," in *Hitchcock's Films Revisited* (New York: Columbia University Press, 1982), pp. 288–302. My focus here is on genre of a different sort, and Hitchcock's use of its conventions to cast a shadow over a cultural ideal. For more along these lines, see Freedman and Millington, eds., *Hitchcock's America*, pp. 3–4.
8 See Dana Brand, "Rear-View Mirror: Hitchcock, Poe, and the Flaneur in America," in Freedman and Millington, eds., *Hitchcock's America*, 123–134.
9 Diane Borden, "Travelogue as Traumalogue: Space, Place, and Memory in *Vertigo*," in Douglas Cunningham, ed., *The San Francisco of Alfred Hitchcock's* Vertigo: *Place, Pilgrimage, and Commemoration* (Lanham, MD: Scarecrow Press, 2012), pp. 153–176.
10 I need to mention here William Rothman's wonderfully perverse argument that Judy (or rather a woman who impersonates both Judy and Madeleine) puts on the necklace precisely to force Scottie to recognize the plot and, ultimately, embrace her for her genius in hatching it. See "Scottie's Dream, Judy's Plan, Madeleine's Revenge" in Katalin Makkai, ed., *Vertigo* (New York: Routledge, 2013), pp. 45–70. I would like to accept Rothman's reading of the film, but ultimately it rests on no evidence other than his conviction that it has to be so – Rothman's dream, as it were.

11 Murray Pomerance, *Alfred Hitchcock's America* (Cambridge, MA: Polity Press, 2013), pp. 190–195.

12 Richard Grusin, *Premediation: Affect and Mediality after 9/11* (London: Palgrave Macmillan, 2010).

13 William Rothman, *Hitchcock: The Murderous Gaze*, 2nd ed. (Albany: SUNY Press, 2012), pp. 315–316.

14 Sidney Gottlieb, ed., *Alfred Hitchcock: Interviews* (Jackson: University Press of Mississippi, 2003), p. 158.

PART I

Hitchcock Encounters America, America Encounters Hitchcock: Roots and Offshoots

I

THOMAS SCHATZ

Hitchcock and the Studio System

Introduction

Alfred Hitchcock was of course a consummate auteur, but also a studio filmmaker and a creature of the production system in which he worked. From the very beginning of his directing career in the 1920s to his last films a half-century later, Hitchcock was engaged in a succession of multi-picture deals with leading studios and producers in Britain and then later in the United States, which afforded him extraordinary resources and also, thanks mainly to the leverage that accompanied his commercial success, an exceptional degree of filmmaking autonomy.[1] Hitchcock was never a staff director per se – that is, he never worked as a salaried employee who was arbitrarily assigned pictures by a studio head. Rather, he played an active role in identifying and developing the films he directed, and he exercised considerable control over the production process. In that sense, he generally functioned as his own producer, and in fact from the late 1940s onward he was credited as producer as well as director of every one of his films.

Looking more closely at Hitchcock's long, prolific career and at this succession of multi-picture deals, we might note a number of rather interesting and somewhat paradoxical trends regarding his relationship with – and his indebtedness to – the studio system. First and foremost, some of these periods of studio engagement were more stable, productive, and successful than others. Moreover, these intermittent periods of stability and success saw Hitchcock develop distinct and in some ways distinctly different cycles of films – the so-called spy cycle of the 1930s, for instance, and the female Gothics of the 1940s. The gestation of these cycles was a complex process that involved Hitchcock's interaction not only with a particular studio or production company but also with key personnel – notably the executives who effectively managed Hitchcock's career at certain points, the screenwriters with whom he developed these cycles, and the production units that formed as these cycles evolved. These units included talent on both sides of the camera, with the star system playing an increasingly significant role in the overall process – and with Hitchcock himself starring in his signature television series in the 1950s and 1960s. These periods of stability and the film cycles that accompanied them marked successive stages and advances in Hitchcock's career, contributing to the increasingly rich, complex, and multifaceted notion of a "Hitchcock film."

The purpose of this chapter is to assess Hitchcock's ongoing, dynamic interaction with the studio system, charting all of these studio deals but paying special attention to the more stable and successful relationships and to the production cycles that coalesced during these periods. More specifically, I intend to focus on four distinct periods and cycles. The first was the run of espionage thrillers in the 1930s during Hitchcock's "British period" – a cycle that began with *The Man Who Knew Too Much* (1934) and culminated with *The Lady Vanishes* (1938), which secured Hitchcock's international stature as well as his passage to Hollywood. The second was a cycle of women's pictures with a decidedly Gothic dimension in the 1940s that began with *Rebecca* (1940) and peaked with *Notorious* (1946). The third and fourth cycles developed concurrently – and along very different lines – in the 1950s. On the one hand, Hitchcock produced and directed a succession of lush romantic thrillers, including *Rear Window* (1954), *Vertigo* (1958), and *North by Northwest* (1959), during what is now considered the most fertile period of his career. On the other, the *Alfred Hitchcock Presents* television series emerged almost in counterpoint, recasting Hitchcock's style in literally hundreds of taut, low-budget, black-and-white episodes of gallows humor, which, for the most part, were even darker (and funnier) than his feature films.

The 1950s marked a sustained peak for Hitchcock as an artist and a commercial entertainer, and a period of near-absolute control as both the author and quite literally the owner of his work. But it was also a period during which he relied more heavily than ever on key associates and creative collaborators to maintain these two production cycles. These cycles converged in 1960 with *Psycho*, by far the biggest box office success in Hitchcock's career and another watershed in terms of his relationship with the studio system. In the wake of that runaway hit, Hitchcock took up permanent residence at Universal Pictures, where he spent the rest of his career and enjoyed unprecedented freedom, authority, and access to filmmaking resources. Despite these advantages, however, the Universal period was one of steady and rather steep decline for Hitchcock due no doubt to a range of personal and professional factors. Chief among them was his failure to utilize those aspects of "the system" that had facilitated his success in earlier periods and were essential to the formulation of Hitchcock's singular filmmaking style.

Hitchcock's British Period and the 1930s Spy Cycle

One remarkable aspect of Hitchcock's development as a filmmaker and his stature as an auteur is how quickly his signature style crystallized in the mid-1930s with the back-to-back hits, *The Man Who Knew Too Much* (1934) and *The 39 Steps* (1935), following a prolific but uneven decade as a director in which "the Hitchcock touch" was only sporadically in evidence. He had started directing in 1925 after a brief apprenticeship (mainly as a title designer and assistant director while in his early twenties), when Michael Balcon of Gainsborough Pictures assigned him two routine melodramas. Five pictures for Balcon and Gainsborough resulted in one notable success, *The Lodger*, in 1927. That year Hitchcock signed a multi-picture contract with John Maxwell at British International Pictures (BIP), resulting in ten pictures of varying types. This period also yielded only one significant success, *Blackmail* (1929), Britain's first sound picture and most distinctive proto-Hitchcock film of the first sixteen that he directed. The next half-dozen projects bore little resemblance to *Blackmail* and were far less successful; a good indication of Hitchcock's foundering career during that stretch was his 1933 film, *Waltzes from Vienna*, a costume musical "operetta" and a most unpleasant experience for its director.

At that point Hitchcock made a timely, career-defining move. *Blackmail* was based on a play by Charles Bennett, who in the wake of the film's success moved into screenwriting and eventually signed with BIP. He and Hitchcock formed a professional and personal rapport, and they collaborated on a screenplay (based on the popular fictional character Bulldog Drummond) involving a couple on holiday in St. Moritz, whose child is kidnapped by a cell of terrorist spies after her parents learn of an imminent assassination in London. The Hitchcock-Bennett project languished at BIP because of Maxwell's concerns about the budget, and in the midst of Hitchcock's unhappy experience with *Waltzes from Vienna*, he and Bennett decided to take their spy thriller to Michael Balcon, now head of production at Gaumont British (a sister studio to Gainsborough). Balcon, still convinced of Hitchcock's talent, opted not only to produce the picture but to sign both Hitchcock and Bennett to five-picture contracts, initiating a most fruitful partnership. Balcon also brought in Ivor Montagu, who had worked (mainly as an editor) on Hitchcock's early Gainsborough films, to serve as associate producer. While Balcon and Montagu assembled the crew – notably cinematographer Bernard Knowles and editor Charles Frend, who worked on the next five Hitchcock-directed pictures – Hitchcock and Bennett finalized the story for their espionage thriller (without Bulldog Drummond) under the title *The Man Who Knew Too Much*. Other writers were brought in for the screenplay, so Bennett took only story credit. He would have screenplay (or co-screenplay) credit on the next four Hitchcock films: *The 39 Steps*, *Secret Agent* (1936), *Sabotage* (1936), and *Young and Innocent* (1937).

Interestingly enough, Hitchcock took writing credit on none of these films, after taking story or screenplay credit (often shared with his wife, Alma Reville) on most of the lackluster BIP productions. But Hitchcock did closely collaborate with Bennett on the Gaumont films, working out the story in minute detail (including storyboards) and developing the shooting script as a veritable blueprint for production – and thus establishing a working relationship with his principal writer that would persist throughout his career. A related trend that emerged during this period was Hitchcock's penchant for taking credit with the press and public for his screen stories, a tendency that generated considerable resentment with Bennett and several of Hitchcock's later key collaborators. "He would never acknowledge any writer," Bennett later wrote. He and Hitchcock may have formed an ideal "writer-director partnership," but the director "could give credit to no one but himself."[2] The credit issue aside, Hitchcock and Bennett embarked on a four-year, five-film run that solidified Hitchcock's popular reputation and his commercial stature, as well as the fundamental elements of his signature style. The most successful of their collaborations were the first two, but even more successful, interestingly enough, was the last of Hitchcock's 1930s spy cycle, *The Lady Vanishes*, which was developed for another director before Hitchcock took it on. Clearly modeled after the Hitchcock-Bennett films and ideally suited to Hitchcock's style, *The Lady Vanishes* was the biggest hit ever in England at the time of its release – and a major hit in the United States as well.

The Hitchcock style was scarcely invented in the 1930s spy films, but it gelled due to the simple fact that these films constituted a *cycle* – that is, a quick succession of pictures that repeated and reinforced certain formal, narrative, and thematic elements that came to constitute the "Hitchcock film" in critical discourse and in the popular imagination of moviegoers. Many of these elements were evident in Hitchcock's earlier work, particularly *The Lodger* and *Blackmail*. Like those two 1920s hits – but few of the fourteen others that Hitchcock directed prior to 1934 – the spy films involved murder or the threat of murder, and they were suspense films utilizing subjectivity to intensify the viewer's identification with a troubled, desperate protagonist. They used deadlines, ticking clocks, and time bombs – quite literally, in the case of *Sabotage* – to build suspense. And they reworked two motifs that first appeared in *The Lodger* and *Blackmail*: the "double chase," with a protagonist fleeing the authorities while trying to solve a crime and prove his innocence, and a female protagonist caught in a troubled, triangulated romance.

The spy films introduced a few important new elements as well – most notably the geopolitical dimension, which exploited the rising threat of fascism and the deepening social turmoil in Europe. On another note altogether, several of these films were essentially romantic comedies, with both *The 39 Steps* and *The Lady Vanishes* clearly tapping into the screwball comedy cycle that was popular in Hollywood at the time. The love story in both films is a lively battle of wits and a battle of the sexes, with the repartee of a spatting couple and the prospect of marriage fueling both narratives. As Andrew Sarris and other critics later noted, many of Hitchcock's best films were comedies of manners – an element that first coalesced in the 1930s spy cycle. Another important aspect was the films' steadily improving production values. This was due to Hitchcock's maturation as a filmmaker, of course, but also to the production unit assembled at Gaumont and to Michael Balcon's readiness to upgrade the budgets and filmmaking resources as Hitchcock's popularity and commercial viability steadily grew. These resources included top stars like Madeleine Carroll and Robert Donat – vital assets that had not been consistently available to Hitchcock prior to the 1930s spy cycle.

Hitchcock experienced the downside of the star system on his last British picture, *Jamaica Inn* (1939), an independent production starring Charles Laughton, who coproduced with his partner Erich Pommer. A stark departure from the spy cycle, *Jamaica Inn* was a period piece about a family of smugglers on the Cornish coast whose ringleader is a local magistrate – a role played by Laughton with his usual scene-stealing relish. Adapted from Daphne du Maurier's 1936 best-seller by screenwriter Sidney Gilliat (who had coscripted *The Lady Vanishes*) and Hitchcock's talented protégé, Joan Harrison, *Jamaica Inn* centered on a young woman torn between her smuggling family and an undercover lawman (and thus a spy of sorts) who infiltrates the gang. The film did display certain Hitchcock qualities, but it was essentially a period melodrama and a star vehicle for Laughton, who along with his partner Pommer battled Hitchcock throughout the production. *Jamaica Inn* did well commercially but not critically, thanks largely to Laughton. Frank S. Nugent's review in the *New York Times* typified the critical response. Nugent deemed the "journeyman melodrama" far below Hitchcock's "standards" and was surprised that the director allowed "a mere actor to run away with the film." Nugent also predicted, accurately enough, that "*Jamaica Inn* will not be remembered as a Hitchcock picture, but as a Charles Laughton picture."[3]

The Selznick Period and the Female Gothic Cycle

When Hitchcock left for America in early 1939 after signing a tentative one-picture deal with major independent producer David O. Selznick, the British film industry was in a state of collapse while Hollywood was in the throes of its Golden Age. Indeed, Selznick's current production, *Gone with the Wind* (released in December 1939), was among the definitive films of that heralded era. And so was *Rebecca*, Hitchcock's debut American film, an early 1940 release that gave Selznick International Pictures back-to-back box office hits and consecutive Best Picture Oscars, while immediately situating Hitchcock in the first rank of Hollywood directors. Interestingly enough, Selznick initially signed him to direct a historical spectacle, *Titanic*, but Hitchcock was determined to do an adaptation of du Maurier's new novel, *Rebecca*. The author had given Hitchcock the galley proofs to her novel while he was directing *Jamaica Inn*, and it soon became a huge bestseller in both England and the United States. The story, which du Maurier readily acknowledged was a reworking of Charlotte Bronte's *Jane Eyre*, struck Hitchcock as terrific motion picture material. It centered on a lovely but naïve and unsophisticated young woman who has a whirlwind romance with an enigmatic aristocrat, marries him and returns to his ancestral estate, and learns that he has a mysterious past and something to hide – his role in the death of his first wife, Rebecca. Selznick eventually agreed to buy the screen rights, and as Hitchcock arrived in Hollywood it was announced that his contract had been renegotiated as a seven-year deal and that his first picture would be *Rebecca*.

Hitchcock soon learned that Selznick was a headstrong and hands-on producer – the antithesis, in fact, of Michael Balcon. When Hitchcock delivered a detailed ninety-page treatment (cum storyboards) of the envisioned film, Selznick dismissed it as "a distorted and vulgarized version of a provenly successful work" and immediately hired Robert E. Sherwood, a high-profile playwright and screenwriter, to work with Hitchcock and Joan Harrison on the adaptation.[4] Selznick also cast the picture, deciding on freelancer Laurence Olivier and Joan Fontaine for the leads – with Fontaine signing a long-term deal with Selznick to secure the costarring role. Hitchcock shot *Rebecca* in late 1939, carefully planning each camera setup and working at a pace that Selznick found maddeningly slow. The producer kept his distance, however, obsessed with *Gone with the Wind* and confident that he would be taking charge of *Rebecca* during postproduction. In fact, Selznick made sure of that by arranging to loan Hitchcock to another independent producer, Walter Wanger, to direct a spy thriller that went into production as soon as Hitchcock finished shooting *Rebecca*. The Wanger film, *Foreign*

Correspondent (1940), was an obvious throwback to Hitchcock's 1930s spy cycle – in fact, Charles Bennett was brought in to write the final draft – and it was a stark contrast in both story and style to *Rebecca*.

Marketed as both a "Selznick production" and a "Hitchcock picture," *Rebecca* was a melding of the two filmmakers' styles and interests. Like *Gone with the Wind*, *Rebecca* was indicative of Selznick's penchant for women's pictures, lavish adaptations, ill-fated love stories, and star vehicles. Hitchcock, meanwhile, was more interested in the film's psychological and atmospheric qualities, and the prospect of infusing the romantic melodrama with a sense of foreboding and suspense. Their collaboration was clearly a success: *Rebecca* was not only a critical and commercial hit but an enormously influential film, spawning a cycle of dark psychodramas centering on isolated, tormented women at the mercy of powerful but disturbed and possibly murderous men. These included a wide range of films from other top directors – *Gaslight* (George Cukor, 1944) and *The Spiral Staircase* (Robert Siodmak, 1945), for instance – but Hitchcock dominated the cycle with *Suspicion* (1941), *Shadow of a Doubt* (1943), *Spellbound* (1945), and *Notorious* (1946).

Significantly enough, these films were more definitively Hitchcock's creations, due to a dramatic change in Selznick's filmmaking role after *Rebecca*. For various personal and financial reasons, Selznick took a four-year break from active production after *Rebecca*, focusing instead on the "packaging" of major motion pictures – projects that invariably had Selznick's own contract talent attached. During this period, Selznick developed an impressive roster of contract talent, with a star stable that included Fontaine, Ingrid Bergman, Gregory Peck, Jennifer Jones, Shirley Temple, and Joseph Cotton. His governing strategy was to assemble the key elements of a film – that is, the script, director, and stars – into a package that was sold to a studio that would finance, produce, and distribute the film, with a share of the revenues going back to Selznick. Seven of the ten films Hitchcock directed while under contract to Selznick were packaged and sold in this fashion, which meant that, regardless of the producer credit on the film, Hitchcock increasingly functioned as his own producer. In fact, on the last of these packages, *Notorious*, which went to RKO, Hitchcock was credited for the first time as both producer and director – which would be standard for the remainder of his career after leaving Selznick in 1947.

Hitchcock's seven-year, ten-film stint with Selznick yielded an array of films, including two spy cycle throwbacks, *Foreign Correspondent* and *Saboteur* (1942); an unsuccessful screwball comedy, *Mr. and Mrs. Smith* (1941); an inventive war drama, *Lifeboat* (1944), scripted by John Steinbeck; and *The Paradine Case* (1947), a courtroom drama that was produced and manhandled by Selznick and was a commercial disaster. But the most successful and significant Hitchcock films of the Selznick period were the Gothic melodramas, beginning with the two very British Joan Fontaine vehicles, *Rebecca* and *Suspicion*, and shifting to an American context with *Shadow of a Doubt*, *Spellbound*, and *Notorious*. These American Gothics took increasingly bold and inventive liberties with the Jane Eyre prototype, and are arguably Hitchcock's best films of the entire decade. All three involved war-related stories and were stylish films noir, centering on a bereft heroine who assumes the role of detective and ultimately prevails. All three end with the death or imminent demise of the lethal male antagonist, although the positive outcome in each case is tinged with irony. All three were hits, although *Spellbound* and *Notorious* were in something of a class by themselves – by far Hitchcock's biggest box office hits of that era and a culmination of Hitchcock's Gothic cycle. Both were developed by Selznick for Ingrid Bergman, just coming off her Oscar-winning performance in *Gaslight* (on loan to MGM), and both were scripted by Ben Hecht, who wrote (or rewrote, often uncredited) most of Selznick's productions in the 1940s. Selznick actually produced *Spellbound*, which co-starred another of his contract players, Gregory Peck; he planned to produce *Notorious* as well, but sold it at the last minute to RKO so that he could concentrate on another of his own mammoth projects, *Duel in the Sun* (1946) – a film on which Selznick utilized a half-dozen directors.

Despite the resources and relative autonomy that Selznick provided, Hitchcock was determined to strike out on his own once he was established in Hollywood. In 1946 he and Sidney Bernstein, an old friend and a major theater owner in England, announced the formation of an independent company, Transatlantic Pictures. They planned to produce pictures in both London and Hollywood, with Warner Bros. handling U.S. distribution. Their first picture was to be *Under Capricorn*, another Hitchcock-directed female Gothic and another Ingrid Bergman vehicle. That project was delayed, however, and consequently Hitchcock's debut picture with Transatlantic was *Rope* (1948), a murder mystery costarring James Stewart and a severe stylistic change of pace: a very male melodrama and Hitchcock's first color film, shot with a purely objective, observational camera and utilizing exceptionally long takes in the creation of a real-time narrative. The technically innovative *Rope* was a commercial disappointment, as was *Under Capricorn* (1949), and so after two years and just two films, Transatlantic folded and Hitchcock signed a multi-picture deal as an in-house independent with Warner Bros. The brief history of Transatlantic was indicative of the travails of postwar Hollywood. When the company was launched in 1946, Hollywood was enjoying its best year ever and both the British and

American markets were booming. But by the time of the first Transatlantic release in 1948, the movie industry was in shambles, ravaged by antitrust rulings and massive social changes that decimated theater attendance.

The subsequent Warner Bros. period (from 1949 through 1953) marked something of a holding pattern for the filmmaker, generating one widely acknowledged masterwork, *Strangers on a Train* (1951), along with three rather middling (for Hitchcock) murder mysteries: *Stage Fright* (1950), *I Confess* (1953), and *Dial M for Murder* (1954). Like most of the major Hollywood studios, Warner Bros. was struggling at the time and clearly was not all that committed to its partnership with Hitchcock. But he formed another alliance that proved far more valuable in the years to come. After Transatlantic's collapse, Hitchcock signed with MCA (the Music Corporation of America), the most powerful talent agency in the entertainment business. By the early 1950s Hitchcock's career was in the hands of MCA's dynamic young president, Lew Wasserman, who put together two deals that impelled Hitchcock's sudden return to form – and to popular and critical favor – and his creation of two concurrent but very different production cycles.

Split Personality: The Paramount Period and *Alfred Hitchcock Presents*

Following the lackluster Warner Bros. period, Hitchcock enjoyed a dramatic career upswing in the mid-1950s that began with *Rear Window*, his most successful film since *Notorious* nearly a decade earlier, which also marked a new phase in his erratic association with the studio system. *Rear Window* was the first film in an unprecedented deal with Paramount Pictures that gave Hitchcock virtually complete creative control (as producer-director) and also, incredibly, ownership of five of the nine pictures after their initial release. Two of his next three pictures, *To Catch a Thief* (1955) and a remake of *The Man Who Knew Too Much* (1956), were equally successful, affirming Hitchcock's comeback and Paramount's readiness to invest in its alliance with the filmmaker. Like *Rear Window*, these were high-profile star vehicles that deftly blended romance and suspense, with budgets – and hence production values – far superior to Hitchcock's films for Warner Bros. A crucial factor here was the formation of a production unit around Hitchcock during the 1950s, most of them MCA clients, who would remain with the filmmaker throughout the Paramount period. Two charter members, cinematographer Robert Burks and editor George Tomasini, came aboard during the Warner period, and they were joined at Paramount by composer Bernard Herrmann, production designer Robert Boyle, costume designer Edith Head, associate producer Herbert Coleman, and title designer Saul Bass. MCA delivered top stars as well, notably James Stewart,

Grace Kelly, and Cary Grant, who headlined these first three Paramount hits. And perhaps most importantly, the first four Paramount productions were scripted by John Michael Hayes, a talented young writer with a background in radio, who was just breaking into film and, like Charles Bennett some two decades earlier, proved an ideal Hitchcock collaborator.

The Hayes-scripted films represent another advance in Hitchcock's career and another distinctive cycle in his body of work. They are noticeably lighter and wittier than the Selznick-era films and the subsequent run of Warner releases, recalling in some respects the comedy-inflected spy films of the 1930s such as *The 39 Steps* and *The Lady Vanishes*. But the romance plot in *Rear Window*, *To Catch a Thief*, and *The Man Who Knew Too Much* is introduced earlier and is a more pronounced and well-integrated narrative element. Hayes's facility with romantic plotting and characterization is perhaps best indicated by the fact that the original Cornell Woolrich story on which *Rear Window* was based, "It Had to Be Murder," did not include a principal female character, let alone a romantic plot line. What's more, all of the various subplots and romances across the courtyard involving Miss Lonelyhearts, Miss Torso, the newlyweds, and others were invented for the film.

In 1954, in the wake of the Paramount deal and the success of *Rear Window*, Wasserman persuaded Hitchcock (with considerable effort) to create an anthology TV series. MCA was moving into television production and distribution via its Revue subsidiary, and Wasserman overcame Hitchcock's misgivings with a deal that he simply could not refuse. The CBS network and sponsor Bristol-Meyers were keen on the idea of a Hitchcock-hosted suspense anthology, and they agreed to put up $129,000 per episode – far above the going rate for half-hour series fare – and to grant Hitchcock full ownership of every series installment after its initial network broadcast. Hitchcock was obliged to host the program and serve as executive producer and script supervisor, and to direct an occasional series episode. While Hitchcock's active involvement in *Alfred Hitchcock Presents* was limited, his contributions to its conceptualization, its style, and its audience appeal were invaluable. He created the silhouette caricature of himself that became the show's logo, and it was his idea to use Gounod's "Funeral March of a Marionette" as the theme song. He conceived the series as a variation on his own style, but with a touch of O. Henry in the payoff of each episode. The stories "should be of the suspense, or thriller, type," Hitchcock wrote to a researcher prior to the series launch, "but there is one important factor that should be common to all of them, and that is that the ending should have a 'twist' almost to the point of shock in either the last line or the last situation."[5]

Hitchcock did approve the stories and scripts, but the main arbiter on such matters was Joan Harrison. After working with Hitchcock early in her career, mainly as a writer, Harrison had gone on to become a successful film and television producer. Hitchcock brought her back to oversee production on *Alfred Hitchcock Presents* (credited as associate producer in the first two seasons and then as producer for the rest of the series run), and she played a crucial role in recasting Hitchcock's style for the series television format. Another key collaborator in the TV series was James B. Allardice, an Emmy-winning comedy writer who scripted all of Hitchcock's material – which was substantial, entailing the opening introduction, commercial segues, and concluding remarks to several hundred episodes. Hitchcock's sardonic, droll commentary was essential to the show's effect, often providing another "twist" to that week's installment. It also situated Hitchcock himself as the star of the series: he was the only recurring figure in the anthology program, whose vaguely familiar visage (thanks to his cameos and press coverage) was now on weekly display in what were, in effect, standup comedy routines.

Alfred Hitchcock Presents debuted in the fall of 1955 and was an immediate hit, reaching the Nielsen top ten in its second season. The original half-hour series ran for seven seasons, and in 1962 it was replaced by *The Alfred Hitchcock Hour*, an upgraded color version, which ran for another three seasons. Subsequent series on network and cable TV would further exploit the Hitchcock brand, while the success of *Alfred Hitchcock Presents* in syndication has kept that vintage series in continuous circulation since its initial run. Although Hitchcock directed only 20 of the 268 episodes of *Alfred Hitchcock Presents*, doing 3 of the 39 season segments in each of the early years, the series did convey his signature style – particularly the gallows humor and iconoclastic eccentricity that had been evident since his earliest films, and that quickly became the defining trait of the TV series. As James Naremore suggests, Hitchcock's entire career can be gauged in terms of the "different degrees or shadings of black humor," which grew more pronounced than ever with the TV series as Hitchcock "became a brand name that signified a refined, black-comic sense of bloody murder."[6]

This issue of humor in Hitchcock's work, particularly during the 1950s, remains one of the most fascinating aspects of his signature style. Hitchcock scholar Donald Spoto, who devotes remarkably little attention to the TV series in his biography, *The Dark Side of Genius*, views comedy as an intermittent Hitchcock trait that surfaced during the 1950s primarily in the "quartet" of Hitchcock-Hayes films. For Spoto, these marked a "breathing space" between the "fearful romanticism" of the 1940s Gothics and the heavy thematic going of the late-1950s masterworks.[7] Naremore, on the other hand, sees a through-line from the Hayes-scripted films through the TV series and directly to *Psycho* (1960) – which is indeed a tour de force of gallows humor and black comedy, and has far more in common stylistically with *Alfred Hitchcock Presents* than with its motion picture predecessors, *Vertigo* and *North by Northwest*. Significantly enough, *Psycho* was produced under the Paramount agreement, but it was shot on the Revue lot at Universal – that is, on Hitchcock's TV series premises – and was staffed predominantly by his television unit. The only key members of Hitchcock's feature film unit involved in *Psycho* were postproduction personnel: editor George Tomasini, composer Bernard Herrmann, and title designer Saul Bass.

North by Northwest and *Psycho* were the most successful films of Hitchcock's entire career, representing a commercial and artistic peak but also a rather acute break from the studio moorings that were vital to his earlier achievements. Wasserman personally set up *North by Northwest*, Hitchcock's most ambitious and expensive production to date (with a budget of $4.2 million), in a one-picture deal at MGM that included the entire Hitchcock unit. Based on an original screenplay by writer Ernest Lehman, *North by Northwest* was conceived as "the Hitchcock picture to end all Hitchcock pictures," as Lehman aptly described it, and an obvious reversion to the 1930s spy cycle – a remake, of sorts, of *The 39 Steps*, although with more fully developed principal characters, a more satisfying romance, and far more spectacular set pieces.[8] *Psycho*, conversely, was shot quickly and inexpensively (on a budget of $800,000), without top stars and devoid of romance or spectacle – an experiment in modern horror and low-grade exploitation, with a macabre sense of humor that put it in a class by itself among Hitchcock's feature films. Its runaway commercial success, which doubled the box office gross of *North by Northwest*, surprised even Hitchcock.

Winding Down: Hitchcock at Universal

Psycho was the last of Hitchcock's Paramount films, and it marked another key transition in his career. In the wake of that monstrous hit, Hitchcock settled in permanently at Universal Pictures, which financed and released all of his subsequent films. Hitchcock turned sixty-one in 1960 and was quite well off financially, but he gave no indication that he was thinking of retirement. He continued to actively develop projects from the now-legendary "Hitchcock bungalow" – actually a self-contained suite of offices on the studio lot – throughout this final chapter of his storied career. But Hitchcock's Universal period was not a fruitful one. Despite being at the top of his game and enjoying greater leverage, creative authority, and access to filmmaking resources than any director in Hollywood, Hitchcock's output in the 1960s and 1970 was one of diminishing commercial and artistic returns. He spent three years between *Psycho* and his initial Universal production, *The Birds* (1963), far longer than he had ever gone between films. And he managed only three more features during the 1960s – *Marnie* (1964), *Torn Curtain* (1966), and *Topaz* (1969) – which evinced a steady decline. There was a falloff in Hitchcock's television output as well. He continued to host his signature series after it was upgraded to an hour-long format in 1962 (as *The Alfred Hitchcock Hour*), but he directed only a single episode during its three-year run.

So although Hitchcock had the vast Universal machine at his disposal, his productivity was nowhere near what it had been in earlier decades. And while his Universal films were reasonably successful at the box office, only *The Birds* warrants serious consideration as one of Hitchcock's masterworks. In fact, the critical response to his work grew increasingly tepid during the 1960s, and by decade's end with *Topaz* it was positively cold. Hitchcock's last two films, *Frenzy* (1972) and *Family Plot* (1976), fared better with critics as well as moviegoers, although both were essentially postscripts to a career that had peaked more than a decade earlier.

Hitchcock's decline during the Universal period underscores the rather obvious fact that a stable, well-financed setup with a Hollywood studio scarcely ensured that he would maintain either the production pace or the quality of his earlier filmmaking. Indeed, all of the other key factors that had fueled his earlier successful cycles were noticeably absent during the Universal phase. One was the consistent, strategic management of his career. The new studio deal was orchestrated by Lew Wasserman, but once Hitchcock was set up at Universal, his relationship with Wasserman and MCA had changed dramatically. In the late 1950s, MCA acquired the Universal studio lot to accommodate its growing production operations, and in 1960 Wasserman decided to purchase Universal Pictures itself – that is, the entire production-distribution company. The Justice Department demanded that MCA divest its talent agency (on rather obvious conflict-of-interest grounds), which Wasserman opted to dissolve rather than sell. Hitchcock, meanwhile, sold the rights to his TV series and several of his films (including *Psycho*) to MCA-Universal, making him one of the largest stockholders in the new company. But Wasserman turned his attention from managing talent to running the sprawling media conglomerate, so once again Hitchcock was on his own and without the kind of guidance and impetus that Wasserman had provided – as had Michael Balcon and David Selznick during earlier peak periods.

Another factor was the demise of Hitchcock's stellar production unit – Robert Burks, Bernard Herrmann, George Tomasini, Herbert Coleman,

Edith Head, and the rest – which disbanded after *The Birds* and *Marnie*. Hitchcock did work with top screenwriters throughout the Universal period, including Samuel Taylor on *Topaz* (who scripted *Vertigo*) and Ernest Lehman on *Family Plot* (who wrote *North by Northwest*). But he failed to find an ongoing creative collaborator on a par with Charles Bennett, Ben Hecht, Joan Harrison, or John Michael Hayes, each of whom had played a crucial role during his earlier peak periods. Nor did Hitchcock develop the kind of rapport with top stars that he had enjoyed earlier with Joan Fontaine, Ingrid Bergman, Cary Grant, Grace Kelly, and Jimmy Stewart. His efforts to make a star of icy blonde Tippi Hedren came up short, although pairing her in *Marnie* with Sean Connery (then starring in the James Bond cycle) undoubtedly contributed to that film's box office, as did pairing top stars Paul Newman and Julie Andrews in *Torn Curtain*. But interestingly enough, Hitchcock opted to work without top stars on his last three films.

Conclusion

A curious irony about Hitchcock's waning years is that, as his career ebbed in the 1960s, he was being heralded by critics and scholars such as François Truffaut, Andrew Sarris, and Robin Wood as the Hollywood auteur par excellence. They were quite right in this assessment, although these and countless others developed a "cult of personality" around Hitchcock that André Bazin warned Truffaut and the other doctrinaire auteurists to avoid.[9] Wood, for instance, struggled mightily in his otherwise excellent landmark study, *Hitchcock's Films*, to argue that *Marnie* was "one of Hitchcock's richest, most fully achieved and mature masterpieces."[10] Sarris, meanwhile, included Hitchcock in his pantheon of Hollywood filmmakers whose "directorial biographies" comprised the basis for studying and understanding American film history, and whose artistic accomplishments were achieved in direct conflict with – and ultimately in spite of – the commercial and impersonal forces of the studio system.[11] Bazin, meanwhile, clearly had Hitchcock in mind when he admonished his critics at *Cahiers du cinéma* to consider the genius not only of individual filmmakers but of the system itself in accounting for film authorship.

Hitchcock's career provides ample evidence of Bazin's thesis, although it encourages us to take a rather nuanced view of it. There were obvious instances during Hitchcock's career when "the system" did not serve him all that well – at British International Pictures in the early 1930s and during his ill-fated Transatlantic Pictures venture in the late 1940s, as well as his long slow fade at Universal. These were periods, significantly enough, when Hitchcock exercised far more control over his career than he did during his peak periods at Gaumont in the mid-to-late 1930s, under contract to Selznick in the 1940s, and in his bifurcated Paramount and TV series trajectories in the 1950s. There was no question of Hitchcock's filmmaking virtuosity throughout his remarkable career. But it is equally evident that, when relying too heavily on his own inimitable genius and working without the full complement of resources the studio system could provide, he created remarkably few definitive "Hitchcock films." His peak periods were characterized by creative and administrative conditions closely attuned to his filmmaking genius – and attuned to the popular and commercial currents of those successive eras as well. Indeed, a striking paradox within Hitchcock's body of work, as I have argued throughout this essay, is that his distinctive authorial voice was actualized in cycles of films with very different narrative and generic tendencies in successive phases of his career. The notion of a Hitchcock film meant something quite different in the 1930s, 1940s, and 1950s, due to his dynamic interaction with a system that, when the necessarily elements were in play – and in equilibrium – enabled his singular genius to find its full expression.

NOTES

1 Discussions throughout the piece of contracts and agreements are based on originals located in the Alfred Hitchcock Collection at the Academy of Motion Picture Arts & Sciences and in the David O. Selznick Collection at the University of Texas at Austin.

2 *The Man Who Knew Too Much: The Memoirs of Screenwriter-Laureate Charles Bennett*, John Charles Bennett, ed. www.labyrinth.net.au/~muffin/bennett_c.html (accessed January 16, 2015).

3 Review of *Jamaica Inn*, *New York Times*, October 12, 1939.

4 See Donald Spoto, *The Dark Side of Genius: The Life of Alfred Hitchcock* (New York: Da Capo, 1999), p. 213.

5 Hitchcock memo to Mary Elson (London story editor), February 24, 1955. In the *Alfred Hitchcock Presents* file, Alfred Hitchcock Collection, Academy of Motion Picture Arts & Sciences.

6 James Naremore, "Hitchcock and Humor," reprinted in *Hollywood: Critical Concepts*, vol II, Thomas Schatz, ed. (New York: Routledge, 2004), p. 323.

7 Spoto, *The Dark Side of Genius*, p. 369.

8 Lehman quoted in Spoto, *The Dark Side of Genius*, p. 392.

9 André Bazin, "De la politique des auteurs," *Cahiers du Cinéma* 70 (April 1957). Reprinted in *Cahiers du Cinema*, Jim Hiller, ed. (Cambridge, MA: Harvard University Press, 1985), pp. 248–259.

10 Robin Wood, *Hitchcock's Films Revisited* (New York: Columbia University Press, 2002), p. 173.

11 Andrew Sarris, *The American Cinema: Directors and Directions, 1929–1968* (New York: Da Capo, 1996).

2

JANET STAIGER

Creating the Brand:
The Hitchcock Touch

When Alfred Hitchcock moved to the United States in March 1939 to work for producer David O. Selznick, the U.S. magazines and newspapers continued the celebrity journalism they had employed for Hitchcock's two previous vacations. Following him around all day and night and probing his attitudes, working habits, and leisure choices (especially in drink and cuisine), profiles and interviews ensured that any film fan had plenty of access to the authentic "Hitch."[1] The response to his arrival was not unusual: it was normal, and it displays the "frenzy of renown" for celebrities that Leo Braudy has described.[2] The response also makes apparent that Hitchcock's image, his brand, is already firmly in place. While his subsequent work in film and television would make him one of the most recognizable directors in the history of cinema, *he* is already present in every sense of what scholars and the public might immediately conjure up. The creation of that brand by the time of his arrival in the United States is the subject of this essay.

Of course, the press was not the only profession that recognized the value of cultivating a recognizable brand. Scholars have already pointed out that Hitchcock early and aggressively was aware that promoting himself might improve his career opportunities. A key proof of this is Hitchcock's declaration at a mid-1920s London Film Society meeting that directors were what counted in making movies. According to Donald Spoto's version, Hitchcock pronounced: "'*We* make a film succeed.... The name of the director should be associated in the public's mind with a quality product. Actors come and go, but the name of the director should stay clearly in the mind of the audience.'"[3] As Robert Kapsis details in his excellent study of Hitchcock's reputation, Hitchcock's actions also indicate a concerted effort to follow that theoretical statement about linking the director's name with quality films through his own behavior of marketing himself – for example, writing a letter in 1927 to the *London Evening News* about himself and about what directors do to make films. Hitchcock also readily participated in studio-produced publicity, his 1930 production company was named

Hitchcock-Baker Productions, and, as he hoped to be hired by Selznick, he "accelerated his promotional activities during the mid-to-late 1930s. The personal idiosyncrasy which he seemed most anxious to exploit at this time was his obesity."[4]

Hitchcock's conduct is not surprising; it makes sense. Moreover, prior to his employment in film, he worked in sales and advertising, so he was primed to think about these matters. However, it is the larger economic context that is also at stake. Capitalist film industries operate in a tension between standardizing product for mass production and differentiating it to create reasons for audiences to return to theaters. This tension for profit maximization encourages workers to be innovative within the bounds of the industry's product. Moreover, individuals negotiate within these bounds to learn how they will create successfully within the system. During the classical Hollywood era, for directors, avoiding unwarranted expressivity was often rewarded, but within some circumstances (such as the genres of musicals, comedies, and the melodramatic film noirs), certain visible stylizations were praised. Other cinema industries have formed their own boundaries and variants (e.g., German expressionism, the French new wave, and Bollywood). As the classical Hollywood system changed during the 1960s into a package-unit mode of production, places for marking individual authorship increased. Furthermore, directors and other workers realized that displays of authorship might further careers as long as the films made profits (e.g., the new Hollywood of 1967 to about 1980 and, later, indie cinema and action-adventure blockbusters). Thus, workers "self-fashioned" their authorship to try to maximize professional and personal benefits such as prestige, power, and money.[5]

Moreover, a much wider culture encouraged this authorial display. Scholars of fame point out that for centuries the elite have exhibited their images on buildings, statuary, and coins as signs of their power, and biographers have conveyed to the masses explanations of what made the elite the elite. By the 1800s, as democratic cultures spread, individuals used the older principles to mark themselves out in their fields. Braudy describes Byron, Disraeli, and Baudelaire as cultivating "fans" to solidify their prominence. Loren Glass points to the author Samuel Clemens as creating a "cultural performance of authorial personality," which included his distinctive pseudonym, Mark Twain. A few people engaged in "ostentatious costuming" to promote an appearance of distinction and individuality (for example, Oscar Wilde). Glass notes that between 1880 and 1920 the number of authors who published their autobiographies increased dramatically. During the same period, the hiring of press agents by "big-city theater owners" spread to other occupations.[6]

Several phenomena encouraged these self-generated articulations: the cultivation of consumerism for its own pleasures, the fashion industry, but particularly mass-circulation newspapers and journals. Historians see the William Randolph Hearst/Joseph Pulitzer battles post-1895 as transitional, with the Hearst papers' "blend of crime, large-scale disasters, small-scale human tragedies, [and] a modicum of national and international political news" as critical in the transition.[7] Press photography complements the printed information. Charles Ponce de Leon wisely counsels that the appearance from the mid-1700s of the printing press for preserving oral gossip and *chroniques scandaleuses* as an underground literature in France foreshadows the modern gossip column, but he also argues that, with the nineteenth-century culture of democratic equality and every person supposedly being a "commoner," the compulsion to find truth and authenticity accelerates, feeding into the proliferation of human-interest stories, interviews, and personal revelations.[8]

For my purposes here, considering what are the typical aspects of an image for someone in the entertainment business by the mid-1920s, when Hitchcock begins his career, will indicate how conventional the building of his brand becomes. It is common in star and celebrity theory to describe people as having several often conflicting facets to their image. Although various schema have been proposed, I split these into four parts under the umbrella term of *image*. The four parts are (1) the *character persona* that is created as an amalgam of clearly asserted performances and roles in films and other media; (2) the *performer* that is "acting ability" or how roles are played; (3) the *worker/laborer* that develops from information about "professional life" and how work situations are negotiated; and (4) the *private persona* that is the "so-called off-camera life."[9] In the development of Hitchcock's brand, by the 1920s all four parts of his image are in play for press coverage or self-revelation. Moreover, the ubiquitous media to disseminate the image are all actively engaged in this.

These publicity media include *biographies* that, according to Leo Lowenthal, shift after World War I to a formula about "idols of consumption" (which certainly benefits Hitchcock!) and increasingly cover people in the entertainment field. Lowenthal's early 1940s content analysis indicates that standard biographies would focus on sociology: the person's "relations to other people, the pattern of his daily life, his relation to the world in which he lives"; psychology: "what the nature of his development has been and the structure of his personality"; history: what she has done and her successes and failures; and evaluation: what the author's conclusion about the person is. Lowenthal writes that biographies describe parents, friends, marriages, hobbies, food preferences, routines of the life, and party preferences, and, surprisingly, one-third mention the person's eyes.[10]

These biographies appear as books but also as short *profiles* in magazines, newspaper articles, and Sunday supplements. Ponce de Leon writes that in this period, to establish credibility, biographers and celebrity profilers needed to create complexity to a character portrait because of the public's skepticism about hagiographical approaches. Thus, making distinctions between public and private lives facilitated more ambiguity in a representation. Additionally, by the 1920s, writers tended to assume that it was in the private life that a person found self-fulfillment.[11] People were often interviewed at home so the reader could supposedly see the authentic person. Celebrity profile visits were "described in laborious detail," and sometimes the writer and celebrity did things together. Unlike in biographies, the profile writer was present in the narrative.

The images of celebrities were also their corporeal *likeness*. While the elite could splatter their visages across an empire, and their successors could spend a great deal of money destroying those, printing and copper engravings were possible from the 1500s, expanding depictions of individualizing physical features further down the economic ladder. Ponce de Leon's research indicates that up to about 1900, a drawing often accompanied a profile. Then photographs became technologically inexpensive to print. By the 1920s, mass-circulation media did photo spreads, and images moved from posed to supposedly candid.

Consequently, in the mid-1920s, when Hitchcock was entering the film industry, how to create an image and a reputation was readily apparent to both him and the public. Documents in the press indicate four phases in the development of the brand of Hitchcock between the early 1920s to 1940.

The Best British Director and His "Touches": From 1926 On

Although Hitchcock directed films for several years prior to the British release of *The Lodger* in February 1927, his third feature-length film was very well reviewed in Britain. The earlier *The Mountain Eagle* (1925) had been described as having "at times brilliant direction," but *The Lodger* drew accolades, including *Bioscope*'s declaration that "it is possible that this film is the finest British production ever made.... Mr. Hitchcock's sense of dramatic values is magnificent ... [It is] a directorial triumph."[12]

This early praise is substantial, and I detail more of it as Hitchcock continues to make films. However, prior to *The Lodger*'s release, his production company's publicity machine was busy. Gainsborough's press agent, Cedric

Belfrage, provided a profile of Hitchcock entitled "Alfred the Great" to a British fan magazine, *The Picturegoer*, in March 1926. The profile describes Hitchcock's childhood family as working class and, with the death of his father, "practically penniless," and his early jobs as earning low wages ("He was grateful for the chance of making good, and in spite of the hardships which the small pay entailed he took the job"). But in Horatio Alger style, "his own grit and endeavour had opened for him, at 19, the magic doors of movie-land, but it was certainly a stroke of good fortune that landed him in such a studio as the Famous [Players] in Poole Street." There, Hitchcock watched important U.S. directors and worked all of the film jobs, learning the craft. Belfrage stresses in the subtitle that Hitchcock is "the youngest director in the world," yet "all who have seen [his first two features] declare [them] to be almost perfect in their technical and artistic perfection." Beyond the studio publicity, Hitchcock is also establishing friendships with the influential people at the London Film Society.[13]

Bioscope's review of *The Lodger* notes what will become distinctive about discussion of Hitchcock's work at this point: "There are numerous shots of a distinctly interesting and original character, and not once is one of these shots used purely for its own sake – on every occasion there is a definite point at issue."[14] Deviating from conventional camerawork and editing, Hitchcock innovated, marking out his authorship for the knowledgeable viewer without (usually) declining into formalism. Subsequent reviews repeat this pattern of describing his work as fresh and mature. *Bioscope* explains that the selling points for *Downhill* (1927) include "the name and clever direction of Alfred Hitchcock"; for *Easy Virtue* (1927), "the established reputation of the author, Noel Coward, and of Alfred Hitchcock, the producer"; and for *The Ring* (1927), "the reputation of the director." *Bioscope* continues to assert that while technique is visible, it is also functional: *The Ring* is a "truthful picture," and "it is presented with an economy of means, a richness of essential detail and the skillful use of every artistic and technical device that makes a picture of outstanding merit" but with no "grotesque trickeries of the camera." *The Ring* earns from *Bioscope* an editorial message addressed "To Alfred Hitchcock, Greatest British Film Director" and the acclamation that *The Ring* has "established beyond doubt your claim to be regarded as one of the greatest directors of films in this or any other country."[15]

The young British film art journal, *Close Up*, is more skeptical about Hitchcock. In reviewing *The Ring*, Robert Herring points out that while people are describing the film as a "masterpiece," perhaps yearning for a British cinema's dominance against its other national competitors, he believes that the techniques praised by some writers are expressionist (read

"German") and uneconomical: "Mr. Hitchcock's method is to depict one simple fact, that a sub-title could have got over, by a long sequence or a number of elaborate tricks. This is worse than a photographic rendering of a story, for it is pretentious." But Hitchcock's work is recognizable: "Mr. Hitchcock's touches and angles misled the public, which had noticed them in German films. And German films are good. Look for the trademark. Yes, Look – don't have someone else's thrust at you. And if you have followed me, you will have found Mr. Hitchcock's trade mark."[16]

"Touches" as trademark: this rhetoric at this historical moment may surprise scholars, but it seems it was somewhat common expressive terminology by the late 1920s in both Britain and the United States for describing characteristics of film directors. I have found this vocabulary in early 1930s U.S. high school manuals educating youth about how to watch films intelligently. Writer Edgar Dale even lists twelve directors, with their photographs, whose "touch" should be easy to spot and includes Frank Borzage, Frank Capra, Ernst Lubitsch, Josef von Sternberg, and eight more of the most well-known American and European directors of the period (but not Hitchcock).[17] In studying what might constitute "the Lubitsch touch," Kristin Thompson locates the application of the language to Lubitsch as early as 1921 and notes that by the mid-1920s it is used in the plural,[18] as it is for Hitchcock in Herring's 1928 essay. The term for Hitchcock is used sporadically thereafter (in singular and plural forms) but is linked usually fairly generally to visual and aural technique. John Grierson summarizes in 1931, "You will have heard before now of 'the Hitchcock touch.' This consists in his great ability to give a novel twist to his sketch of an episode."[19] Helen Brown Norden writes in *Vanity Fair* in 1935 about *The Man Who Knew Too Much* (1934):

> For touches like the click of the first bullet on the hotel window-pane and that stunned instant of hesitation before Louis realizes that he has been fatally shot; for someone's cough, clearing the throat just before the choral sequence at the concert; for the opening of the scene in the hotel dining-room, with that stupendous view of the mountains, fading in, through the window panes, to the dance floor; for the moment when the rescued child, hysterical with fear, instinctively shrinks back from her mother ... for these touches alone, I say, Mr. Hitchcock should be awarded all the directorial palms of the year.[20]

Or *News-Week*'s praise in 1936 for "the same skillful touches of humor, subtlety, and suspense" in both *The 39 Steps* (1935) and *Secret Agent* (1936).[21]

Thus, Hitchcock's touches generally refer to great noticeable moments of cinematic skill and eventually to affective experiences associated with the outcome for his techniques. Although some films excited reviewers more than others, from *The Lodger* on, expectations were that audiences were

45

watching the best British director working, and he displayed specific touches as his trademark. Even *Close Up* comes around occasionally, remarking for *Blackmail* (1929) that it exhibits the "most intelligent mixture of sound and silence we have yet seen," "Hitchcock's Cockney humour adds to its appeal," and while "not a masterpiece" or "an artistic triumph," "it is a first [sound film] effort of which the British industry has every reason to be proud."[22]

Experimenter or Realist? From 1928 On

A major dichotomy in evaluating films is apparent in Herring's initial criticisms of *The Lodger*. Cinematic skill was expected, but the norms for both British and U.S. fictional filmmaking emphasized transparency rather than reflexivity for most movies. Symbolism or flash had its place, but "realism" was also treasured. Embedded within realism for the British reviewers – at least for the criticism of Hitchcock's work – was an assumption of a humanistic display of people's tribulations. When a director worked in genres more associated with drama, the technical bravado could disrupt, but this distraction could also occur in lighter fare. At times, Hitchcock succeeded in providing both innovations and realism; at other times, reviewers believed he had failed. For the romantic comedy/drama *The Farmer's Wife* (1928), *Bioscope* complains that Hitchcock is "led away by his tendency to fantastic angles of photography," but it lauds the very dramatic *The Manxman* (1929) for its "unflinching realism" and characters who are "real and human."[23]

The reviews for *Murder!* (1930) display the mixed critical consequences for emphasizing only the experimental half of this tension. The British paper *Spectator* claims no "amount of intelligence" could have "made a good film of this story" and concludes that it is neither cinematic nor realistic: "none of the characters in this production had any resemblance to real people." *Close Up* decides it is "quite the best thing this country has done," for Hitchcock can "think cinema." The *New York Times* notes that "Mr. Hitchcock rather likes to experiment, but in doing so he is often inconsistent."[24]

In fact, Hitchcock seems to be planting the image of the innovator. According to Spoto, in 1930 Hitchcock hired a publicist to keep "his name before the public." Although profiles and Hitchcock's own authored articles had previously been published, Oswell Blackeston interviews him for *Close Up* about the inventive sound techniques in *Murder!*. Blackeston does little actual interviewing, at least in the published article; mostly he just quotes Hitchcock, who is ready to talk. Hitchcock describes his theory of "advance monologue" and describes several unusual shots he created. Hitchcock claims, "'such touches, of course, can only be added to a good story.'" The article carries on, "'*Potemkin*'," he continued with a twinkle in his eye, 'is the only Russian film I have seen.'"[25] As though his eye reveals his playful soul, the interview reinforces Hitchcock's image of cultivating an experimental side.

The other side of the tension is realism, not a characteristic normally considered an aspect of Hitchcock's brand. However, at this point, his work occasionally earns that description, partially as the studios for which he is working assign him films in genres that demand it. The *Spectator* thinks that Hitchcock likes the challenge: "There are few British directors with his pictorial sense, but he is not one of those screen pastrycooks who are at their happiest when human realism makes no demand on them." Yet, such a depiction for Hitchcock is rare as British film critics attempt to analyze where he goes wrong. C. A. Lejeune believes that Hitchcock lacks "human understanding"; he is an "observer" of people. Grierson opines, "He knows people but not things; situations and episodes, but not events."[26] This image of personal distance from his characters will also persist into Hitchcock's later career.

At times Hitchcock will assert that he wants realistic representations in his films, but it seems to be that he envisions producing them through situations (as Grierson observes). Although it is a couple of years later, Barbara J. Buchanan begins a 1935 interview with "I asked Alfred Hitchcock point-blank, 'Why do you hate women?'" Hitchcock's publicity people may not have prepared him well. He replies: "'I don't exactly hate them,' he protested. 'But I certainly don't think they are as good actors as men.'" He then goes on to argue that he does not want glamour and beauty from females; "'Glamour,' he told me defiantly, 'has nothing to do with reality, and I maintain that reality is the most important factor in the making of a successful film.'"[27] He justifies the stories of his handling of female stars as attempts to make them behave more naturally.

Hitchcock's concern to argue that he is seeking realism is not necessarily at odds with his desire to be known as an experimenter. The tension can be negotiated if realism is found in some aspects of a film, say character development; experiments, applied elsewhere. It is doubtful, however, that Hitchcock's move to thrillers and screwball comedy provided opportunity for extensive exploration of complex characters.

The Artist of Suspense and Comedy: From 1934 On

Scholars concur that Hitchcock's move in 1934 to British Gaumont and a team of writers with whom he worked well resulted in an outpouring of films that were not only highly praised but better distributed (and reviewed) in the United States.[28] Moreover, these melodramatic thrillers[29] consistently used a subplot with qualities of the screwball comedy, a genre described by Steve Neale as "an energetic mix of slapstick, wisecracks, intricately plotted farce and the comedy of manners combined with vividly eccentric character-ization and a disavowable undercurrent of sexual innuendo."[30] This shift in genres and their concentration produced review after review that associated Hitchcock with the affective pleasures of suspense and comedy.

For instance, for *The Man Who Knew Too Much* (1934), *Film Daily*'s subheading for its review states: "Swell melodrama with plenty of exciting action plus human interest and comedy touches." Andre Sennwald of the *New York Times* writes that, with one exception, "it is the swiftest screen melodrama this column can recall," is "distinctly Mr. Hitchcock's picture," and is "the raciest melodrama of the new year." Norden of *Vanity Fair* liked the "light banter ... [presented] in a smart and natural way." "It is not only exciting melodrama; it is, in its way, a work of art."[31] *The 39 Steps* (1935) fared the same. Sennwald of the *New York Times* is again impressed: "A master of shock and suspense, of cold horror and slyly incongruous wit, he uses his camera the way a painter uses his brush, stylizing his story and giving it value which the scenarists could hardly have suspected.... [It has] sinister delicacy and urbane understatement." After comparing Hitchcock to Anatole France, Sennwald describes the movie as a "blend of unexpected comedy and breathless terror."[32]

Again, the Hitchcock publicity machine attempts to reinforce the pub-lic response. Aside from the interview with Buchanan in the fall of 1935 about his authentic attitudes toward women, Hitchcock engages in a series of articles explaining his methods. For *The Picturegoer*, he expounds on "Why 'Thrillers' Thrive." He provides a five-part autobiography for *Film Weekly*, an account that has become the source for many stories about Hitchcock's life. For New York City readers in the summer of 1936, in an essay entitled "Close Your Eyes and Visualize!," he reviews his career and expounds on "'the 'Hitchcock touch'," the importance of stories being told visually even though sound is now available, the mistaken notion that he loathes women when in fact his desire is for "reality" first and comedy next, and the function of the comedy "to relieve the tension."[33] Because his films do provide both suspense and humor, thereafter these two terms are almost joined at the hip.

His Body and Ours: From 1935 On

As the U.S. mass media began paying attention to Hitchcock's films and pub-licity generated attention to him and his work, it is typical for this era that arti-cles would start not only trying to describe and define his public and private image but providing readers the sort of background that would personalize the man into a celebrity. Even when Hitchcock is an assistant working for Famous Players, a London film magazine includes him in its profile on the

Figure 2.1. A sketch of Alfred Hitchcock in 1923.
The Motion Picture Studio [journal], London, 1923.

company, providing both words and drawings depicting the men and women working at the studio. The sketch for Hitchcock is remarkably prescient of his future iconic image in its brief outline from the side and a body stance of his stomach thrust forward, hands in his pocket (Figure 2.1).[34]

His own attention to his visual form appears in the choice in 1927 to send Christmas cards that were a jigsaw puzzle of an "eight-stroke profile caricature." By the mid-1930s Hitchcock was becoming sufficiently physically identifiable that the *Sunday London Times* reviewer of *The 39 Steps* mentions seeing Hitchcock in his cameo role in the movie. Likely supplied by his studio, an image accompanying a 1938 interview is his film appearance in *Young and Innocent* (1937).[35]

It was not just Hitchcock's body, of course; it was its size. By *Secret Agent* (1936), Hitchcock weighed more than 300 pounds, according to Spoto. Kapsis claims that "Hitchcock accelerated his promotional activities during the mid-to-late 1930s. The personal idiosyncrasy which he seemed most anxious to exploit at this time was his obesity."[36]

Although it may have occurred earlier, the first article mentioning the escalating size of Hitchcock's body appears to be *McCall's* review in September 1935 of *The 39 Steps*, written by Pare Lorentz who refers to him as "the chubby Cockney." In a British interview, Norah Baring jokingly writes, "in more ways than one he is an outstanding figure in British films. A big man, his height is dwarfed by his huge girth," and when he replies, it is "with a twinkle in his eye." Another U.S. periodical produces the next reference. *Time* writes in June 1936 that "England's pudgy master of melodrama, Alfred Hitchcock" directed *Secret Agent*.[37]

This descriptive practice begins to become routine in reviews and often includes not only his weight but his eyes: "Alfred Hitchcock, England's jovial and rotund master of melodrama"; "England's roly-poly, impish-eyed Director." When Hitchcock visits the United States in August 1937, the *New York Times* headlines the news story "Falstaff in Manhattan: Alfred Hitchcock Tests Our Kitchens and Our Tastes in Melodrama" and engages in detailed description of him in physical terms, including "eyes that peek elfishly."[38]

Not only were Hitchcock's physique and eyes becoming of significance as of 1935; so were ours. Undoubtedly an upshot of the sort of films he was directing, language in the reviews begins more routinely to describe the movies' affective and *physical* effects on the audience. Hitchcock is "a master of shock and suspense" and produces "breathless terror." "Mr. Hitchcock has an amazing and almost unanalyzable [sic] gift for creating and prolonging suspense." *Young and Innocent* "will have [audiences] sitting on the edge of their seats" with its "nerve-tingling suspense." *The Lady Vanishes* (1938) is "exciting" and the "audience is sitting breathless."[39]

Again, Hitchcock's publicity feeds this. His explanation of why thrillers thrive for *The Picturegoer* emphasizes that in contrast to the theater where the audience members are mere spectators, in movies "we participate." In "Close Your Eyes," he states that he wants to "jolt cinemagoers in their seats with stories that move – with unexpected thrills, with comedy, with reality." He clearly wants to provoke, and as celebrity journalism devoted to him increases, he has opportunities to do so outside of the films themselves. The interviews themselves become entertainment.[40]

Hitchcock and the "Cineastes"

The profiles and articles published in the United States as a result of his visits in 1937 and 1938 and then his move to Los Angeles in 1939 solidify these image facets of character, performer, worker, and private individual to create Hitchcock's brand. As I described about the celebrity context, the conventions for these human-interest and gossip stories required emphasizing personal facts while constructing and evaluating the public biography. The second paragraph of the *New York Times* essay, "Falstaff in Manhattan," about his first U.S. visit, fulfills this duty:

> Mr. Hitchcock is a walking monument to the principle of uninhibited addiction to sack and capon, prime beef and flowing ale, and double helpings of ice cream. His free-floating, unconfined waistline is a triumph in embonpoint, and he scrutinizes the world, catching its moods and manners and filing them away for future availability, through bright, piercing eyes that peek elfishly out of a rubicund face. When he smiles, his chins all smile with him, one after another.... It is reassuring to be able to report that the future of melodrama, as long as it remains in his expansive custody, will never suffer for lack of attention.[41]

This article individualizes him physically and focuses on both his private and his public lives. It marks out what he contributes artistically to film-making and describes his work behaviors. When Hitchcock returns in June 1938, Eileen Creelman of the *New York Sun* dutifully begins with her experience of dining with him at Twenty-One when he is describing to a waiter the sort of lamb chop he can have on his new diet.[42]

Yet, the fall 1938 four-page *New Yorker* profile by Russell Maloney indicates how developed the reputation is becoming while reinforcing it. Mahoney begins the essay: "The vogue for Alfred Hitchcock's cinema melodramas is mainly a local phenomenon. 'The 39 Steps,' his best-known job of direction, has, in the past three years, been revived thirty-one times by various theatres on Manhattan Island." Mahoney continues that some people would rather re-watch a Hitchcock movie than take a chance with a new film. So a small cult is developing. (Other writers mention these Hitchcock "fans" and are becoming so familiar with him that Frank S. Nugent of the *New York Times* often refers to him in reviews simply as "Hitch.")[43]

Maloney runs through standard biographical information such as Hitchcock's amusing escape in Zurich without enough money while filming one of his early movies, his Catholic background, the two-month writing conferences, the "editing" of a film before shooting, the manipulation of the actors, the habit of throwing his cup over his shoulder when he finishes drinking his afternoon tea, his marriage and "small flat in London," his love of horticulture. Hitchcock's promotion of what is occurring is marked by Mahoney recounting that "Hitchcock is the soul of amiability and has been known to begin an interview, after offering the reporters a drink, with 'I suppose you want something grotesque.'" The essay is nearly three-quarters complete before Maloney addresses the weight (and diet): "His fatness seems to buoy him up. Spiritually and physically, he might be a kin to a

Macy balloon. His large, close-set ears, bright-blue eyes, scrubby black hair, and double chin give him the air of one of his own likable cinematic villains." A line-drawing of Hitchcock accompanies the "Profile."[44]

With Hitchcock's move to Los Angeles in 1939, profiles in mass-market magazines proliferate. These articles continue the trends already described and begin to include photographs of Hitchcock in his pajama robe and at play with his dogs. The only new thematic angle, which has been slightly set up previously, is the beginning of the *chroniques scandaleus* twist of Hitchcock's behavior as impish into something more akin to cruelty. For *Life*, Geoffrey Hellman opines: "the director ... is never happier than when seeing someone writhe" and a favorite target is "fair-haired girls."[45]

When *Rebecca* (1940) is released, U.S. reviews consistently describe it as Hitchcock's picture due to its "masterly" and "superb" direction while also usually mentioning Selznick as a producer who will provide good production values and a faithful adaptation of the original source.[46] From the perspective of celebrity journalism and creating Hitchcock's brand, it is valuable to note that the reviewers were sensitive to matters of authorship, attributing specific features of the film to each man while describing the total result as outstanding.

Moreover, the reviewers determine that Hitchcock has succeeded in maintaining his brand while meeting up alongside another powerful Hollywood author. Nugent exclaims:

> Hitch has it ... the English master of movie melodramas, rounder than John Bull, twice as fond of beef ... The question being batted around by the cineastes (hybrid for cinema-esthetes) was whether his peculiarly British, yet peculiarly personal, style could survive Hollywood, the David O. Selznick of "Gone with the Wind."[47]

Nugent's evaluation is yes, "his famous and widely publicized 'touch' seems to have developed into a firm, enveloping grasp" to produce "a brilliant film."

Certainly this cineaste sensitivity to fine details of authorship is something not apparent to average moviegoers, but the reviewers are glad to help them see it. Thus, by 1940, authoring behaviors in the films directed by Hitchcock, publicity activities, and celebrity journalism have established the brand of "Hitchcock" so that cineastes could speculate on and evaluate sources and results of authorship. "He" existed.

Acknowledgments

Thanks to Anne Petersen for help on the history of celebrity journalism, Casey McKittrick for discussions about Hitchcock's obesity, Anne Morey and the UT Film Faculty for close readings of the essay, Tom Schatz for evaluations of the literature on Hitchcock, and Peter Staiger for companionship watching the movies.

NOTES

1 "Alfred Hitchcock: England's Best Director Starts Work in Hollywood," *Life*, 19 June 1939, 66; Katharine Roberts, "Mystery Man," *Colliers*, 5 August 1939, 22; Geoffrey Hellman, "Alfred Hitchcock: England's Best and Biggest Director Goes to Hollywood," *Life*, 20 November 1939, 33–43.

2 Leo Braudy, *Frenzy of Renown: Fame & Its History*, rev. ed. (New York: Oxford University Press, 1997).

3 Emphasis in the original; Donald Spoto, *The Dark Side of Genius: The Life of Alfred Hitchcock* (Boston: Little, Brown and Company, 1983), p. 73. Spoto dates the event as occurring in 1925. Patrick McGilligan provides a similar account and cites Ivor Montagu's memoirs that date the remark to early 1927; *Alfred Hitchcock: A Life in Darkness and Light* (New York: Regan Books, 2003), pp. 86–87 and 799. Also see Robert Kapsis, *Hitchcock: The Making of a Reputation* (Chicago: University of Chicago Press, 1992), p. 16.

4 Kapsis, *Hitchcock*, 18–23. The quotation is from p. 23.

5 Janet Staiger in David Bordwell, Janet Staiger, and Kristin Thompson, *The Classical Hollywood Cinema: Film Style and Mode of Production to 1960* (London: Routledge & Kegan Paul, 1985), pp. 108–110; Janet Staiger, "Authorship Studies and Gus Van Sant," *Film Criticism* 29, no. 1 (Fall 2004): 1–22; Janet Staiger, "Analysing Self-Fashioning in Authoring and Reception," in *Ingmar Bergman Revisited: Performance, Cinema, and the Arts*, ed. Maaret Koskinen (London: Wallflower, 2008), pp. 89–106; Janet Staiger, "'Because I Am a Woman': Thinking Identity and Agency for Historiography," *Film History* 25, nos. 1–2 (2013): 205–214.

6 Braudy, *Frenzy*, 481–83; Loren Glass, *Authors Inc.: Literary Celebrity in the Modern United States, 1880–1980* (New York: New York University Press, 2004), pp. 57–60.

7 Richard Schickel, *Intimate Strangers: The Culture of Celebrity* (Garden City, New York: Doubleday, 1985), p. 30.

8 Charles Ponce de Leon, *Self-Exposure: Human-Interest Journalism and the Emergence of Celebrity in America* (Chapel Hill: University of North Carolina Press, 2002), pp. 15–18, 33–36.

9 Janet Staiger, *Media Reception Studies* (New York: New York University Press, 2005), pp. 115–124.

10 Leo Lowenthal, "The Triumph of Mass Idols" [1944], rpt. in *Literature, Popular Culture, and Society*, ed. Leo Lowenthal (Englewood Cliffs, NJ: Prentice-Hall, 1961), pp. 109–140.

11 Ponce de Leon, *Self-Exposure*, 33–40, 57–58; also see Richard deCordova, *Picture Personalities: The Emergence of the Star System in America* (Urbana: University of Illinois Press, 1990), pp. 119–120.

12 "The Mountain Eagle," *Bioscope* [U.K.], 7 October 1925, 48; "The Lodger," *Bioscope*, 16 September 1926, 39.

13 McGilligan, *Alfred Hitchcock*, pp. 85–86; Cedric Belfrage, "Alfred the Great," *The Picturegoer* [U.K.], 11, no. 63 (March 1926), 60.

14 "The Lodger," *Bioscope*, 39.

15 "Downhill," *Bioscope*, 26 May 1927, 43; "Easy Virtue," *Bioscope*, 1 September 1927, 67; "The Ring," *Bioscope*, 6 October 1927, 43; "Without Prejudice," *Bioscope*, 6 October 1927, 27.

16 Robert Herring, "The Latest British Masterpiece," *Close Up* 2, no. 1 (January 1928), 35–36.

17 Janet Staiger, "The Revenge of the Film Education Movement: Cult Movies and Fan Interpretive Behaviors," *Reception: Texts, Readers, Audiences, History* 1 (Fall 2008), http://receptionstudy.org/files/Staiger.pdf.

18 Kristin Thompson, *Herr Lubitsch Goes to Hollywood: German and American Film after World War I* (Amsterdam: Amsterdam University Press, 2005), pp. 127–131.

19 John Grierson, "Rich and Strange," *Everyman*, 31 December 1931, rpt. in *Grierson on Documentary*, ed. Forsyth Hardy (New York: Harcourt, Brace, 1947), 51.

20 Helen Brown Norden, "Hollywood on Parade," *Vanity Fair*, 44 (May 1935), 45.

21 "Secret Agent," *News-Week*, 13 June 1936, 41.

22 Hugh Castle, "Elstree's First 'Talkie,'" *Close Up* 5, no. 2 (August 1929), 133. Beyond his "touches," Hitchcock has a formula by 1938; see "The Hitchcock Formula," *New York Times*, 13 February 1938, 158.

23 "The Farmer's Wife," *Bioscope*, 8 March 1928, 75; "The Manxman," *Bioscope*, 23 January 1929, 38. U.S. reviewers were not impressed with *The Manxman*, nor did they consider the issue of realism.

24 Celia Simpson, "The Cinema," *Spectator* [U.K.], 11 October 1930, 489; Hugh Castle, "Attitude and Interlude," *Close Up* 7, no. 3 (September 1930), 184–189; Mordaunt Hall, "A Grandeur Production," *New York Times*, 2 November 1930, 8: 5.

25 Spoto, *Dark Side*, 123; Oswell Blackeston, *Close Up* 7, no. 2 (August 1930), 146.

26 Stephen Watts, "Alfred Hitchcock on Music in Films," *Cinema Quarterly* [Edinburgh], 2, no. 2 (Winter 1933), 80; Charles Davis, "The Cinema," *Spectator*, 9 March 1931, 370; Caroline Alice Lejeune, *Cinema* (London: Alexander Maclehose, 1931), p. 11; Grierson, "Rich and Strange," 50.

27 Barbara J. Buchanan, "Alfred Hitchcock Tells a Woman That Women Are a Nuisance," *Film Weekly* [London], 20 September 1935, 10. For earlier remarks by Hitchcock about female stars, see Alfred Hitchcock, "How I Choose My Heroines," in *Who's Who in Filmland*, ed. Langford Reed and Hetty Spiers (London: Chapman & Hall, 1931), pp. xxi–xxiii.

28 Ryall, *Alfred Hitchcock*, pp. 102–105; McGilligan, *Hitchcock*, p. 167; Kapsis, *Hitchcock*, pp. 21–22.

29 As Steve Neale has shown, the term "melodrama" in this period is used to describe action films (Westerns, suspense, detective, gangster movies) rather than social or family dynamics. "'Melo' Talk: On the Meaning and Use of the Term 'Melodrama' in the American Trade Press," *The Velvet Light Trap*, no. 32 (1993): 66–89. In the reviews to follow, Hitchcock is as often labeled the master of melodrama as of suspense. The words should be considered interchangeable at this historical moment.

30 Steve Neale, *Genre and Hollywood* (London: Routledge, 2000), p. 70.

31 "The Man Who Knew Too Much," *Film Daily* [U.S.], 22 March 1935, 7; Andre Sennwald, "The Screen," *The New York Times*, 23 March 1935, 11; Andre Sennwald, "Peter Lorre, Poet of the Damned," *The New York Times*, 31 March 1935, 11: 3; Norden, "Hollywood on Parade," 45.

32 Andre Sennwald, "The Screen," *The New York Times*, 14 September 1935, 8.

33 Alfred Hitchcock, "Why 'Thrillers' Thrive," *The Picturegoer*, 18 January 1936, 15; Alfred Hitchcock with John K. Newnham, "Screen Memories," *Film Weekly*, 2 May 1936, 16–18; 9 May 1936, 7; 16 May 1936, 28–29; 23 May 1936, 28–29; 30 May 1936, 27; Alfred Hitchcock, "Close Your Eyes and Visualize!" *Stage* [New York], 13, no. 10 (July 1936), 52–53.

34 "Paris in Poole Street: Graham Cutts Busy at Famous Players – Lasky Studios," *The Motion Picture Studio* [London], 28 April 1923, 6.

35 Spoto, *Dark Side*, 103–104; Ryall, *Alfred Hitchcock*, 105–106; Leslie Perkoff, "The Censor and Sydney Street," *World Film News* [London], 2, no. 12 (March 1938), 4.

36 Spoto, *Dark Side*, 154; Kapsis, *Hitchcock*, 22. Also see McGilligan, *Alfred Hitchcock*, 204.

37 Pare Lorentz, "Movies," *McCalls* [U.S.], 63 (September 1935), 17; Norah Baring, "The Man Who Made *The 39 Steps*: Pen Portrait of Alfred Hitchcock," *Film Pictorial*, 23 November 1935, 14–15, rpt. in *Alfred Hitchcock: Interviews*, ed. Sidney Gottlieb (Jackson: University Press of Mississippi, 2003), p. 10; "The New Pictures," *Time*, 15 June 1936, 56.

38 Frank S. Nugent, "The Screen," *New York Times*, 11 February 1938, 27; "The Girl Was Young," *Time*, 14 February 1938, 32; "Falstaff in Manhattan," *New York Times*, 5 September 1937, 122. The analogies for Hitchcock's body became amusing. See later in the chapter for Russell Maloney's equation of him to a Macy balloon. Also see Frank S. Nugent's "rotund spider" in "The Screen in Review," *New York Times*, 26 December 1938, 29.

39 "The New Pictures," *Time*, 15 June 1936, 56; Andre Sennwald, "The Screen," *New York Times*, 14 September 1935, 8; Frank S. Nugent, "There's Always a Topic," *New York Times*, 28 February 1937, 167; "The Girl Was Young," *Film Daily*, 19 January 1938, 6; "The Lady Vanishes," *Film Daily*, 5 October 1938, 6.

40 Hitchcock, "Why 'Thrillers' Thrive," 15; Hitchcock, "Close Your Eyes," 53.

41 "Falstaff in Manhattan," 122.

42 Eileen Creelman, "Picture Plays and Players: Alfred Hitchcock, English Director, to Take a Look at Hollywood," *New York Sun*, 15 June 1938, 26.

43 Russell Maloney, "Profiles: What Happens After That," *New Yorker*, 10 September 1938, 25. "Steady revivals" are mentioned in "The Lady Vanishes," *Time*, 21 November 1938, 53. *Time* writes about "fans of Director Alfred Hitchcock" in "The New Pictures," 30 October 1934, 49, as does Katharine Roberts, "Mystery Man," *Colliers*, 5 August 1939, 22. Frank S. Nugent, "The Screen in Review," *New York Times*, 26 December 1938, 29; Frank S. Nugent, "The Screen in Review," *New York Times*, 12 October 1939, 33.

44 Maloney, "Profiles," 24–28.

45 "Alfred Hitchcock: England's Best Director Starts Work in Hollywood," *Life*, 19 June 1939, 66; Katharine Roberts, "Mystery Man," *Colliers*, 5 August 1939, 22; Hellman, "Alfred Hitchcock," 33–43.

46 "Reviews," *Film Daily*, 26 March 1940, 6; Frank S. Nugent, "The Screen," *New York Times*, 29 March 1940, 28; John Mosher, "The Current Cinema: From Rebecca to Ellie May," *New Yorker*, 30 March 1940, 63–64; "Entertainment," *Newsweek*, 8 April 1940, 34–35; Otto Ferguson, "Sight Cases of Marriage," *The New Republic*, 102, no. 15 (8 April 1940), 474–475; Philip T. Hartung, "The Stage & Screen," *The Commonweal*, 31, no. 25 (12 April 1940), 534; "The New Picture," *Time*, 15 April 1940, 96 and 98.

47 Frank S. Nugent, "The Screen," *New York Times*, 29 March 1940, 28.

3

SARA BLAIR

Hitchcock on Location: America, Icons, and the Place of Illusion

Of all the effects that make movies uniquely powerful as a form of illusion, none is so foundational as its uses of space. From its very beginnings as a mass medium, cinema self-consciously explored its twinned powers of indexicality – capture of the traces left behind by actual bodies and objects in actual spaces at a given instant – and of iconicity – conjuring fantastic beings of light and shadow made, through the magic of cinematic technique, to appear lifelike, as if real, before our very eyes. These two modes of film point to a critical, if relatively unexplored, issue: What role does location – actual material place – play in the making of cinematic illusion? How does the design of cinematic space – the illusory, nonexistent world of the film and its sites, into which the viewer imaginatively enters – make use of, and even reanimate, actual space? What *makes up* the relationship between cinematic space and social space, governed in real time by myths and special effects and illusions of its own? Oddly enough, however, the effects of location have rarely been considered in the annals of film theory, apart from their resonance in specific film texts or diegetics; and standard encyclopedias and histories of film practice tend to omit discussion of location altogether.[1] So what place might place have in understanding the effects of film as a form of illusion, or of critical apprehension?

No director gives us more room to maneuver on these grounds than Hitchcock does. Noted from his earliest ventures as a proponent of location shooting, yet legendary for his frame-by-frame construction of the world and look of his films, Hitchcock was keenly attuned both to actual spaces as sources of cinematic suggestion and to film as a site of entry into their cultural and psychic resonances. Given the defining themes of his work and the tenor of his *auteur*-ial pronouncements about them, Hitchcock's films are often celebrated as experiments with narrative genres, or as stagings of psychosexual drives and desires. But actual sites turn out to play a critical role in their own right in Hitchcock's work, particularly in key American films concerned with American icons and American identities.[2] In what follows,

I want to consider the place of place in Hitchcock's cinema, and to consider the way it maps onto other territories of fantasy and illusion.

In the wake of Hitchcock's canonization as a quintessentially contemporary, artist, it is easy to forget that he was born in 1899, a subject of the not-yet-twentieth century and the unamused Queen Victoria. The early cinema into which he threw himself, first as a young spectator and later as an apprentice filmmaker, still reflected the double origins of film and its distinctive logic of place. With respect to those origins, biographer Donald Spoto identifies the work of British filmmaker William Haggar as a notable precedent for Hitchcock. Haggar's 1905 biopic about the real-life nineteenth-century British murderer (and longtime folk hero) Charles Peace remained one of the most popular and widely viewed films in Britain throughout the early years of cinema.[3] Highly theatricalized, *The Life of Charles Peace* starred members of Haggar's own family enacting Peace's criminal escapades: cat-burgling, ogling women, committing murder, leading police on a breathless chase across city rooftops, and throwing himself from the carriage of a train.

Haggar's film hardly aims for the documentary quality of early film's *actualités*. The mise-en-scène is clumsy; so, too, the protagonist's stage makeup, which has been said to resemble that of a music-hall clown.[4] But Haggar's unprecedented use of location shooting for dramatic action sequences – cops chasing the streetwise criminal in vain across open fields and railway yards – lent striking dynamism to the eleven-minute film, and it spoke volumes to Haggar's working-class audience, for whom, as film historian David Berry has noted, actual spaces of work, church, and traditional leisure were still dominated by repressive authorities and codes.[5] (Notably, a dynamic rooftop chase scene anticipates the famous opening sequence – another breathtaking rooftop chase – of Hitchcock's *Vertigo* [1958].)[6] True to life, Haggar's Peace gets hanged in the end, but not before literally thumbing his nose at the cops while disguised as a vicar, all in a daring close-up. Inviting identification, Haggar's camera bridges the fantasmatic space of cinematic adventure with the everyday social world of his audience. The film's effects – its play with juridical power and the thrill of criminality, its use of heights and speed to augment suspense and dislocate the viewer: all recognizable as trademarks of Hitchcock's work – depend not only on innovative editing but on the self-conscious use of location and cinematic space to connect with real spaces of lived experience.

If Haggar provides a benchmark for thinking about the power of place in Hitchcock's work, another set of filmmakers served as an acknowledged and durable model: the pioneering German artists of the post–World War I era. In 1924, when Hitchcock took on the role of assistant director, he worked at the world-class, state-of-the-art production facilities of UFA (Universum Film-Aktien Gesellschaft). A year later, for his directorial debut, Hitchcock was sent by the British production company Gainsborough to the Emelka Studios in Munich. He would later describe the directors he observed at both sites as the makers of "the modern German films, to which we owe so much artistically."[7]

Yet even under the sway of German Expressionism, with its emphasis on artifice and distortion in a fantasy world made in the studio, Hitchcock insisted on significant location work. His first film, *The Pleasure Garden* (1925), employed on-site shooting in Genoa, San Remo, and Lake Como.[8] His second, *The Mountain Eagle* (1926), made striking use of sites in the Ötztaler Alps in the Austrian Tyrol, if only to tell an unlikely story of revenge and sexual scandal among backwoods folk in Kentucky. In a certain sense, Hitchcock's apprenticeship in Germany, with the whole of continental Europe as his back lot, constituted a kind of location work. His earliest films experimented purposively with the uses of familiar sites as narrative elements, a resource for enhancing affective logic as well as the reality effect.

Hitchcock did not begin working in the United States until 1939. By then, Hollywood had long since become *Hollywood*, a place so steeped in myth-making and self-mythologizing that it was downright unreal. Dorothy Parker, who worked there throughout the 1930s and 1940s as a scriptwriter (including her work on the 1937 industry-insider film *A Star is Born* as well as a stint for Hitchcock on *Saboteur* [1942]), later refused to refer to the company town by name; she simply called it "'Out there.' "[9] If, as Parker suggested, Hollywood was empty as a lived site, it was heavily trafficked in terms of fantasy. Comedian Bob Hope, who moved there in 1938, quipped in 1965, "There'll always be an England, even if it's in Hollywood."[10]

The distinctive character of Hollywood as a space – empty yet dense; emblematic of the founding logic of American westering and shot through with fantasies of European empire – was what had helped grow it as a site of cinematic commerce to begin with. So attests a 1927 location map created by Paramount Studio and shared with potential investors in the studios' campaign to expand the American film industry (Figure 3.1). Sherwood Forest and the coast of Malaysia, Siberia and Bret Harte's pioneer landscape, the French Alps and the Israelites' Red Sea: Hollywood, expanding its reach throughout the state and beyond, looked to encompass them all, ranging freely across history and continents alike – no locale too exotic, temporally distant, or far-flung. In the industry view, "location," space outside the studio, is always already a space of fantasy and myth-making. Material sites in a territory still being colonized, mapped, and imagined as provinces of American settlement and industry lend themselves with

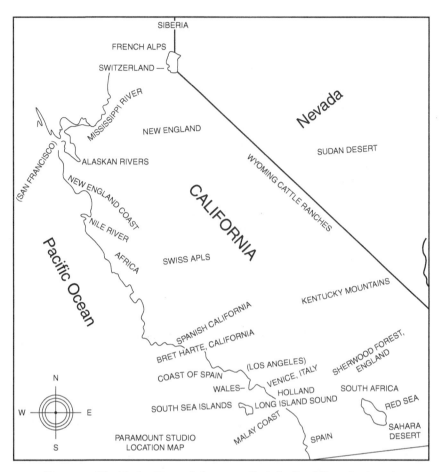

Figure 3.1. *The Motion Picture Industry as a Basis for Bond Financing* (1927).
Halsey, Stuart and Co. Available online at http://archive.org/details/motion00hals
(posted 20 July 2013). Accessed 31 July 2013. Cf. http://kottke.org/13/07/
paramount-studio-location-map-of-california

special force to cinematic representation, itself a definitively modern form
of industrial-technological production. And that representation in turn confirms the availability of the land and the landscape for projections of all
kinds. Ultimately, Paramount's map documents Hollywood's most durable
achievement: suturing the reality effect of cinema to bedrock fantasies of a
virgin land, infinitely available for American ingenuity.

In this context, Hitchcock's evolving relationship to location work and
questions of cinematic effect is striking. When he moved to the United States
to begin working under contract to mogul David O. Selznick, he already
had a reputation for effective use of visually arresting locations, including

the dome of the British Museum (*Blackmail*, 1929), the Royal Albert Hall (*The Man Who Knew Too Much*, 1934), and the Forth Bridge and muirs of eastern Scotland (*The 39 Steps*, 1935). In these British-made films, however, Hitchcock's dramatic location shots make limited use of their subjects, mobilizing landmark sites in service of suspense and visual effect. Paradoxically, it is his meticulously crafted studio spaces that resonate with viewers' social experience and the felt constraints of social identity.

The back lots of Hollywood studios and the fantasy land that was California provided Hitchcock with vastly heightened resources for exploring these kinds of tensions. For the 1943 thriller *Shadow of A Doubt* (which he later identified as his favorite among his films), Hitchcock chose Santa Rosa, fifty-five miles north of San Francisco, as a key site for filming. In a notable first, he also made his primary location the setting of a film and in an important sense its subject. Santa Rosa of the early 1940s was a quiet town of 12,600, little changed since the turn of the century.[11] Nestled in the Sonoma Valley below Hood and Sonoma Mountains, it was the very image of apple-pie America. With its historic central square, gracious residences, and orderly landscaping, it could, as film reviewer Roger Ebert noted, "have modeled for Normal Rockwell's *Saturday Evening Post* covers."[12]

Hitchcock being ... well, Hitchcock, we might predict that his engagement with this idyllic place was perverse, a calculated choice allowing him to take on key myths of American national identity. But the resonances of place and location in *Shadow* are decidedly more mixed. Shot in late 1941 and the summer of 1942, the film coincided with the onset of World War II. Lumber and other building materials were being strictly rationed by the new War Production Board; Hitchcock's usual elaborate sets, costing as much as $100,000, were out of the question. The historic home on Santa Rosa's McDonald Avenue, with its cake-bread ornamentation, multiple thresholds, and front and back staircases, offered itself as a useful resource for his distinctive mise-en-scene.[13] There was also a sharp publicity angle: no studio had shot a film on location in decades. Always alert to the main chance, Hitchcock's studio (Universal) convinced *Life* magazine to do a feature on his work in Santa Rosa. As he rolled the movie cameras, *Life* photographers avidly documented his newsworthy use of " 'the real thing.' "[14]

Beyond the photo ops, American men were being conscripted by the tens of thousands, women were taking their places in the workforce, and U.S. factories were retooling for wartime production. Under these conditions, everyday America as a field of representation was irresistible. The context invited nostalgia, and Hitchcock was not immune; his mother was dying in London and wartime restrictions prevented him from visiting her. It was no accident that he hired Thornton Wilder – whose theatrical look back at small-town

Figure 3.2. *Shadow of a Doubt* (1943).

American life, *Our Town*, had premiered in 1938 – to write the first draft of the script of *Shadow*. The Newtons' dinner-table conversations, the organic life of Santa Rosa's Main Street, the traffic cop (shot at heroic low angles) who knows every passerby by name – all reflect an urge to forestall personal and social change, loss, the march of time. In this sense, Hitchcock's uses of location, his framing of a way of life under threat whether its citizens know it or not, mark *Shadow of a Doubt* as a definitively American film.

Hitchcock being Hitchcock, *Shadow* self-consciously explores this condition. Indeed, the central conflict of the film comes down to radically opposed ways of seeing the twentieth-century United States – for Charlie, as an organic collective of "citizens" and neighbors; for her uncle, as a filthy urban stockyard of "fat, wheezing animals." What kind of space was mid-century America? Which vision of it were we fighting for? Santa Rosa was not the only location Hitchcock employed in *Shadow* to dramatic effect. The first shot of the film, produced by a newsreel crew under his direction, is a grimly panoramic view of New Jersey's Pulaski Skyway complete with belching smokestacks, a "No Dumping" sign, and homeless men prominently on view in the foreground (Figure 3.2). Diagetically, this view of urban decay back East prepares us to know the worst about Uncle Charlie (who is at one point described as a "New York man"). But it also suggests an interest in the repertoire of icons – material sites with deep symbolic resonance – on which Hitchcock was building his oeuvre and his American career. Shadowing the psychic doubles of *Shadow of a Doubt* is an evolving experiment with the iconography of America, and the way iconic spaces of the American nation might lend themselves to cinematic experience and illusion.

The film immediately preceding *Shadow* had already afforded Hitchcock a signal opportunity to test the cinematic possibilities of a range of iconic American spaces, repurposed for his aims. *Saboteur* tells a classic Hitchcockian story of the wrong man. Barry Kane, a worker in a Southern California defense plant, is accused of sabotage and murder when a fire breaks out at the plant and his friend is killed. To clear himself, Kane must evade the cops as he pursues the real saboteurs – a group of American fascist fifth columnists – across the United States to their rendezvous point in New York City. *Saboteur* began production less than two weeks after Pearl Harbor was bombed on December 7, 1941. Because of heightened security, location shooting planned for Boulder Dam and other sites had to be revised or conducted largely with second crews (producing still photos or shots of the landscape without actors) and supplemented with matte paintings – familiar tricks of the cinematic trade.

Hitchcock still managed extensive location shooting, and he still managed to build the arc of the narrative as a movement through a series of resonantly real and symbolic spaces: the harsh scrub of the high desert West (the fictive Soda City in which Kane finds evidence of the fascists' plot); that new institution of automobile America, the highway; the towering skyscrapers and landmarks (Rockefeller Center, Radio City Music Hall) of New York. But he was forced to move into the studio to shoot the climax of the film, whose visual logic had been his starting point for the entire project: the final confrontation between Kane and the saboteur Fry on the torch of the Statue of Liberty, from which, in a by-now familiar motif, Fry falls to his death (Figure 3.3). Restrictions imposed since an actual sabotage attempt at the Statue in 1916 meant that the torch would never have been available as a location site. This, it turned out, was a serendipity. For in replicating the most instantly recognizable of American icons on a sound stage, Hitchcock began to experiment in earnest with a resistance to realism, a resistance he would employ both to manipulate viewer response and to probe the relationship between viewer identification and the nature of America.

The replica of Liberty's torch head, torch, and arm that Hitchcock had his production team build has generally been described as a mimetic venture – an accurate rendition of the original, lending some ballast to a vertiginous, high-wire melodramatic scene.[15] But accuracy here is a MacGuffin – to borrow Hitchcock's pet term for a misleading plot element that allows the real business of the film to unfold – and it served its purpose well. On closer viewing, the structure that appears in the film as the context for the

Figure 3.3. *Saboteur* (1942).

literally gripping standoff between Kane and Fry is less than realistic – more papier-mâché fantasy prop than massive stainless steel and copper construction (Figure 3.4). And it is in just this way that Hitchcock's sound-stage work recalls the historical life of America's icon coming into being as such.

Liberty's right arm and torch, a gift to the United States from France on the occasion of the American Centennial, first appeared publicly at the Centennial Exposition in Philadelphia in 1876. Circulation of popular images of the "colossal arm and hand" helped persuade the American public of the symbolic fitness of the planned statue to their nation and its evolving modernity. The prosthetic quality of that original object – uncanny, disembodied, available for the fantasies of a rapidly changing social body – gives us a helpful context for reading Hitchcock's studio-made version and his use of the site of Liberty. Quite improbably, the American fascist Fry falls to his death from the statue's "hand" because the stitching on his jacket sleeve, by which Kane grasps him, gives way, as we see in tantalizing cuts to close-up of the bursting thread. (Quipped legendary screenwriter Ben Hecht, soon to collaborate with Hitchcock on *Spellbound* and *Notorious*, "He should have had a better tailor."[16]) Dramatic death spiral aside, this plot point figures something important about Hitchcock's use of space: that the seams here, on this site of struggle, are meant to show. Even as viewers are being sutured to an ideal of Liberty by the dramatic effects

64

Figure 3.4. Colossal hand and torch, Bartholdi's state of "Liberty," 1876.
Robert N. Dennis Collection of Stereoscopic Views, New York Public Library.

of locatedness, Hitchcock makes visible the cinematic technique, the sleight of hand, that creates them.

Such antirealism, as it has sometimes been called, is all the more striking in juxtaposition with the straight shooting that precedes it. En route to the Statue of Liberty in a cab, Fry has a clear view of a sinking battleship in the Brooklyn Navy Yard, the result of his team's just-accomplished act of sabotage. The devastation on which he gazes, in terms of visual scope and texture, offers itself as transcriptive, the result of some kind of documentary recording; so it was. During the filming of *Saboteur,* the former luxury liner SS *Normandie*, seized by the United States after France's fall to the Nazis and impounded on Manhattan's Pier 88, caught fire during work to transform it into a U.S. troop transport; the ship overturned, quite spectacularly, in New York Harbor (Figure 3.5). Always quick on the draw, Hitchcock dispatched a film crew the following day to get a traveling shot, made from a taxi, of the foundered ship, which he linked to his own plot with intercut close-ups of a sneering Fry.[17] Clearly not involving special effects, miniatures, or matte painting, this brief outbreak of actuality clarifies the logic of place and location in Hitchcock's scheme. In *Saboteur*'s movement between actual sites and the studio, between documentational codes and reconstructions subtly marked by their status as such, Hitchcock finds the rhythm that would come to characterize his distinctive mode of cinematic illusion.

The achievement of what has sometimes been called Hitchcockian realism, equal parts expressionism and fidelity to the materiality of everyday modern life, is not just a matter of camera angles and (or versus) mise-en-scène. With all their epic scale and symbolic power, icons of postwar America – the

Figure 3.5. Burning of SS *Normandie* (USS *Lafayette*). www.youtube.com/
watch?v=erTNmB4dXhU (2:29/3:21). Accessed June 11, 2014.
"Accident or sabotage? The world may never know... one of the major catastrophes of our day"

American way, the American dream, the American century – offered themselves up as rich sites of engagement with the power of illusion, cinematic
and social. For the rest of his career, Hitchcock would continue to press the
illusory effects of camera work and studio enhancements (a key example
being *Rope*, made entirely in the studio with only a handful of shots). But
he was also keenly attuned to the affective power of iconic places, and to
the way their cinematic uses might bind the viewer to a heightened experience of illusion making. Later films – including *To Catch a Thief* (1954),
The Wrong Man (1956), and *Vertigo* (1958) – explore the synergies of site
and cinematic seeing in various registers. None does so to greater effect
than the film that has often been reckoned Hitchcock's most iconic, whose
impact depends critically on its uses of intersecting icons of mid-century
America: *North by Northwest*.

By 1959, Hitchcock himself had become an American icon. His bejowled
face was instantly recognizable to popular audiences from cameo appearances in his films and from the groundbreaking television show *Alfred
Hitchcock Presents*, whose opening title sequence featured a clever line
drawing of his rotund silhouette. In the dawning post-studio era, he com-
manded unprecedented directorial power – reflected in his production's bottom lines, which swelled in direct relation to the costliness of his epic sets.
Over the previous decade, Hitchcock had ordered up, among other things,
a minutely detailed miniature reproduction of some 35 miles of New York

City skyline, lit by 8,000 incandescent lightbulbs and 200 neon signs powered by 150 transformers; a meticulously constructed amusement park, down to the lighting systems and working amusements; and a Greenwich Village–style courtyard housing block of 31 apartments (most of them fully habitable) with running water, electricity, and steel girder support, the whole raised on a foundation sunk so deep on Paramount's back lot that the builders actually struck water.[18]

Such creationist schemes, if we can call them that, index a relentless drive not toward realism but toward the illusion of it. Whichever mise-en-scene Hitchcock's viewers encountered, they understood they had entered into the world of the movies, where, as one critic puts it, "stylistic consistency is the basis of knowledge and pleasure" and every space "promises to be both more interesting and more coherent, more deserving of the name world, than the world outside the frame."[19] No Hitchcock film more successfully realizes its cinematic space than *North by Northwest* (1959), and no other so cannily enlists actual spaces and sites in that achievement. Here, the project of illusion making by way of reality effects coincides with purposive movement through locations defined by America's own project of world-making in the American century.

The working title for this cinematic extravaganza was, of all things, "The Man in Lincoln's Nose"; the film began its life a decade before the cameras rolled, Hitchcock later reported, as the mental image of a man dangling from the sculptured eyebrow of that president on the face of Mount Rushmore. Iconic, affording massive elevation (the highest on the North American continent east of the Rockies) and the prospect of a dramatic drop from the stark granite cliffs of the Black Hills, Rushmore was the perfect setting for a Hitchcock film – particularly one intended, as screenwriter Ernest Lehman put it, to be "the Hitchcock picture to end all Hitchcock pictures."[20] Critics have made much of the film's uses of monumental space; indeed, *North by Northwest* has provoked some of the most elegant readings of cinematic visions of America and of film qua film that we have, from distinguished philosophers and theorists like Stanley Cavell and Fredric Jameson.[21] But these readings tend to overlook (pun intended) the historical dimensions of the spaces the film employs, which bring into relief the mixed effects with which Hitchcock's cinema engages the project of myth-making.

To begin with, Hitchcock's generative image of the rugged individualist on the brink was as unoriginal as his design for a studio-sited prosthesis of Lady Liberty. Throughout the construction of Mount Rushmore, which began in 1927 and ended when funds ran out in 1941, a photographer employed by the monument's designer and the National Park Service was on hand to document the epic undertaking. Working with scaffolds, slings, and

Figure 3.6. Charles D'Emery, Mt. Rushmore in the making. Courtesy Mount Rushmore. National Park Service Portfolio.

rapelling equipment, Charles D'Emery recorded and mythologized the labor of monument-building; he was not above staging images for the desired effect, including one that foreshadows Hitchcock's germ (Figures 3.6 and 3.7). The very face of Rushmore, scored by geophysical compression and carving techniques, anticipates *North by Northwest*'s title sequence of moving grids, with its suggestion of spatial systems, natural as well as cultural, from which the protagonist must escape.[22] More to the point, D'Emery's camera poses the heroism of westering against the backdrop of a transcendental eyeball, whose impassivity prefigures a modern state of surveillance. If D'Emery's image holds open the possibility of some kind of meaningful gaze between the descendent of pioneers and the Founding Father, it also acknowledges the interpenetration of land, landscape, and fantasies of a manifestly destined modern nation. Long before Hitchcock's project,

68

Figure 3.7. Charles D'Emery, Mount Rushmore, 1937. Staged photo with Jefferson's eye.
Courtesy Mount Rushmore, National Park Service Portfolio.

D'Emery produces, in a kind of VistaVision, an image that signals its own role in the production of icons for twentieth-century America.

Admittedly, Hitchcock would take this signaling to a whole new pitch and frequency. Beyond extensive scouting and background shooting, one of the few Rushmore location shots to make it into *North by Northwest* is our first view of the monument. Strikingly, it is made visible to us not in all its uncanny presence as a (near) natural feature of the landscape, but rather as an effect of cinematic mediation. Using a slow-fade dissolve, Hitchcock superimposes Rushmore on the screen-filling face of a worried Thornhill, who has just learned that his public censure of Eve Kendall ("for using sex the way some people use a flyswatter") has exposed her to Vandamm (Figure 3.8).

The superimposition gives way to a pull-in shot of the monument that brings it closer as we – and Thornhill – peer through a telescope in the

Figure 3.8. Two national monuments, Cary Grant and Mt. Rushmore.
North by Northwest (1959).

Figure 3.9. Mount Rushmore, framed and reframed. *North by Northwest.*

park's welcome center (Figure 3.9). Paradoxically, the real location so critical to suturing the viewer to the stakes of the action in the diegetic world
shows itself as a product of the machinery of illusion that makes it so.
And it is that machinery (which belongs to the plot of the film, the film's
self-understanding, and the viewer alike) that exposes the monumentality of

this actual location as an effect of *its* cultural framing. Which, finally, is the space of illusion, and which is real? Where does mise-en-scène leave off and social landscape begin?

The artful confusion extends significantly further. Not only is the object in view, Rushmore, an icon – or rather, a film image of a material site conditioned by its cultural status as an icon. So too is the man who views it. For the figure whose face fills Hitchcock's meticulously designed VistaVision frame, and who peers through the telescope, is never really Roger Thornhill so much as the larger-than-life movie star Cary Grant. Throughout *North by Northwest*, Grant's outsize status remains a comic touchstone, as when he attempts to shave with a tiny travel razor that is risibly under-scaled ("Big face, little razor"), or escapes from a locked hotel room by climbing into the bedroom of a lone female guest who ejaculates first with fright ("Stop!") and then with seductive pleasure ("Stop..."). By 1960, Grant reigned as the number-one box office attraction in the United States, and this was not just an effect of Hollywood's celebrity machine. His appeal was distinctive to its context and unique in the history of cinema. Both John F. Kennedy and Lucky Luciano – the president and the gangster – thought he should star in their life stories; the actor himself once noted to an interviewer, "Everybody wants to be Cary Grant. Even *I* want to be Cary Grant."[23] What made that figure such a labile fantasy object for mid-century American dreaming?

The answer has, it turns out, much to do with America as a location, in the cinematic sense – that is, as a space of mobility and illusion. Born Archibald Leach, the son of a Jewish pants-presser, Grant had climbed his way up from British vaudeville, stilt-walking on Coney Island, and bit parts in the U.S. theater, transforming himself on film as the quintessential urban(e) man for the unfolding twentieth century. He became, as film critic Pauline Kael put it in a trenchant tribute, published in 1975 (just shy of the American bicentennial), "the Man from Dream City" – an emblematic figure of so-called class and classlessness, whose "romantic elegance" was "wrapped around the tough core of a mutt."[24] Critical to this effect, viewers and scholars agree, were not only Grant's cool sartorial elegance and impeccable physicality but his distinctive accent – neither British nor American, both cultivated and Cockney, entirely sui generis, its rhythms laced "with the swift patter of baseball talk."[25] By the time Grant's face filled the screen in *North by Northwest*, he was playing not a dramatic character but his own invention. None other than C. L. R. James, the Trinidadian writer and founding figure of postcolonial theory, called Grant "a new social type": the very embodiment at mid-century of the American project of making oneself up while making the world over in America's image.[26]

This is the figure who eyes Mount Rushmore through the telescope's lens, whose "big face" joins those monumental icons of American power, one Grant (invented and cinematic) juxtaposed with another (General Ulysses S.). The tale Hitchcock tells in *North by Northwest* is far from politically radical – it ends, after all, in a defense of marriage act, with the new Mrs. Thornhill hoisted onto the top bunk of a train's sleeper car before it barrels all too obviously through a tunnel. But Hitchcock's signature interest in cinematic illusion and its production of collective identity had special resonances in the context of Cold War gamesmanship. Indeed, in that context, Hitchcock's filmmaking itself became an act of camouflage and stealth. When he was refused permission to shoot a critical sequence on location at the United Nations – that of Grant's arrival on a mission to track down the owner of the Long Island estate that had been the staging grounds for the "play-acting" of a spy-on-spy encounter – Hitchcock simply stole the shot. His first attempt, using a camera hidden in a van, failed (his producer was recognized by UN security staff). Undaunted, he sent a cameraman with a long focal-length lens into a nearby building. The result was a shot tracking Grant across the iconic UN plaza designed by famed modernist architects Oscar Niemeyer and Le Corbusier. Enhancing suspense and the viewer's visceral sense of the monumentality of Cold War power, the sequence also bespeaks an urgent continuity between real and fictive (or social and cinematic) forms of illusion.

That synergy, or confusion, of location only grows more urgent as *North by Northwest* and its plot play out. By the time Eva Marie Saint and Cary Grant dangle from an escarpment below George Washington's nose in the climactic scene, Hitchcock has revealed (or unreeled) the sleight of hand by which the United States itself – like the heartland crossroads where Thornhill is crop-dusted; like the Edenic lodgepole pine wood where the lovers meet; like the Vandamm house, a faithful rendition of the ultra-modernist Frank Lloyd Wright style, purpose-built not on the ecologically fragile outcroppings of the monument site but on a location near the studio, in Culver City; like the stark vertical face of Mt. Rushmore as reconstructed on the sound stage – is nowhere and everywhere, a space emptied of the inconvenient truths of settlement and nation-building to make room for an image repertoire in which Americans could see themselves and the late capitalist, Cold War version of their cherished ideals. That Rushmore itself was designed by a sculptor known for his belligerent nativism and his ties to the Ku Klux Klan only makes our sense of Hitchcock's investments in the place of illusion clearer.[27] What *North by Northwest* gives its mid-century viewers is not a critique or an ideological schooling but a compass, a confident locatedness, embodied in a hero who can move through sites of illusion without being taken in by them. Finally, Hitchcock suggests to mid-century viewers, there is no better place to see America – to locate its illusions clearly – than at the movies.

NOTES

1 For example, the *Schirmer Encyclopedia of Film*, ed. Barry Keith Grant (New York: Schirmer Reference, 2007), has no entry for "location" per se; the entry under "Realism" for "Making Movies Real" (vol. 3, 385–394) lists a variety of necessary "technical elements," beginning with "historical accuracy of wardrobe" and "[e]xtra-diegetic music" and focusing on shooting and editing practices (fades, dissolves, shot/reverse shot, the 180-degree rule, etc.).

2 For a broad view of this argument, see Jonathan Freedman and Richard Millington, eds., *Hitchcock's America* (New York: Oxford University Press, 1999).

3 Donald Spoto, *The Dark Side of Genius: The Life of Alfred Hitchcock* (Boston: Little Brown, 1983), p. 52; Noël Burch, dir., *What Do These Old Films Mean?* Vol. 1, *Great Britain 1900–1912, Along the Great Divide* (London: Channel Four Television, 1981).

4 Noël Burch, *Life to Those Shadows*, tr. Ben Brewster (London: BFI Publishing, 1990), p. 101.

5 Berry, "Haggar, William," *Directors in British and Irish Cinema: A Reference Companion*, ed. Robert Murphy (London: BFI Publishing, 2006), p. 264.

6 Some commentators have suggested that the rooftop chase was shot on location, although it clearly was made in the studio – an index, perhaps, to the broad powers of early film's reality effects. For additional details and rare stills from the film, see Peter Yorke, *Walter Haggar: Fairground Filmmaker* (Abercynon: Accent Press, 2007).

7 Spoto, *Dark Side*, p. 68.

8 *Bioscope* review, cited in Maurice Yacowar, *Hitchcock's British Films* (Hamden, CT: Archon Books, 1977), p. 281.

9 "The Art of Fiction: No. 13. Dorothy Parker." Interview by Marion Capron. *Paris Review*. Summer 1956. Reprinted in *The Paris Review Interviews*, vol. 1 (New York: Picador, 2001), pp. 1–16; citation, p. 15.

10 Hope's quip was part of his introductory remarks at the Academy Awards of 1965, in which the London-set *Mary Poppins* was a standout winner. Richard Stirling, *Julie Andrews: An Intimate Biography* (New York: Macmillan, 2008), p. 79.

11 "Historical U.S. Census Populations of Places, Towns, and Cities in California, 1850–2000." http://www.google.com/url?sa=t&rct=j&q=&esrc=s&source=web &cd=1&ved=0CCsQFjAA&url=http%3A%2F%2Fwww.dof.ca.gov%2Fhtml% 2Fdemograp%2Freportspapers%2Fcensussurveys%2Fcensus-historical%2Fdocu ments%2Fcalhist2.xls&ei=pQZxUuzTK4mW2QXM_4CABg&usg=AFQjCN E69owCGKN9xx7uGVHgyJZ_RLvymQ&sig2=I75kBQGpWdxwDJe6r9ER UQ&bvm=bv.55617003,d.b2I. California Department of Finance. Accessed 30 October 2013.

12 Roger Ebert, Reviews: "Great Movie: *Shadow of a Doubt*," http://www.rogerebert .com/reviews/great-movie-shadow-of-a-doubt-1943. Posted 9 November 2011. Accessed 22 August 2013.

13 Bill Krohn, *Hitchcock at Work* (London: Phaidon Press, 2003), p. 56.

14 Krohn, *Hitchcock at Work*, p. 56.

15 Krohn, *Hitchcock at Work*, p. 50.

16 Norman Lloyd, cited in Tom Weaver, *I Was a Monster Movie Maker: Conversations with 22 SF and Horror Filmmakers* (Jefferson, NC: McFarland Company), p. 168.

17 Hitchcock, *Hitchcock/Truffaut* (New York: Simon and Schuster, 1984), p. 147. Hitchcock notes here that the United States Navy "raised hell" about these shots because they suggested "that the *Normandie* had been sabotaged" as a result of the Navy's "lack of vigilance in guarding it"; they appeared in the film nonetheless.

18 For details of earlier film sets, see Spoto, pp. 230, 306, 325.

19 Thomas Leitch, "Games Hitchcock Plays," in *Perspectives on Alfred Hitchcock*, ed. David Bond (New York: G. K. Hall and Co./Simon and Schuster Macmillan, 1995), pp. 51–68; citation, 59.

20 Ernest Lehman, cited in Leland Poague, "'Tell Me the Story So Far': Hitchcock and His Writers," in *A Companion to Alfred Hitchcock*, ed. Thomas Leitch and Leland Poague (London: Blackwell, 2011), pp. 141–161; 159.

21 See, for example, Stanley Cavell's wonderful reading of the return to a cinematically constructed "Nature" as the setting and context for a recovery of the remarriage plot, in Cavell, "*North by Northwest*," *Critical Inquiry* 7:4 (Summer 1981), pp. 761–776, and Fredric Jameson's analysis of "Spatial Systems in *North by Northwest*," in *Everything You Always Wanted to Know about Lacan (But Were Afraid to Ask Hitchcock)*, ed. Slavoj Žižek (London: Verso, 2010), pp. 47–72.

22 *North by Northwest*'s title sequence, designed by Saul Bass, famously begins with running lines against a green background – reminiscent of green-screen technology, a special effect available since 1939 – that dissolve into the reflecting façade of the actual C.I.T. building in midtown Manhattan, where Thornhill's ad agency is located. Not only is the city here a space of image -making; it is itself inseparable from the image world it creates. Indeed, the façade of the building becomes a surface for the projection of moving images of city life on the streets below. Even on the ground, where crowds of city dwellers rush through real city spaces (like Fifth Avenue, where Hitchcock, in his cameo moment, has a bus door closed in his face), cinematic effects assert themselves. Hitchcock's footage of the crowd, a close observer will notice, is actually looped, so that the same woman in a blue dress exits the Plaza hotel at the beginning of the sequence and at the end. Innumerable theorists of urban modernity – most prominently Georg Simmel and Walter Benjamin – had long since suggested that cinema not only captures the felt effects of urban experience but shapes the very act of perception to its own rhythms and intensities.

23 Cited in Graham McCann, *Cary Grant: A Class Apart* (New York: Columbia University Press, 1995), p. 5.

24 Kael, "The Man from Dream City," reprinted in *When the Lights Go Down* (New York: Holt, Rinehart and Winston, 1980; orig. 1975), p. 9.

25 Benjamin Schwartz, "Becoming Cary Grant," *The Atlantic Monthly*, 299.1 (January 1, 2007), pp. 132, 134–136; 134.

26 C. L. R. James, *American Civilization* (Oxford: Blackwell, 1993), p. 245, quoted in Schwartz, p. 134.

27 On sculptor Gutzon Borglum's political affiliations and cultural sympathies, see John Taliaferro, *Great White Fathers: The Story of the Obsessive Quest to Create Mount Rushmore* (New York: Public Affairs, 2002), particularly pp. 183–194.

4

HOMER B. PETTEY

Hitchcock, Class, and Noir

> Despite our public embrace of political and judicial equality, in
> individual perception and understanding – much of which we refrain
> from publicizing – we arrange things vertically and insist on crucial
> differences in value.... It's as if in our heart of hearts we don't want
> agglomerations but distinctions. Analysis and separation we find
> interesting, synthesis boring.
> – Paul Fussell, *Class: A Guide Through the American Status System*

Class was always a particularly dark obsession with Alfred Hitchcock. His
British thrillers of the 1930s often depicted narrative antagonism and thematic oppositions in terms of social hierarchies. In his American noirs beginning in the 1940s, he often leaves class issues hanging, literally suspended
or in danger from high places, especially monuments and public spaces,
as though class were always a suspended dilemma of American culture.
For the Hitchcockian noir hero, class was a barrier to be crossed, a new
American frontier to be subdued. Highbrow culture flourishes in conspicuous extravagance of wealth that divides haves from have-nots, as well as in
the egotistical pleasure of looking down upon others – a privileged distance,
segregated, aloof, and wholly undemocratic. The Hitchcockian noir enacts
this dichotomy visually with vertical and horizontal axes that denote class
distinctions and with illusion of depth comments upon the delusion of class
separation. Noir, then, for Hitchcock is an aesthetic of class that synthesizes
genre and style to create a visual critique of the darker side of American
culture.

Hitchcock's contributions to film noir developed from his own marginalized class origins. From his school days, through his artistic apprenticeship,
to his move to Hollywood, Hitchcock understood that social conditions
for class were not simply determined by ancient rites of heritage. In his
early British films, he translated familiar, even stereotypical class gestures,
manners, and movements into his mise-en-scène in order to expose, often

satirically, the drawbacks to a system of social hierarchies. America offered Hitchcock an opportunity, both economically and artistically, to explore the visual and narrative dimensions of high- and lowbrow allegories of social rank within modern democracy.

It is, then, essential to differentiate Hitchcock's émigré British films from his American noirs, among them: *Saboteur* (1942), *Shadow of a Doubt* (1943), *Spellbound* (1945), *Strangers on a Train* (1951), *I Confess* (1953), *The Wrong Man* (1956), and his final American noir, *Psycho* (1960). Common film noir themes appear among these films, such as the wrongly accused man in *Saboteur, Spellbound, Strangers on a Train, I Confess,* and *The Wrong Man*; psychological imbalance and psychotic reactions in *Shadow of a Doubt, Strangers on a Train,* and *Psycho*; psychosexual predicaments in *Shadow of a Doubt, Spellbound, Strangers on a Train, I Confess,* and *Psycho*; and entrapped self-victimization for both the male and female protagonists in *Shadow of a Doubt, Spellbound, I Confess,* and *Psycho*. In all these American noirs, Hitchcock relies on the class conflict as narrative, thematic, and especially aesthetic dimensions of his filmmaking. As Murray Pomerance has pointed out, social class and vertical hierarchy "underlie the visible relations" in Hitchcock's films, and, along with depth of field to mark social separation, Hitchcock relies on setting and camera angles to promote spatial distance as class distinctions.[1] Hence, Hitchcock's penchant for climactic scenes of height and separation, such as the British Museum chase in *Blackmail* (1929), the Statue of Liberty in *Saboteur*, the merry-go-round calamity in *Strangers on a Train*, the train death in *Shadow of a Doubt*, and Mount Rushmore in *North by Northwest* (1959).

Certainly, Hitchcock's Hollywood films with British plots and locales display what might be termed noir techniques, among them the numerous chiaroscuro compositions of Mrs. Danvers (Judith Anderson) plaguing the new Mrs. De Winter (Joan Fontane) in *Rebecca* (1940); the famous scene of Johnnie Aysgarth (Cary Grant) carrying the glass of milk up the staircase among the spiderweb shadows in *Suspicion* (1941); and shadowy dangers backstage for Eve Gill (Jane Wyman) as she tries to protect psychotic killer Jonathan Cooper (Richard Todd) from the clutches of the constabulary. Noir and class elements intermingle in *Foreign Correspondent* (1940), with Stephen Fisher's (Herbert Marshall) erudite, almost foppish philanthropic poses in opposition to the newly arrived American reporter Johnny Jones (Joel McCrea). The film also relies on the chilling use of high places and potentially lethal descents: Johnny Jones hiding from international thugs in the ruined windmill; Rowley (Edmund Gwenn) murderous attempt to push Johnny off Westminster Cathedral; and the plane crash and subsequent rescue by the American ship, ironically named *Mohican*. Hitchcock's true noirs, however, are American in plot, theme, and setting, precisely because the director sought to explore and to expose social-class problems with an American sensibility for his new American audience.

Often, British fiction of the nineteenth and early twentieth centuries couched class in terms of individual self-sacrifice, morbid suffering, a melancholy outlook on life, and the stoic, honorable, and ultimately moral stance of enduring pain as a badge of social status. Hitchcock's favorite boyhood reading included such imperialistic novels by Sir Walter Scott, G. K. Chesterton, Arthur Conan Doyle, Wilkie Collins, and John Buchan.[2] Of course, these novelists are also the sources for much of the hard-boiled detective fiction of 1930s American culture. Like the hard-boiled detective, Hitchcock's heroes undergo pain, but he transformed the highbrow form of aristocratic values into a parodic, outsider's democratic sensibility. Even more so, Hitchcock abandons the aristocratic, masochistic self-sacrificing melancholia of the previous age for a modern, individual sense of personal justice. Most of Hitchcock's heroes, especially his American noir heroes, initially fight to save their own skins or to prove their innocence before their fight expands to the international concerns of the culture at large. Reading the Hitchcock noir plots as microcosms of the macro-sociopolitical narrative reveals his ethical critique of the destructive nature of self-interest over American self-reliance.

To be sure, American comedies of the 1930s, such as the films of Frank Capra, often relied on class antagonism, but not merely for "denouncing or satirizing the upper class than in finding common ground between the classes, or at least in suggesting that the rich are capable of learning humility and humanity from their working-class and middle-class counterparts."[3] British comedies also promoted "the all-embracing ethos of consensus."[4] Such saccharine democratization hardly appealed to Hitchcock's sense of social critique, since satirizing aristocratic conceits is at the very heart of his filmic representation of American culture. In this respect, Hitchcock was the anti-Capra. As Hitchcock admitted to J. Danvers Williams in 1938, "I have always wanted to make films with some sociological importance," as evidenced in the class considerations in most of his silent films, especially *The Lodger* (1929).[5] In some respects, the MacGuffin of Hitchcock films was not the incidental object, but rather the love-story adventure plot that misdirected filmgoers from the class satire, as James Leach perceptively remarks about his pre-Hollywood films: "In the thrillers of the late 1930s, he deftly evaded the censor's watchful eye by becoming a kind of 'secret agent' himself, hiding 'violent things' beneath a surface of light entertainment."[6]

If Hitchcock's noir vision has any counterpart, it is to be found in the work of the émigrés who accompanied him to these shores, many joining him in Los Angeles, including Nobel laureate Thomas Mann; subversive theatre genius Bertolt Brecht; modernist writer Alfred Döblin; Dadaist Man Ray; choreographer George Balanchine; actors Marlene Dietrich, Greta Garbo, Paul Henreid, and Peter Lorre; film directors Max Reinhardt, William Dieterle, Josef von Sternberg, Erich von Stroheim, Anatole Litvak, Max Ophüls, Douglas Sirk, Jean Renoir, Fred Zinnemann, and Ernst Lubitsch; and composers Miklós Rózsa, Franz Waxmann, and Dimitri Tiomkin. Conductor of the Los Angeles Philharmonic, the German émigré Otto Klemperer transformed the musical landscape of America with his impressive Hollywood Bowl concerts in the 1930s by attracting the superb talents of Angelino exiles Arnold Schoenberg and Igor Stravinsky.[7] So cosmopolitan and so very artistically and intellectually stimulating was Hollywood during this period that Thomas Mann remarked that it was a greater city "than Paris or Munich had ever been."[8] Certainly, this incredible influx of world-class artistic talent elevated the film industry and contributed to the development of what is erroneously considered a home-grown American genre – film noir.

Many notable émigré film noir directors of the pre- and early postwar period had Jewish heritage, among them Fritz Lang, whose mother was Jewish before converting to Catholicism; Billy Wilder, who claimed that Hitler made him a Jew; as well as Otto Preminger, Michael Curtiz, and Robert Siodmak. Trying to avoid being too monolithic, Vincent Brook makes an intriguing argument about the creative influence on film noir of Jewish émigrés, particularly the pervasive adapting of Jewish social marginality, reliance on Expressionist emotional and psychological visual style, adoption of German *Kammerspiel*, and Weimar street film lighting effects, and the cumulative artistic force of what R. Barton Palmer has termed "group auteurist" collaboration among Jewish actors, set designers, composers, and editors.[9] Hitchcock arrived in Hollywood with similar training as most other émigré directors: apprenticeship in Germany, knowledge of continental modernism, directorial transition from making silent to talking films, and a special outsider's perspective on both his native British and his adopted American cultures.

Hitchcock had been an émigré twice in his life: once to work at UFA (*Universum Film-Aktien Gesellschaft*) in 1924 and then to direct features in Hollywood in 1939. The two periods of artistic exile forged Hitchcock's cinematic sensibilities and his experimental aesthetic. Moreover, Hitchcock retained from his UFA training elements of Expressionism as a means of interrelating visual and thematic content. *Lustmord*, particularly in the works of George Grosz and Otto Dix, fascinated Hitchcock, especially the conceit of serial sexual murders à la Jack the Ripper, which were certainly elements in *The Cabinet of Caligari* (1920) and *Waxworks* (1924). From *Caligari* in particular, throughout his career, Hitchcock would translate the abstract, Expressionist shapes into a realistic yet stylized mise-en-scène "using light, shadow, and camera angles, to express moods of foreboding, feelings of anguish, and confinement," all elements of film noir aesthetics.[10] Hitchcock's own propensity for the theme of *lustmord* exhibits itself in the numerous plots that rely on sexually motivated killing, from *The Lodger* through *Shadow of a Doubt* and *Psycho* to *Frenzy* (1972). Hitchcock's hanging-man theme is an adaptation of Conrad Felixmüller's *The Death of the Poet Walter Rheiner* (1925), with the artist's right hand clutching the drapery, his cocaine hypodermic in his left hand, as he is suspended in an open window frame above a hallucinatory Berlin nightscape illuminated by neon signs, street lamps, and apartment windows.[11] German Expressionist content, techniques, and style were integral to Hitchcock's experimental vision throughout his career.

Biographers of Hitchcock often point to his time in 1924 as an assistant director on *Blackguard* (1925), a British-German production at UFA studios, and particularly to the influence of F. W. Murnau's comments on perspective in film, Hitchcock's observations of Murnau's technique during the making of *The Last Laugh* (*Der letzte Mann*, 1924), and how Hitchcock named the German filmmakers of 1924–1925 as his mentors throughout his career.[12] Most impressive for Hitchcock must have been Murnau's insistence on no intertitles for *The Last Laugh*, thereby demanding that all content, emotion, and narrative be conveyed visually. Murnau's virtuosity impressed Hitchcock, especially his experimental camera movements, lighting and shadow effects to register psychological and emotional states, and his play with illusions of perspective in order to create a reality on screen that was not actually there on the set.

Murnau's liberation of the camera from the tripod transformed film: by mounting the automatic camera on a bicycle; strapping it to his camera-man's belly; moving it up and down by means of an extension ladder; or, as in *The Last Laugh*, achieving the "flying tone" when the doorman awakens from his dream to the sound of a trumpet: "The camera was mounted in a gondola hung on tracks that could travel across the entire courtyard on a downward slant for about twenty meters – from the ear of the sleeping Jannings to the mouth of the trumpet."[13] What is essential about this cinematic liberation for Hitchcock is not so much mere experimentation, but what he learned so well from Murnau: that all efforts from mise-en-scène to camera angles were to produce what appeared on the screen. Hitchcock's noir aesthetic developed alongside his American use of Murnau and the German Expressionists, which had already been adapted into his early work.

What Hollywood offered him was a technological advantage during the war years that European and British film companies could not hope to exploit.

Such devotion to the cinematic can be observed in Hitchcock's major films, which invariably include lengthy scenes that contain virtually no dialogue. James N. Bade focuses on four types of subjective shots in Murnau that became part of Hitchcock's style: the static shot from the subject's point of view; the mobile tracking shot, especially directing attention to details; the pan that reveals the subject's gaze; and the distorted shot to reveal the subject's state of mind.[14] These subjective techniques can be seen in Hitchcock's noirs, such as, in *Spellbound*, Gregory Peck's fixation on the parallel lines made by the fork marks on the white table cloth; Ingrid Bergman's review of the books in the library, until she spots *The Labyrinth of the Guilt Complex*; Leo G. Carroll's revolver panning Ingrid Bergman's movement through his study; and the hallucinatory Salvador Dali dream sequence. *Spellbound* is really a *film blanc*, a psychological noir whose aesthetic concentrates on whiteness for its effects. Of course, Hitchcock would have been aware of such subjective camerawork in early 1940s films noir, such as the drug-induced hallucination in *Murder, My Sweet* (1944) or the camera tracking Barbara Stanwyck's ankle bracelet down the stairs in *Double Indemnity* (1944). To compose the score for *Spellbound*, Hitchcock hired Miklós Rózsa, who impressed the director with his moody, experimental, and controversial noir music for Wilder's *Double Indemnity*: "Rózsa's signature sound, unabashedly sensuous yet curiously stark ... suited *Spellbound*'s narrative, one that combines high dementia with high romance."[15] Bade's fourth distinction can be extended to Hitchcock's fascination with musical distortion in noir. Indeed, Hitchcock had an astute knowledge and appreciation of film noir techniques of the period.

Hitchcock adopted the UFA style of *Kammerspielfilme*, which were "naturalistic dramas about the lower middle-class or servants, and they usually have a tragic ending, for example, involving a protagonist's being murdered or committing suicide."[16] Hitchcock's filmic interest in the American middle-class themes was an extension of *Kammerspielfilme*, with the exception that the death or imprisonment occurred to those undemocratic figures harassing the protagonist. German Expressionist films, like later film noir, employed cinematic techniques that Hitchcock relied on throughout his early and especially his American filmmaking career: chiaroscuro lighting effects correspond to paradoxes and binary oppositions; the sinister foreboding is rendered by extreme shadows and shadow movement; the claustrophobic or entrapment sensation is produced by horizontal and vertical shadows; stairs serve as one of his signatures for spatial references for mystery and horror; "mirrors heighten the sense that characters are split and relentlessly and painfully self-conscious; and startling camera angles (sometime unusually high, or low, or oblique) and quick changes in camera position have a destabilizing effect, signaling the inner and outer world of the main characters as precarious and volatile."[17]

Hitchcock acquired from Weimar filmmaking more than just technique. The star power of Weimar directors in the 1920s must have seemed all-too-attractive an aspiration for the young director, since Fritz Lang, G. W. Pabst, and especially F. W. Murnau were not only regarded as stars, but their films were often "marketed solely on the drawing power of the director's name and his reputation for artistic quality and versatility."[18] Certainly, Hitchcock's marketing of himself sprang from his observations of Murnau as an artist and as a star, as well as the UFA conception of the director as *auteur*.

Before beginning *The Last Laugh*, Murnau wrote a short manifesto on mobile camerawork for the first issue of *Die Filmwoche* in 1924. The mobile camera would result in a pure filmmaking and "does not imply the creation of a new technically complicated apparatus, in artistic terms it means rather the opposite, i.e. the regaining of a simplicity and finality of the technical process."[19] Murnau also placed subjective camera techniques in relationship to architectural perspectives, a key element in Hitchcock's later penchant for monumental structures for climatic scenes in his films. Murnau's combination of Emil Janning's subjective distortion and urban architecture in *The Last Laugh* exposes the menacing position of man entrapped within class hierarchies of a dystopic and heterotopic cityscape:

> Also, in a drunken vision, he dreams that his (private) tenement block and (public) hotel façade blend into one distorted structure, wherein the hotel's revolving door rises to gigantic (again, threatening) stature: this time, however, the dream permits him to exist as a tiny cog within the logic of the massive doorway. Here the dream corresponds to the film's spatial dialectic: it was noticed right away in 1924 that these two massive structures, both of which were built actual-size on the set by Murnau's architects, Herlth and Röhrig, were inversely related social spaces.[20]

Hitchcock often envisioned the American noir urban landscape as a dystopia of social constraints, as exemplified by dangers of New York City's tourist attractions in *Saboteur*, the oppressive, claustrophobic lanes of Québec City in *I Confess*, and psycho-neurosis inducing streets, commercial interiors, and the Tombs in *The Wrong Man*.

In *I Confess*, Father Michael Logan's (Montgomery Clift) vows, including that of poverty, place him at odds with the ruling class. The film's intrigue involves his supposed assignation with a wealthy Parliament member's wife (Anne Baxter) and his subsequent blackmail by an unscrupulous lawyer, who is murdered. Two young Catholic schoolgirls have seen the murderer, dressed in a priest's cassock and hat, leave the victim's house. This night-for-night scene exhibits all the cinematographic elements of film noir: narrow lanes and alleyways irregularly reflecting light from water pooled after a recent rain; rich contours of shadows and intermittent harsh light to accentuate the priest-figure's silhouette; and shifting camera angles to sustain the tension of this fleeing culprit's plight. That same night, Father Logan hears the confession of the real murderer, the rectory handyman Otto Keller (O. E. Hasse), whose guilt he cannot reveal without breaking his vows and damning his soul. Hitchcock maintains a rather classic studio approach to filming all of the characters save Otto Keller, whose courtroom perjury is shot in oblique angles, thereby stylistically connecting Keller with the priest-murderer of the opening scene. In the film's opening montage of Québec City, interspersed horizontal *DIRECTION* signs serve as apocalyptic omens for the spatial separation that portends Father Logan's ordeal with upper-class authorities. Later, another city montage sequence intercuts church steeples at vertically oblique angles, as a visual reminder of the detached, hierarchical social status of the police and court officials, even the absence of the Church to aid Father Logan's lonely agony in the city. For Hitchcock, this imperiled hero represents a constant struggle in America, whereby oppressive actions always lurk behind the façade of justice and right erected by the dominant class and authorities. Hitchcock's most religious film to date would be followed two years later by his most distinctly noir film and his second Catholic film, *The Wrong Man*.

The Wrong Man can be viewed ideologically as film noir because it serves as "an indictment of the false promises of the emerging consumer society of the 1950s in America."[21] Hitchcock's silhouetted figure in a backlit triangle of light within a sound stage announces to the audience that the film is based on a true story. Two elements visually suggest a noir aesthetic for the film: the semi-documentary techniques of *The Naked City* and other noirs, and the shadowy figure of Hitchcock at the film's beginning. Unlike *The Naked City*, Hitchcock never reduces this noir to a God's eye point of view, as though he were refuting that formula in the subgenre of the semi-documentary noir. Interestingly, Hitchcock does employ just such God's-eye POV shots at disruptive moments in other noirs, such as young Charlie's hand on the banister as she descends to peril in *Shadow of a Doubt*. or the high angle of Arbogast's (Martin Balsam) gruesome murder on the stairs in *Psycho*, both of which are moments of gender and class jeopardy.[22]

The Wrong Man opens with Manny Balestrero (Henry Fonda) playing bass in the band for wealthy patrons, then leaving the Stork Club, followed ironically by two NYPD patrolmen, and Manny entering the subway, where he catches a train and sits reading the newspaper. He examines the horse races, looks at a Ford automobile advertisement enticing buyers to enjoy "family fun," and at a new account offer from "The New York Savings Bank." All of these economic incentives – gambling, purchasing, saving money – are beyond Manny's means, which is exactly Hitchcock's point. His lower-middle-class family life is constrained financially, but for the opening scenes of the Balestrero household Hitchcock uses classic studio lighting and camera movement. The same is true for the tense scene of Manny's misidentification as the robber by the neurotic secretaries at the insurance company. In fact, film noir techniques do not enter into *The Wrong Man* until the police take Manny from his front doorstep and place him in their car. At that point, the night scene in the claustrophobic police car, the harsh, realistic lighting of the interiors of stores, and the literally barred shadows of entrapment in the jail indicate a shift to a noir aesthetic that reinforces the dark, oppressive fate of the protagonist. When Manny is finally confronted with the horror of his incarceration, a Murnau-like hallucinatory whirling of the camera transforms the entire screen into an ever-increasing spiral of disorientation. Here, the class anxiety is determined by power structure (the police, district attorney, and court system) set against the low-paid wage earner, Manny, the bass player at the Stork Club. Moreover, Manny is a pious Catholic, and like Father Logan, his outsider status and his faith ultimately both free and torment him. After the real culprit is rightly and miraculously identified by the detectives, Manny is left with a nearly catatonic spouse (Vera Miles), whose prognosis is questionable. Hitchcock's happy ending, however, with the entire family now strolling along a Miami ocean-front bathed bright sunlight, reinforces the director's earlier conscious shift to noir techniques to express class domination.

Saboteur (1942) was Hitchcock's first American film, that is, the first Hitchcock film entirely set in the United States. *Saboteur* stands in between *39 Steps* (1935) and *North by Northwest*, with a noir-like plot convention of an incident precipitated by chance, accident, or fate that leads the protagonist to become both detective and victim simultaneously, whereby the solution to the murder scheme frees him from suspicion. The narrative, then, becomes a labyrinthine journey tale into the darker (social, economic, and political) side of modern life. Film noir has employed variations on this thematic and narrative convention, among them: Fritz Lang's *The Woman in the Window* (1944), George Marshall's *The Blue Dahlia* (1946), Delmer Daves's *Dark Passage* (1947), John Cromwell's *Dead Reckoning* (1947), and Robert Aldrich's *Kiss Me Deadly* (1955). In these noirs, the protagonist, usually middle-class, must confront and then overcome hypocrisy, malfeasance, intrigue, and criminality of upper-class villains, who often represent

American values. Hence, Hitchcock's *Saboteur* sets a standard for many ambivalent noir plots and conventions.

From the beginning *Saboteur* evinces class distinctions. Fry's (Norman Lloyd) haughty disdain for the two fellow workers, even when they return his letter and $100 bill, visually associates him with the sinister. His assistance with the fire extinguisher, really filled with gasoline, is out of character, out of his class. In what appears to be a moment of unity among the workers, Fry – an ironic name for an arsonist – feigns help by handing them a fire extinguisher, but that only exacerbates the conflagration. Fry's betrayal is a political allegory for Hitchcock: the disdain of fascist übermen is disguised insidiously by feigned moments of democratic unity. This pattern sustains itself throughout the film, as it does throughout much of Hitchcock's career. The aesthetics of the fire rely on noir stylistics, as the screenplay denotes:

SEMI CLOSE-UP OF A BLANK WALL

It is the stained wall of the paint shop. From the bottom corner of the picture we see a wisp of smoke as it begins to curl, slowly at first, then with more volume. Soon it is a full cloud of smoke, making its way across the screen.[23]

This description indicates the use of ever-more-enveloping blackness as a noir motif that signals the major event that will precipitate the protagonist's adventure. This spreading smoke is similar to the animated maps of Nazi conquests in Europe, as a spreading of the black death of the swastika across the land. Moreover, the smoke is the invidious treason of American sympathizers with fascism, all of whom are associated with the upper class.

Barry Kane (Bob Cummings) pursues Fry as he eludes capture by the police. He must travel the workingman's route, among the truckers and along the back roads of America. His journey is similar to outsider (Canadian) Richard Hannay's (Robert Donat) in *The 39 Steps* and to middle-class executive Roger Thornhill's (Cary Grant) in *North by Northwest*. Both Hannay and Thornhill must adapt to, sometimes adopt, patterns of behavior of a lower class. Both find a kind of harmony, yet alienation, among that other class: Hannay with the Crofter's wife (Peggy Ashcroft) and Thornhill among alien corn. Like Thornhill's saga, Kane's journey takes him across the American landscape, although unlike Thornhill's westward progress, Kane moves from the wide-open freedom of Western spaces to the confinement of New York City.

Kane's adventure, moreover, is a journey through American social classes, punctuated by a series of escapes from menacing, aristocratic figures and the police authorities. Kane flees Los Angeles with the help of a working-man trucker who gives him a lift to the Tobin Ranch, an exclusive, sprawling Western dude estate of tycoon Charles Tobin (Otto Kruger), equipped with its own Olympic-sized swimming pool. Tobin, Kane soon learns, is in cahoots with Fry, but before he can escape with this knowledge, Tobin has him arrested. Once again, with the help of the same working-class trucker, Kane effects a getaway. He finds himself in the wilderness at a deluxe log cabin, the home of a blind musician, Phillip Martin (Vaughan Glaser), and his overly suspicious niece, Pat Martin (Priscilla Lane). Pat is a perfect foil to and eventual partner for Kane, since her successful career as a model for billboard advertisements visually associates her with mainstream American market capitalism. On the road, Kane and Pat Martin squabble as they fall in love, in a typical Hitchcockian romance, during the wonderfully absurd, accidental encounter with a truck caravan of circus freaks. The single democratic moment of the film occurs with a vote taken among the circus freaks whether or not to spare the couple from the apprehension by the police. The mustachioed dwarf, garbed in a smoking jacket, furiously squeaks his dissent in a parody of Hitler, but also a comic slap at antidemocratic aristocratic views. Eventually, the couple arrives at the ghost town of Soda City, where Kane uncovers yet another sabotage plot, this time against the Hoover Dam, a symbol of American ingenuity and democratic progress.

Three New York locations are central to class and aesthetic issues in *Saboteur*: the society mansion; the Radio City Music Hall theater; and the Statue of Liberty. Arriving in New York, Kane is led through a Drug Store, out an alley, and into the upper-class mansion of society hostess Mrs. Sutton (Alma Kruger), where Pat Martin is being held. Hitchcock accentuates the couple's plight with long shots of spatial separation during the highbrow gala in the mansion's expansive ballroom. Kane disrupts the dance in a moment of class revenge by announcing that, unbeknown to the society matron, Mrs. Sutton, her expensive necklace will be auctioned off. As Kane searches for Pat, ascending an enormous staircase, he discovers Tobin in an ornate drawing room. Hitchcock reserves only long shots for Tobin to accentuate the class distance between Kane and this brand of upper-class fascism. Tobin sits on a French settee, centered between two nineteenth-century portraits of aristocratic ladies hung on a baroque wallpaper backdrop, theatrically displayed with proscenium-like curtains framing the scene. Tobin's cool, detached demeanor makes his vicious class condescension and his undemocratic lust for power all the more terrifying:

> You're one of the ardent believers, a good American. Oh, there're millions of you. People that plod along without asking questions. I hate to use the word 'stupid', but it seems to be the only one that applies.
>
> The Great Masses.
>
> The Moron Million.

Well, there are a few of us who are unwilling to just troop along. A few of us who are clever enough to see that there is much more to be done than live small, complacent lives. A few of us in America who desire a more profitable type of government.

Tobin's sinister dismissal of American democratic life includes familiar aristocratic disdain for hard work and middle-class values. Kane's response, before he is blackjacked by Tobin's butler, reduces Tobin's superiority to a psychosocial dis-ease: "You really hate *all* people."

After the bombing at the Brooklyn Naval Yard, the now fugitive Fry enters the Radio City Music Hall theater pursued by police, while on the giant silver screen an upper-class romantic comedy plays. The darkened theater, the reflected light from the screen, the silhouetted figure of the gun-toting Fry on the screen – all contribute to Hitchcock's noir style. Typical of Hitchcock's "tonal ambiguity," film audiences are caught up in a film-within-a-film paradox whereby the characters on the screen speak dialogue that correlates self-reflexively to the shootout in the auditorium: "Get out of here, he has gone mad ... murder ... run for your life."[24] The choice of a romantic comedy of class distinction adds to the irony of laughter and murder combined; the script's description indicates Hitchcock's intentional visual and aural punning in this scene: "Throughout we hear occasional conventional phrases that have an ironic parallel with the real scene that is taking place in the theater" (#680, p. 149). This parallel also refers to *Saboteur* itself, whereby the plot against America is both a fictional device and an all-too-real possibility. Moreover, the irony of the upper-class figures on the screen literally speaking down to Fry produces a typical Hitchcock serio-comic social inversion. In this respect, the final scenes with Fry are self-reflexive of the American wartime conditions: the public's escapism into class comedies in film (movie theater); the political escape from class realities in Europe to America (Statue of Liberty). In both scenes, Hitchcock reverses verticality so that the representative of aristocratic, totalitarian power becomes the victim. The slow tearing-away of Fry's coat sleeve on the torch-wielding arm of the Statue of Liberty visually provides Hitchcock's commentary on the failure of the threadbare ideology of fascism.

In *Shadow of a Doubt* (1943), Santa Rosa, California is the backdrop for an American *Our Town* in film noir, the dark side of the American Dream of middle-class prosperity. Santa Rosa is also a mixture of social classes, with working-class figures (policemen, telegraph operator, librarian, and barmaid), middle-class types (bankers, federal agents, country club patrons), and a villainous pseudo-aristocrat (Uncle Charlie). Many scenes in the film depict the melting pot of classes, such as several crosswalk scenes, where the social classes intersect. One scene of Uncle Charlie (Joseph Cotten), in a dapper high-class outfit, and Young Charlie (Teresa Wright) heading to the bank even includes a young Army soldier (who was my father, in a cameo!) among the milling, middle-class townsfolk. At the bank, Uncle Charlie jokes and flaunts his money with the bank president, all the while embarrassing his brother-in-law, Joseph Newton (Henry Travers), the middle-class bank clerk. Hitchcock relies almost exclusively on class status as the motivation for Uncle Charlie's serial murders, as evidenced by his famous dinner table "brooding" soliloquy of "deep, inner resentment":

UNCLE CHARLIE

Women keep busy in towns like this. In the cities it's different. The cities are full of women ... middle-age ... widows ... their husbands are dead ... the husbands who have spent their lives making thousands ... working ... working ... and then they die and leave their money to their wives ... their silly wives. And what do the wives do? These useless women? You see them in ... hotels, the best hotels, by the thousands ... eating the money, drinking the money, losing the money at bridge ... playing all afternoon and all night ... smelling of money ... proud of their jewelry ... proud of nothing else ... horrible, faded, fat and greedy women.[25]

Too often Uncle Charlie's speech has been reduced to sexism, which is only part of his demented, morbid view of American culture. Uncle Charlie lives between two class extremes – the impoverished lower class and the aristocracy. In the opening scene, as a fugitive, he lies, "meticulously neat" on a bed, "not even ruffled," in a "shabby and ill-kept" boardinghouse, one of a "number of meanlooking wooden houses," and scattered about floor are notes that have fallen from his wad of money (#1, 2). As a *faux* nobleman, he casts an embittered, contemptuous gaze upon the working world of middle-class men and the conspicuous consumption of middle-class wives of the leisure set.

In the noir setting of a lower-class dive bar, the neon-lit 'Til-Two Lounge, Louise (Janet Shaw), the barmaid and former high-school classmate of Young Charlie, observes the ring that Uncle Charlie has given to his niece. Louise offers in a weary monotone: "I'd die for a ring like that." Louise, the working-class woman, whom Uncle Charlie ignores, defeats his argument against women, since she too is lured by jewelry. Uncle Charlie, however, attacks Young Charlie's bourgeois views:

UNCLE CHARLIE

(he takes the ring and puts it in his pocket)

What do you really know? You're just an ordinary little girl living in an ordinary little town. You get up every day of your life, and you know there's not going to be a thing in the world to trouble you.

...

What do you know about the world? Do you know that it's a foul sty? Do you know that if you rip away the fronts of house you'll find swine? The world is a hell.

(Shadow #276, 124)

Uncle Charlie's nightmarish vision of the filthy world contrasts with Young Charlie's blindness, her optimism, her American Dream of reassurance and security. Once again, at a table, Uncle Charlie pontificates about the world, but this time, the "ordinary" world is one that he had just praised. Once again employing a reverse verticality, the aristocratic villain lowered to the dregs of a low-life lounge fittingly encapsulates Hitchcock's critique of American polarized class. Uncle Charlie's death scene aboard the train is also an apt Hitchcockian social commentary. Like Fry, Uncle Charlie falls from the illusory status of class superiority to his death. For both *Saboteur* and *Shadow of a Doubt*, class despotism is vanquished by means of a *pseudo-deus ex machina*, whereby the antidemocratic false idols descend to their necessary and deserved ends.

Hitchcock's early American noirs show his fascination with postwar American class issues, as evident in his later 1950s and 1960s films. *Rear Window* (1954) makes clear class distinctions along same-gender lines, with working-class Stella (Thelma Ritter) contrasted to modern corporate entrepreneur Lisa Carol Fremont (Grace Kelly) in dress, manner, and language. *Marnie* (1964) pits the psychosexual kleptomania and frigidity of Marnie (Tippi Hedren) against the aggressive landed gentry of Mark Rutland (Sean Connery), so that marriage between classes ultimately results in an uneasy, albeit desired, reconciliation between social spheres. Still, Hitchcock's greatest achievement in film noir class critique must be *Psycho* (1960). There, his signature visual vertical and horizontal axes for class division begin with the open panorama of Phoenix, Arizona, moving in a single shot descending through a hotel window to the longing, partially dressed couple, Marion (Janet Leigh) and Sam (John Gavin), lying on a bed as they kiss and discuss the financial constraints that preclude their marriage. Marion steals funds from the wealthy rancher and flees to the Bates Motel, where she meets her death. The axes of class are never more apparent than in the contrast of elevation between the opulent Victorian house on the hill and the postwar modernist ranch-style layout of the cabins of the motel. The feigned, now ruined aristocracy looks down upon the forfeited, now ruined capitalist enterprise, both of which reveal not so much a collapse of class teleology as a cultural impasse. Norman's (Anthony Perkins) cross-dressing, cross-dating murders have as much to do with his rejection of an older system of hierarchy as they do with his inability to cope with a newer system of value.

In the end, using stark high contrast lighting and mise-en-scène, Hitchcock pokes darkly satiric fun at American class values as Norman completely transforms into the aristocratic maternal figure. Hitchcock concludes with the new, upper-class visage of Norman-as-Mother superimposed, overlaid, almost de-evolutionarily, on an image of a sardonic skull against the background of the swamp. In that image, Hitchcock culminates his views of the paradoxical American system of class ambivalence.

NOTES

1 Murray Pomerance, *An Eye for Hitchcock* (New Brunswick, NJ: Rutgers University Press, 2004), p. 139.
2 Patrick McGilligan, *Alfred Hitchcock: A Life in Darkness and Light* (New York: Regan Books/HarperCollins, 2003), p. 14.
3 Christopher Beach, *Class, Language, and American Film Comedy* (Cambridge: Cambridge University Press, 2004), p. 68.
4 Sarah Street, *British National Cinema* (London: Routledge, 1997), p. 38.
5 Interview with J. Danvers Williams in *Monthly Film Bulletin* 6.65 (May 1939), p. 93, as quoted in Stephen C. Shafer, *British Popular Films, 1929–1939: The Cinema of Reassurance* (London: Routledge, 1997), p. 89.
6 James Leach, *British Film* (Cambridge: Cambridge University Press, 2004), p. 43.
7 Dorothy Lamb Crawford, *A Windfall of Musicians: Hitler's Émigrés and Exiles in Southern California* (New Haven, CT: Yale University Press, 2009), p. 44.
8 As quoted in Joseph Horowitz, *Artists in Exile: How Refugees from Twentieth-Century War and Revolution Transformed the American Performing Arts* (New York: HarperCollins, 2008), p. 49.
9 Vincent Brook, *Driven to Darkness: Jewish Émigré Directors and the Rise of Film Noir* (New Brunswick, NJ: Rutgers University Press, 2009), p. 21. R. Barton Palmer, "'Lounge Time' Reconsidered: Spatial Discontinuity and Temporal Contingency in *Out of the Past* (1947)," in Alain Silver and James Ursini, *Film Noir Reader 4* (New York: Limelight, 2004), p. 54.
10 Bettina Rosenblatt, "Doubles and Doubt in Hitchcock: The German Connection," in *Hitchcock: Past and Future*, eds. Richard Allen and Sam Ishii-Gonzáles (London: Routledge, 2004), p. 44.
11 Stephanie Barron, "Introduction," in *German Expressionism, 1915–1925, The Second Generation*, ed. Barron (Los Angeles: Prestel for the Los Angeles County Museum of Art, 1988), p. 37.
12 Donald Spoto, *The Life of Alfred Hitchcock: The Dark Side of Genius* (London: Collins, 1983), p. 68; François Truffaut, *Hitchcock* (Rochester, NY: Simon and Schuster, 1967), p. 19.
13 Klaus Kreimeier, *The UFA Story: A History of Germany's Greatest Film Company, 1918–1945* (Berkeley: University of California Press, 1999), p. 107.
14 James N. Bade, "Murnau's *The Last Laugh* and Hitchcock's Subjective Camera," *Quarterly Review of Film and Video* 23 (2006), p. 259.
15 Jack Sullivan, *Hitchcock's Music* (New Haven, CT: Yale University Press, 2006), p. 108.
16 Joseph Garncarz, "German Hitchcock," *Hitchcock Annual* 9 (2000): 86.

17 Sidney Gottlieb, "Early Hitchcock: The German Influence," *Hitchcock Annual* 8 (1999): 104.

18 Joseph Garncarz, "The Star System in Weimar Cinema," in *The Many Faces of Weimar Cinema: Rediscovering Germany's Filmic Legacy* (Rochester, NY: Camden House, 2010), p. 118.

19 As quoted in Dietrich Scheunemann, "Activating the Differences: Expressionist Film and Early Weimar Cinema," in *Expressionist Film: New Perspectives*, ed. Scheunemann (Rochester, NY: Camden House, 2003), p. 15.

20 Janet Ward, *Weimar Surfaces: Urban Visual Culture in 1920s Germany* (Berkeley: University of California Press, 2001), p. 189.

21 Nicholas Haeffner, *Alfred Hitchcock* (London: Pearson/Longman, 2005), p. 63.

22 Thomas Elsaesser, "Too Big and Too Close: Alfred Hitchcock and Fritz Lang," in *The Hitchcock Annual Anthology: Selected Essays from Volumes 10–15*, eds. Sidney Gottlieb and Richard Allen (New York: Wallflower Press, 2009), p. 162.

23 Peter Viertel and Joan Harrison, *Saboteur* (Script No. 768; October 30, 1941): #14, 5.

24 Richard Allen, *Hitchcock's Romantic Irony* (New York: Columbia University Press, 2007), 18, 168.

25 Thornton Wilder, Sally Benson, and Alma Reville, *Shadow of a Doubt* (Changes, August 10, 1942): #241 MED. SHOT, 110.

5

CARL FREEDMAN

American Civilization and Its Discontents: The Persistence of Evil in Hitchcock's *Shadow of a Doubt*

Hitchcock from London to Hollywood

On March 1, 1939, Alfred Hitchcock – accompanied by his wife and daughter, a personal assistant, a cook, and a maid – boarded the *Queen Mary* in Southampton in order to set sail for New York. Britain would never again be home for the London-born Hitchcock. Allowing for numerous international trips, he remained in the United States for the rest of his life, residing in California, making movies in Hollywood, and eventually taking American citizenship.[1] He thus became one of those modern artists, like Henry James, T. S. Eliot, or W. H. Auden, who cannot be described as unambiguously either British or American. Like them, he was neither – or, more accurately, both. Also like them – and unlike such more extreme instances of cultural "extraterritoriality" (George Steiner's term)[2] as Joseph Conrad, Vladimir Nabokov, or Samuel Beckett – Hitchcock crossed no linguistic barriers and instead went on to engage, in his work, the Shavian (or pseudo-Shavian) paradox that Britain and America are two nations divided by a common language. From 1939 on, the relation between the culture of his original homeland and that of his adopted one is a frequent presence in Hitchcock's cinema.

In the following pages I examine *Shadow of a Doubt* (1943) as registering a crucial moment in the process of Hitchcock's Americanization.[3] It is, I maintain, the first film in which he emerges as predominantly an American filmmaker and creates a major work deeply rooted in the American cultural tradition. Like many of his great American precursors, Hitchcock takes as his central concern the persistence of evil in American civilization.

Yet, before examining the American character of the film, it is important to make clear that Hitchcock's roots in the culture of late Victorian Britain are by no means effaced in *Shadow of a Doubt*. On the contrary, the film is built on a theme that was a prominent component of the British culture into which Hitchcock was born in 1899, namely that of the half-good and half-evil double, presented here through the juxtaposition and interaction of the benevolent, virginal teenage girl Charlie Newton (played by Teresa Wright, and hereafter referred to as Young Charlie) and her murderously sinister uncle, Charlie Oakley (played by Joseph Cotten, and hereafter referred to as Uncle Charlie), after whom Young Charlie is named. In addition to numerous other works now mostly forgotten, this motif is central, for instance, to Robert Louis Stevenson's *The Strange Case of Dr. Jekyll and Mr. Hyde* (1886), to Oscar Wilde's *The Picture of Dorian Gray* (1891), and to Bram Stoker's *Dracula* (1897). These authors – Wilde most overtly – were in revolt against the stark ethical dichotomies of an earlier Victorian moralism, and their insistence that good and evil are more implicated in one another than Britain's quasi-official moral guardians were inclined to allow struck a responsive chord with the reading public of the United Kingdom. These works were popular during Hitchcock's formative years, and the young Hitchcock is known to have read both *Jekyll and Hyde* and *Dorian Gray* multiple times before embarking on his filmmaking career. *Shadow of a Doubt* continues the main theme of such texts – the ethically divided double.

It is not just a matter of formal or mathematical doubling. In their 1957 book on Hitchcock – one of the foundational texts of Hitchcock studies – Eric Rohmer and Claude Chabrol flatly declare (explicitly following the suggestion of François Truffaut) that "*Shadow of a Doubt* is based on the number two."[4] The first example they give has become one of the most widely discussed formal elements of the film: the way that the two Charlies are introduced in "rhyming" shots that show each of them, on opposite sides of the country (Uncle Charlie in Philadelphia, Young Charlie in her hometown of Santa Rosa, California), stretched out fully clothed on a bed. Rohmer and Chabrol offer many further instances of such duality, to which later commentators have added still more, and which any attentive viewer can multiply almost indefinitely. Thus, for example, Uncle Charlie is one of two suspects that the police are investigating in the Merry Widow Murders, and both are ultimately killed, accidentally, by two transportation machines (Uncle Charlie by a train, his unnamed counterpart by an airplane propeller). Two police detectives turn up at the Newton residence to investigate the crimes. Young Charlie's father, Joe Newton (Henry Travers), and his neighbor Herbie Hawkins (Hume Cronyn) make up an informal club of two devoted to the rather Hitchcockian hobby of wittily inventing various ways to murder one another. In the relatively late scene where the two Charlies confront one another – Young Charlie having figured out her uncle's murderous ways – the bar in which they sit is called the 'Til-Two, and Uncle Charlie orders a *double* brandy from a waitress who, it turns out, has been on the job for two weeks. The search for such instances of doubling can continue almost indefinitely, and it might well be difficult to name another movie in which the number two is more prominently featured.

But to say that the film is *based* on the number two may be subtly misleading, for it might be taken to reduce the structure of *Shadow of a Doubt* to the sort of quantitative formalism that, though certainly at work within the film, is only incidental to Hitchcock's main purpose. As with his Victorian predecessors, Hitchcock's interest in doubling is fundamentally moral, not just mathematical.[5] For him as for Stevenson or Stoker, the ethical duality of good and evil is a genuine dialectic, not a mere dichotomy; or, to put the matter another way, the binary opposition of good to evil, which is fundamental to all ethical thought, can always be deconstructed, as Nietzsche showed, in order to demonstrate that neither term is genuinely independent of the other, or even opposed to the other in any completely simple way. Good and evil always "interinanimate" (Donne's brilliant coinage) one another.

In Stevenson's novella, for example, it should be remembered that Dr. Jekyll undertakes his pharmacological experiments because he is uncomfortably aware of the way that virtuous and vicious impulses coexist and mingle within his own moral being. He hopes to purify himself as Dr. Jekyll by chemically creating (or releasing) a separate personality, Mr. Hyde, in whom all his evil tendencies can be concentrated (and enjoyed). The experiment ultimately fails precisely because evil cannot, in fact, be so neatly separated from its dialectical antithesis. Mr. Hyde refuses to play the subordinate and strictly limited role assigned to him, becoming the dominant personality within the Jekyll/Hyde double; and the drug Dr. Jekyll has concocted to release Mr. Hyde loses its power to restore Jekyll. In the end, Dr. Jekyll is rid of his evil twin only when both are annihilated through Hyde's suicide.

Shadow of a Doubt is only very slightly inflected by the Gothic mode that dominates Stevenson's novella (as well as the novels by Wilde and Stoker), so that Hitchcock's two Charlies are not the same person in the precisely literal sense that applies to Jekyll and Hyde. But the connection between them is weirdly and unnaturally close. In Young Charlie's first lines of dialogue, she begins by expressing some typically teenage boredom and dissatisfaction with her family's conventional middle-class existence, but then soon hits on an idea that she feels certain will solve everything. She determines to send a telegram to Uncle Charlie, explicitly casting him as a savior whose mere presence among the Newton family will somehow make life exciting and worthwhile. Exactly how Uncle Charlie can accomplish such "miracles" (Young Charlie's own term) is left unclear – it seems an almost magical belief on his niece's part – but, upon finding that Uncle Charlie has already sent a telegram of his own, announcing his imminent arrival, Young Charlie concludes that the two of them must be bonded by mental telepathy. Shortly after Uncle Charlie's arrival in the Newton home, Young Charlie tells him that she's glad that her mother (Uncle Charlie's older sister) named her after Uncle Charlie and that her mother thinks the two Charlies are "both alike." "I think we are too. I know it," Young Charlie adds, going on to maintain that the two are not just uncle and niece but "something else" and "sort of like twins" – a chillingly bizarre line (for how can two people of different generations be twins?) that Uncle Charlie will quote back to his niece during the tense scene at the 'Til-Two.

The extraordinary affinity between the Charlies – so deep that it seems to verge on actual identity, as the constant iteration of the name itself keeps reminding us – means that no simple dichotomy is tenable between the cheerful, beneficent Young Charlie and her cynical, misogynistic, multiply murderous uncle. On one level, the implication of each Charlie in the other is figured in their (symbolic) incestuous sexual union. It is not just that the strange intensity of the mutual attraction, especially on Young Charlie's side, necessarily conveys an erotic connotation. The latter is also suggested in one visual turn after another. The introduction of the Charlies lying on their respective beds – a double shot that will be repeated later in the film – naturally invokes the possibility of their being in bed together; and it is no accident that, when Uncle Charlie arrives at the Newton home, Young Charlie's bed and bedroom are, at her own insistence, assigned to him (though she temporarily moves in with her younger sister). In the scene where Young Charlie, along with her father, sister, and brother, picks up Uncle Charlie at the Santa Rosa train station, the meeting of niece and uncle is shown in a cinematographic turn nearly always used in Hollywood film to represent the reunion of lovers: the camera switches from one to the other as each is shown rushing toward the other, both faces beaming with joy and anticipation. During the first extended tête-à-tête conversation between uncle and niece, Uncle Charlie takes Young Charlie's hand and slips a ring on her finger, like a suitor formalizing his engagement to be married to his beloved.

The ring turns out to have belonged to one of the rich widows that Uncle Charlie has romanced, robbed, and murdered. Young Charlie's acceptance of it, together with her (barely) unconscious but intense sexual desire for her uncle, thus establishes the fresh-faced teenage virgin as not only in symbolic violation of the incest taboo so fundamental to the moral order of nearly all civilizations but also as an unwitting accomplice to Uncle Charlie's career as a serial killer, the loot from which she agrees to share. Like Dr. Jekyll, the formally upright and virtuous Young Charlie cannot be wholly acquitted of moral responsibility for the actions of her evil "twin." And, just as Dr. Jekyll is ultimately destroyed by Mr. Hyde, so Young Charlie only barely escapes several attempts on her life by Uncle Charlie.

In fact, as the plot of *Shadow of a Doubt* plays out, Young Charlie eventually shows herself willing to become an accomplice (after the fact) to her uncle's murders in a straightforward, fully conscious, and perhaps legally culpable sense. Despite her strong attraction to her uncle, Young Charlie soon begins to sense that there is something wrong about him: an insight possibly enabled by their strange affinity. She is taken into the partial confidence of one of the police detectives (who will become her fiancé by film's end), but also undertakes some shrewd research on her own (Young Charlie, as her father proudly notes, was the smartest girl in her class at the high school from which she has recently graduated). Before long, she has concluded with near certainty that her uncle is the Merry Widow Murderer. Though horrified, she nonetheless decides to withhold some of what she knows from the detectives and to advise Uncle Charlie to leave town. She is thus prepared to help him perhaps escape justice and perhaps kill again. One can, to be sure, feel sympathy for Young Charlie here. Awareness of Uncle Charlie's terrible crimes cannot instantly cancel her powerful affection for him; and, moreover, Young Charlie is worried that learning the truth may literally kill her mother, who has always adored and idolized her younger brother. Young Charlie is trapped in the classic Antigone position (the paradigmatically tragic situation, according to Hegel), caught between the demands of personal and familial feeling on the one hand and the transpersonal requirements of her society's ethical and legal order on the other. Yet this is, in a way, precisely the point. In the theme of the dialectical twinship of good and evil that Hitchcock has carried on from Stevenson, Wilde, Stoker, and other late Victorian storytellers, the twin poles of ethics are always more involved with one another than superficially appears; and choosing between them is therefore by no means the simple task that the earnest moralists maintain it to be.

The Americanization of Alfred

In *Shadow of a Doubt*, then, Hitchcock appears as the heir – perhaps the last heir of major artistic stature – to a narrative tradition rooted in the late-Victorian Britain into which he was born. But the further project of the film is thoroughly to *Americanize* this tradition and, in so doing, to set not only this particular movie but also Hitchcock himself in a profoundly American intellectual and artistic line. If the *auteur* of the film is still British, he is also, and even more deeply, already American.

Although Hitchcock made important films right after moving from London to Hollywood, the culture of his new homeland is not immediately registered, to any great extent, in his work. *Rebecca* (1940) and *Suspicion* (1941) offer British stories with British settings, and are in many ways the direct successors to such masterpieces of Hitchcock's London period as *Murder!* (1930), *The 39 Steps* (1935), and *The Lady Vanishes* (1938). *Rebecca*, in particular, proclaims its British roots partly by giving a starring role to the deeply English Laurence Olivier, the preeminent actor on the London stage of his (and Hitchcock's) era. *Foreign Correspondent* (1940) – perhaps one of the most underrated films in the Hitchcock oeuvre – is a somewhat different case, since it begins in New York and stars the quintessentially American actor Joel McCrea. Yet, as the title suggests, the film is not strongly tied to any particular place. The espionage plot moves from one locale to another, and much of the action is set in London, Amsterdam, the Dutch countryside, and even in the Atlantic Ocean. *Saboteur* (1942) has an American setting and cast, but, as William Rothman has pointed out, is best understood as "an Americanized remake of *The 39 Steps*."[6] Despite its veneer of pro-American war propaganda – and its somewhat ostentatious visual use of such American landmarks as the Boulder Dam, the Brooklyn Navy Yard, Radio City Music Hall, and, above all, the Statue of Liberty – the project of *Saboteur* is, as Rothman suggests, more to parody than seriously to engage America. It is only with *Shadow of a Doubt* that Hitchcock first seems not only fully comfortable with his American surroundings but determined to establish himself as a genuinely American artist rather than just a British artist living in the United States.

The moment in *Shadow of a Doubt* that most clearly stresses the newly American quality of Hitchcockian cinema – the most overt signal of Americanization – concerns a ruse that the two police detectives employ to gain access to the Newton home in their investigation of Uncle Charlie. They pose as researchers for something called the "National Public Survey" and proclaim themselves interested in interviewing and taking photographs of the Newtons, who have purportedly been found to constitute the "typical American family."[7] The claim seems plausible enough, for the Newtons live in a modest but ample suburban house and consist of a father who works at a mid-level position in the local bank, a stay-at-home mother who manages the housekeeping and child-rearing, and three lively children. Mrs. Newton (Patricia Collinge), who is pleased for her family to be thought so normal, looks the perfect American housewife and mother as she poses for the camera while making a cake. It is quite true that, as Jonathan Freedman and Richard Millington have observed, this "normativeness is being demonstrated to be wholly simulacral, both a pose for and the creation of the media who ostensibly record it."[8] Indeed, the American typicality of the Newton family is a *double* simulacrum, since the "National Public Survey" that constructs it is itself a simulacrum constructed to conceal the detectives' true motives. But then, as Hitchcock in Hollywood (the world capital of simulation) was surely well aware, the simulacral construction of reality, especially cultural reality, is itself as American as apple pie (or as maple cake, one of Mrs. Newton's specialties). The very defining characteristic of American national identity is that it is, as Benedict Anderson demonstrates in his influential study of nationalism, the original and paradigmatic "imagined community," whose felt cultural integrity was deliberately and synthetically constructed.[9]

Hitchcock also takes pains to make *Shadow of a Doubt* emphatically American on levels more fundamental, if less explicit, than the signal sent by the "National Public Survey." In casting, for example, the point is not just that the stars Teresa Wright and Joseph Cotten are in fact American actors. The pretty but fairly ordinary-looking brunette Wright is allowed no glamorous clothes or makeup, and is presented, in both appearance and manner, as the bright, perky all-American girl. She radiates a girl-next-door kind of attractiveness that contrasts with the spectacular beauty of the "cool blondes" (Ingrid Bergman, Grace Kelly, Kim Novak, Eva Marie Saint, Janet Leigh, and Tippi Hedren, inter alia) who would become Hitchcock's most famous leading ladies – and who often seem at least vaguely European and "un-American," even when actually meant to be of U.S. nationality.

As for Cotten, he too appears more as pleasant-looking in a mundane American way than as stunningly handsome. It is worth noting that, in Cotten's most important roles prior to *Shadow of a Doubt*, Orson Welles had used him to portray deeply sympathetic American types. In *Citizen Kane* (1941), Cotten is the amiable, honest drama critic – and hero's best friend – Jedediah Leland; in *The Magnificent Ambersons* (1942), he plays the kindly inventor and businessman Eugene Morgan; and in each case the likeability of Cotten's character is emphasized by being contrasted with a much less sympathetic sort, namely the ruthless tycoon Charles Foster Kane (Welles) and the spoiled, mean-spirited aristocrat George Minafer (Tim Holt), respectively. Hitchcock, in effect, inherits from Welles the persona of Cotten-as-American-good-guy and keeps this persona superficially intact while also revealing the character to be, just below the surface, a sociopathic serial murderer. Of course, Wright as an all-American girl is, as we have seen, not so innocent as she may initially appear either.

Much the same pattern – of evil hidden beneath attractive all-American surfaces – appears on the all-important level of setting. Prior to the shot that introduces Uncle Charlie lying on his bed, the camera shows us his Philadelphia surroundings: hobos eating lunch underneath a large suspension bridge; smokestacks belching black pollution into the air; rusted-out cars in a junkyard; children playing ball in the street; lines of row houses; and, later, desolate vacant lots and more piles of junk. This is, of course, a version of America, specifically the urban America as featured in the film noir that, as Hitchcock was making *Shadow of a Doubt*, was just beginning to emerge as one of the major genres in the Hollywood repertoire (and a genre to which Hitchcock would, of course, later make important contributions of his own with such films as *Rear Window* [1954] and *Vertigo* [1958]). Yet, despite the occasional popularity of a few urban aesthetic forms like film noir (and jazz), the main cultural temper of America has always been essentially anti-urban: and the noir-like dreary bleakness with which Uncle Charlie's Philadelphia is portrayed ratifies the dominant ideological notion that a big city cannot be regarded as *truly* American in the strongest and most eulogistic sense.

Accordingly, Hitchcock's camera soon moves to the other side of the North American continent, not only to introduce Young Charlie lying on *her* bed but also to show us the far more agreeable and more "authentically" American locale of Santa Rosa (near which Hitchcock himself actually bought a house while *Shadow of a Doubt* was in production). If Uncle Charlie's Philadelphia resembles the settings of film noir, the move out west to California necessarily recalls the Western genre, which in the 1940s was still the bedrock not only of Hollywood cinema but of American popular culture as a whole. Indeed, as Robin Wood has pointed out, Hitchcock's Santa Rosa "can be seen as the frontier town [of the Western] seventy or so years on."[10] In the seven intervening decades, the town has progressed beyond the roughness and danger associated with Western films and now seems not only quintessentially American, as in the Western, but also virtually idyllic.

Before meeting Young Charlie, we see, first, an aerial view of Santa Rosa as a whole, carpeted with abundant green trees and nestled among the foothills of some mountains in the background. Then the camera moves in to show such details as attractive, relatively compact downtown buildings; a smiling policeman directing traffic and allowing pedestrians to cross a bustling but not excessively crowded street; and then the quieter residential street on which the Newtons live, with a large leafy oak in the foreground and a small bus going past, its bell cheerfully ringing. The camera zooms in to show the Newtons' own residence, a well-maintained two-story white frame house, with bay windows and the kind of big front porch on which small-town Americans are stereotypically wont to relax and socialize with their neighbors. It would be difficult to imagine a more profoundly and seductively American setting: and this initial impression is confirmed and deepened as the movie progresses and we see that Santa Rosa includes such further American icons of the period as a telegraph office, a railroad station, a diner, a clock tower, and a free public library.

Now, since evil, in the person of Uncle Charlie, invades Santa Rosa from the big city of Philadelphia – he comes ostensibly for a friendly family visit but actually, of course, in order to elude the police – the film's apparent preference for the small town, and its concomitant endorsement of American anti-urban ideology, do carry some genuine weight. The visual attractiveness of Santa Rosa in contrast to the desolation of Philadelphia is real enough. Murder is fairly routine in the urban metropolis, as both film noir and Uncle Charlie's career as a serial killer make evident, while Santa Rosa appears to be nearly crime-free: jaywalking is the most serious offense with which we see the local police (as opposed to the detectives from back east who are following Uncle Charlie) having to deal. Furthermore, and with particular ingenuity, a clear contrast is conveyed between the interest in murder on the part of the small-town denizens Joe Newton and Herbie Hawkins – an interest that is harmless, humorous, basically literary, and implicitly presented as very much like Hitchcock's own cinematic interest in the subject – and the actual practice of multiple cold-blooded murder by the urban (and comparatively urbane) Uncle Charlie.

Yet the matter is, of course, also more complicated than that. Just as the two Charlies cannot be so easily differentiated or divided from one another – morally, erotically, and otherwise – so no simple ethical dichotomy can be sustained between small-town innocence and big-city corruption in America. Just as Young Charlie connives in – indeed, enthusiastically welcomes – Uncle Charlie's evil presence in her home, and even to some degree connives in his capital crimes, so Santa Rosa is not exactly innocent of the monster in the town's midst: for it is the town as a whole, not just his niece, that enthusiastically welcomes Uncle Charlie. Joe Newton's bank is naturally more than happy to accept the $40,000 that Uncle Charlie deposits, all of it presumably stolen from the widows he has murdered. Beyond that, there is something about Uncle Charlie that almost everyone in Santa Rosa finds tremendously exciting and enthralling. A local civic association begs him to deliver a lecture about his travels ("We don't get many American speakers," as one member significantly comments), and is thrilled by his performance. With almost unbearable irony, a local affluent, attractive widow thinks that Uncle Charlie might be a good match for her. After his death, the town gives him a hero's send-off, with the funeral procession rolling down the main downtown streets, big crowds of Santa Rosans in attendance, and a deep-voiced clergyman recalling Uncle Charlie's presumed virtues at interminable length. The deep evil of American society that Uncle Charlie represents cannot be confined to the mean urban streets of Philadelphia; it also infects the more "truly" American village of Santa Rosa. In an interesting twist, the characters in *Shadow of a Doubt* who are *least* implicated in what Uncle Charlie stands for are the two detectives: outsiders in Santa Rosa like Uncle Charlie himself, who belong to the same metropolitan world from which he has emerged.

Hawthorne to Hitchcock and Beyond

That Hitchcock, in his most American film to that point, should thus find evil in the most deeply American of settings and characters – in a way that somewhat contrasts with the comparative benignity of British society assumed in many of the films of his London period – might well be thought to derive, at least in part, from the cold eye of the outsider. Paradoxically, however, it is in his insistence on occluded but powerfully persistent American evil that Hitchcock really shows himself to be working in the American grain.

The most obvious American connection is to Thornton Wilder's *Our Town* (1938). Hitchcock admired the representation of small-town American life in Wilder's play and recruited Wilder to work on the script for *Shadow of a Doubt*. Yet the link between Wilder's stage drama and Hitchcock's film is more tenuous than might initially appear. For one thing, though Hitchcock and Wilder spent some friendly time together planning the movie, and though Hitchcock included in the introductory credits an unusual slide reading, "We wish to acknowledge the contribution of Mr. Thornton Wilder to the preparation of this production," it is unclear how much – if any – of the actual writing Wilder did.[11] More important, the two small towns – the Grover's Corners, New Hampshire, of Wilder and the Santa Rosa, California, of Hitchcock – are fundamentally different in more than just geographic (and chronological) ways. Though Grover's Corners is not necessarily just the innocuous slice of wholesome Americana that countless high-school and community-theater productions have taken it to be – death, after all, is the central theme of *Our Town*, which strongly hints at a certain existential futility in all human endeavor – Wilder's town *is* almost entirely innocent of actual evil. The darkness in *Our Town* is caused, rather, by human limitation in an ultimately indifferent universe. In *Shadow of a Doubt*, Hitchcock does not copy Grover's Corners. He produces a roughly comparable American small town and shows it to be, unlike Grover's Corners, infected with the terrifying evil of serial murder.

In so doing, Hitchcock demonstrates himself to be at one with American storytellers greater – and more centrally American – than Wilder. Though there is no space here for more than a few notes in substantiation, it seems clear that the chief foundational figure of the tradition to which *Shadow of a Doubt* belongs is Nathaniel Hawthorne. In "Young Goodman Brown" (1835), for instance – perhaps as deeply typical a product of Hawthorne's genius as any particular work that one could name – the society of Salem, Massachusetts, which understands itself to be a theocracy of strict virtue, is shown to be secretly brimming with diabolical evil in something like the literal sense. Whether the extended sequence in the forest be read as hallucination or as actual revelation of Satanic worship, Hawthorne clearly exposes and condemns such vicious practices as the mass murder of Indians and the persecution of Quakers (the latter something for which the author's seventeenth-century ancestor, Major William Hathorne, was particularly known). A subtler exposure is enacted in "The Minister's Black Veil" (1836), in which the Puritan divine of the title takes to wearing a black veil that obscures most of his face and that he refuses to remove under any circumstances. The garment does wonders for his stature as a clergyman, because he soon acquires an awesome reputation for special insight into veiled evil, into secret sin. But the story itself suggests that the real evil is hidden in plain view: that is, the minister's own spiritual pride that cuts him off, for life, from all real human contact, including with the young woman to whom he had been engaged before taking the veil.

The tale thus somewhat foreshadows Hawthorne's greatest treatment of evil hidden within America's New England foundations, *The Scarlet Letter* (1850). While the dominant religious ideology of seventeenth-century Boston takes the adulterous love of Hester Prynne and Arthur Dimmesdale to be damnable and (on Hester's side) open sin, the novel demonstrates at length the actual, if occluded, evil to be the Bostonians' own self-righteousness – the latter condensed in the cold-blooded determination with which Roger Chillingworth (who is secretly Hester's husband) slowly tortures Dimmesdale to death. Though their killing methods are different, the cynical misanthrope and misogynist Chillingworth is a direct ancestor of Uncle Charlie.

Hawthorne's (qualified) admirer Edgar Allan Poe ought also to be mentioned in connection with the American tradition in which *Shadow of a Doubt* places itself. Whereas little is known of Hitchcock's reading of Hawthorne, the filmmaker spoke quite openly about Poe's importance for him. In a 1961 essay, Hitchcock explicitly credits Poe with inspiring him to make movies, noting that, like the American short-story writer, his method was to try to create "a completely unbelievable story told ... with such a spellbinding logic that you get the impression that the same thing could happen to you tomorrow."[12] Though Poe's settings are often nominally (but only nominally) European, he is as American as Hawthorne in his excavations of evil at work beneath society's smooth surfaces: and it seems all but certain that this aspect of Poe's fiction had its impact on Hitchcock.

In "The Cask of Amontillado" (1846), for example, unspecified and presumably trivial insults lead one friend to murder another in a particularly grotesque way, chaining him up alive behind a brick wall; and, as in "The Black Cat" (1843) and "The Tell-Tale Heart" (1843), the realization of evil is deepened by Poe's telling the story from the viewpoint of the murderer, who in all three cases is a monomaniacal sociopath somewhat like Uncle Charlie. In "The Masque of the Red Death" (1842), evil is manifest in the form of an imaginary disease clearly based on the bubonic plague but meant to be even more horrifying; and the red death demonstrates its ability to penetrate into even the most apparently secure locations. In "The Fall of the House of Usher" (1839), as in *Shadow of a Doubt*, sociopathic murder within a family is shown to be a concrete possibility. Poe frequently insists that evil can strike anywhere, that there are no safe havens; and this structure of feeling is integral not only to *Shadow of a Doubt* but also to Hitchcock's depiction of American civilization in such varied later films as *Rear Window* (1954), *The Wrong Man* (1956), *Psycho* (1960), and *The Birds* (1963).

Even to mention the other major writers that might be placed alongside Hawthorne and Poe in this tradition would be to revisit much, probably most, of American literary history. William Faulkner, America's preeminent twentieth-century novelist (and an almost exact contemporary of Hitchcock's), devoted his career to undermining the moonlight-and-magnolias self-image of the American South and exposing a legacy of evil marked by slavery, war, poverty, ignorance, racism, and violence. Arthur Miller, arguably the nation's finest playwright, was no less astringently critical, and, in *The Crucible* (1952), Miller returns to Hawthorne's Salem in order to examine the origins of American corruption. The literary impulse to excavate evil beneath the apparently innocuous appearances of American society is crucial to current writers as various as Cormac McCarthy (arguably the most critically respected American novelist at work today) and Stephen King (perhaps the most commercially popular). This is the American tradition that Hitchcock joins with *Shadow of a Doubt* and to which, as noted earlier, he continues to contribute in many of his best later films. Poe would have instantly recognized a mild-mannered motel clerk who turns out to be a matricide and serial killer, and Miller would have perfectly understood how America's much-praised justice system imprisons those innocent of any crime. Hawthorne would not have been the least bit surprised by an apparently normal American husband who, observed closely from one's rear window, is seen to have murdered his wife. The greatest American storytellers have generally been most American in their radical discontent with American civilization; and the fact that it is with *Shadow of a Doubt* that

Hitchcock joins this company may not be the least reason that he counted it as his own favorite among his films.[13]

Acknowledgments

I should like to thank Annette Freedman, Elsie Michie, and Stephen Peltier, each of whom carefully read this essay in manuscript form and made valuable suggestions for its improvement.

NOTES

1 Donald Spoto, *The Dark Side of Genius: The Life of Alfred Hitchcock*, Centennial Edition (New York: Da Capo, 1999) and Patrick McGilligan, *Alfred Hitchcock: A Life in Darkness and Light* (New York: IT Books, 2003) are my chief authorities for all biographical references to Hitchcock.

2 The allusion is to George Steiner, *Extraterritorial: Papers on Literature and the Language Revolution* (New York: Atheneum, 1971).

3 All references to and quotations from *Shadow of a Doubt* are based on the digitally remastered DVD version released by Universal Studios in 2006.

4 Eric Rohmer and Claude Chabrol, *Hitchcock: The First Forty-four Films*, trans. Stanley Hochman (New York: Frederick Ungar, 1979), p. 72. The collocation here of the names of Rohmer, Chabrol, and Truffaut is of course indicative of the immense importance of Hitchcock for French New Wave cinema; it would be only a slight exaggeration to describe the New Wave as a project of French Hitchcock critics who decided to implement in actual filmmaking what they had learned from watching and writing about the Hitchcock oeuvre.

5 This is not, of course, to say that the mathematical and moral senses of doubling are unrelated; Freud's 1919 essay, "The 'Uncanny,'" provides the classic psychoanalytic account of the connections.

6 William Rothman, *Hitchcock: The Murderous Gaze*, Second Edition (Albany: SUNY Press, 2012), p. 185.

7 The notion of the Newtons as the typical American family points to a theme of domesticity as well as to one of nationality. The former, which lies slightly outside the concerns of the present essay, is well treated in James McLaughlin, "All in the Family: Alfred Hitchcock's *Shadow of a Doubt*," in Marshall Deutelbaum and Leland Poague, eds., *A Hitchcock Reader* (Ames: Iowa State University Press, 1986), pp. 141–152, and in Elsie B. Michie, "Unveiling Maternal Desires: Hitchcock and American Domesticity," in Jonathan Freedman and Richard Millington, eds., *Hitchcock's America* (New York: Oxford University Press, 1999), pp. 29–53.

8 "Introduction" to Freedman and Millington, eds., *op. cit.*, p. 3.

9 See Benedict Anderson, *Imagined Communities: Reflections on the Origin and Spread of Nationalism*, Revised and Extended Edition (London: Verso, 1991), especially chapter 4, "Creole Pioneers."

10 Robin Wood, *Hitchcock's Films Revisited*, Revised Edition (New York: Columbia University Press, 2002), p. 293.

11 Wilder joined the U.S. Army early in the preproduction of *Shadow of a Doubt* and, according to Spoto, "did little more than help scout locations and work on a prose treatment" (p. 257); the actual screenplay, in Spoto's account, seems to have been produced by Hitchcock himself, his wife Alma Reville (always Hitchcock's most trusted colleague), and the short-story writer Sally Benson. McGilligan suggests a larger role for Wilder, at one point quoting the film scholar Bill Krohn to describe what Wilder produced as "a very rough draft" (p. 313). J. D. McClatchy, the editor of the Library of America edition of Wilder's *Collected Plays & Writings on Theater* (New York: Library of America, 2007), includes a complete screenplay in his volume (although the dialogue is by no means identical to that of the actual film) and, in the notes, refers to it as "the screenplay he [Wilder] wrote in 1942 for Alfred Hitchcock's film *Shadow of a Doubt*" (p. 835); McClatchy also quotes a letter in which Wilder explicitly takes credit (p. 870). Given the intrinsically collaborative nature of cinema – not to mention the size of the egos often involved – it can of course be notoriously difficult to determine exactly who did what.

12 Quoted in Dana Brand, "Rear-View Mirror: Hitchcock, Poe, and the Flaneur in America," in Freedman and Millington, eds., *op. cit.*, p. 123.

13 McGilligan says, "[M]ore than once, [Hitchcock] called [*Shadow of a Doubt*] his favorite." He also points out, however, that, "speaking for posterity, he pointedly told François Truffaut it *wasn't* his favorite, and told Peter Bogdanovich it was merely '*one* of his favorites'" (p. 327; emphasis in the original). But Hitchcock's daughter Patricia flatly declares *Shadow of a Doubt* to have been her father's favorite film in an interview included on the DVD cited earlier.

PART II

Hitchcock: Sexualities, Genders, Theories

6

SUSAN WHITE

Alfred Hitchcock and Feminist Film Theory (Yet Again)

In an insightful essay appearing in another volume devoted to Hitchcock's work, "Hitchcock and Feminist Theory from *Rebecca* to *Marnie*," Florence Jacobowitz writes,

> I agreed to write this chapter on the significance of Hitchcock to feminist film theory and criticism following the completion of a course I taught on women and film that included films by Hitchcock and other classical-era Hollywood directors, including Dorothy Arzner. The students' ambivalence toward these films extended beyond a particular auteur; for them, the problem with seeing any value in classical realism overrides a problem with specific directors like Hitchcock. Students are familiar with the basic tenets of feminist theory established in [Laura Mulvey's] "Visual Pleasure and Narrative Cinema" and hold firm to them: classical realist films construct a male viewer and women, symbolizing castration "and nothing else," are investigated, saved or punished, or fetishized as pure spectacle.[1]

My own experience over the past decades has been quite different. I present early feminist criticism like Mulvey's, generally referred to as "second wave," that is, as a feminism extending beyond political issues like winning the franchise or achieving equal rights to questioning the dynamics of power in cultural and intimate life, by inviting students to see the advantages and disadvantages of its theoretical perspectives.[2] My students almost never react without ambivalence to psychoanalytic approaches to film that frequently characterized work of this vintage, and which are brilliantly epitomized by Mulvey's pivotal essay. Invocations of Oedipus complexes make them crazy; the word "castration" sends them flying out the door. They are also loath to break down the codes of realism, unless they find a film "hammy" (or melodramatic). So, the challenge is to show why the early feminist work on Hitchcock, which may seem to them obviously "wrong," was nevertheless so influential, and why it may still have something to say to us today.

These changes in approaches to genre films and to gendered spectatorship have taken place gradually. I think that this evolution, like our own critical practice, would benefit from a rigorously historical presentation, although I grant that this is very hard to do in undergraduate classes or even via essays like this one. But it is the fear of second-wave feminist theory like Mulvey's triggering some kind of intellectual or affective stasis – a tone that pervades recent feminist film theory well beyond Jacobowitz's – that alarms me, and that looking back to its origins may help us overcome. What follows, then, is an attempt, even at this third-wave moment, to frame feminist criticism of Hitchcock's films with respect to the intellectual traditions from which it springs as an attempt to see where it might lead all of us – teachers, students, readers and writers – in the future.

As feminist criticism moved toward the vanguard of film theory, Hitchcock's reputation as a serious and complex director had been on the rise, first in France and England and then across the Atlantic. François Truffaut, Jean-Luc Godard, and Robin Wood militated in favor of a substantial critical evaluation of Hitchcock's body of work. Instead of considering the films trivial, mere entertaining genre pieces by "the master of suspense," they convinced the scholarly world of their worth as objects of close study. The subsequent 1970s surge in critical and theoretical work on Hitchcock's films, and the specific configuration of this period's feminist film theory, were determined by 1950s intellectual and political movements in Britain, France, and the United States. Out of these conflicting currents of late 1950s and early 1960s political and aesthetic discourses, there emerged a complex relationship between Hitchcock studies and feminist theory.

It is important to realize that both feminist film theory and a newly politicized cinephilia worked through the conflicting views of mass or popular culture taken by the Marxist social theorists of The Frankfurt School and their pre–World War II associates. Whereas Adorno and Horkheimer express deep cynicism about any potential for social change or revolutionary thought in the products of the "culture industry," Walter Benjamin's work took a more subtle and more ambivalent view of new forms of cultural productions. Bertolt Brecht's influential approach to the theory and practice of theater, cinema, and literature also envisioned (a reconfigured) popular culture as a locus for revolutionary reflection on social conditions, but demanded that the spectator rupture his or her pleasurable relationship of identification with characters and narrative.

The Gramsci-influenced cultural Marxism of The Centre for Contemporary Cultural Studies in Birmingham (The Birmingham School), which began its work on popular culture and "subcultures" in 1964, was already carrying out something like the work both critics called for. Without abandoning the Frankfurt School critique of Enlightenment notions of progress,

Stuart Hall and his colleagues explored the emancipatory potential of popular culture. The Birmingham School's cultural theory slowly grew more influential in film theory, as it continued to hammer out the problem of human agency in culture in the context of British post-colonialism and to develop the vocabulary of critical race theory. But for Hitchcock studies of the early 1970s, the French Marxists were prime movers of the theoretical discourse on cinema spectatorship. Something like a Frankfurt School approach to the technological basis of cinema marked the widely influential 1970s theories of the "basic cinematic apparatus," which may include any physical aspect of film production and distribution. According to this logic, cinema is not a technologically "neutral" tool, but is positioned within in the context of the relations of power governing the invention, manufacture and use of the "cinema-as-apparatus." In 1971 and 1972, *Cahiers du cinéma* editor-in-chief Jean-Louis Comolli wrote a series of articles calling for a materialist history and practice of cinema, one that would take into account those power structures associated with the cinematic "apparatus." In 1974–1975, Jean-Louis Baudry detailed how the cinematic "apparatus" brings ideological constraints to the act of spectatorship, marshaling a Marxist sensibility concerning the relations of production, and described the ideological modeling of the spectator in terms that added Lacanian psychoanalysis to the mix.

From the perspective of current thinking on gender and film, this Lacanian bent – brought to all the figures I have discussed earlier through the influence of Louis Althusser – presents a real stumbling block, in that Jacques Lacan's account of the work of gender casts the pall of inevitability on the plight of human subjects, although it is not the case that he is universally read in this way; certainly Althusser and other cultural Marxists saw ideology as a historical phenomenon. Lacan, a rather histrionic fellow, declared himself the representative of a (perhaps oxymoronic) radical Freudian orthodoxy and painted a portrait of the work of phallocentrism that positions women (or, what's worse, "woman") outside signification, unable to seize the signifier – the word, the film text. As Mary Ann Doane wrote, regarding Freud's "investigation" of "woman as other," Lacan's woman may be a "pretense, haunted by the mirror effect by means of which the question of woman reflects only the man's own ontological doubts."[3] Whether Lacanian-inflected gender theory places itself outside history, and in this way undermines its potential for effecting political change in cultural products, has become an even more difficult question since Slavoj Žižek's provocative work on Hitchcock made it once again difficult to ignore the signification of the phallus, and since critics with an acute sense of historical contextualization have made good use of Žižek's work.

The leftist traditions that influenced the rise of feminist film theory were not, generally speaking, especially concerned with women as material, political beings. Nevertheless, the point to stress here is that feminist theorists *used what was at hand to forge a political weapon*, one with which they hoped to reveal what Fredric Jameson would later term "the political unconscious" of mainstream cinema. As we will see, such deconstructions of bourgeois ideology, however limited in scope, would come to play an overtly political role in feminist and queer critiques of the hegemony of white masculinity in Hollywood and Hitchcock.

While, in the early 1960s, the journal *Movie* had already gone forth with a program of Marxist and psychoanalytically inflected studies of Hitchcock, one member of the group of British critics and academics associated with the radical British film journal *Screen* was responsible for articulating a paradigm shift in film and gender theory. Laura Mulvey's extraordinarily convincing essay, "Visual Pleasure and Narrative Cinema" (1975), seemingly created contemporary feminist film theory in one fell swoop.[4] In her essay, Mulvey posed the provocative question as to whether the "gaze" in cinema is "male." Male spectators would presumably be able to identify with the masterful gaze of his onscreen surrogate, while women could only find themselves and their own interests by reading through and around the phallocentric style and contents of film. Mulvey's essay launched the opening salvo in a conflict about how, and even if, feminist criticism could usefully engage with classical cinema, and as the debate continued, what white, heterosexual (in practice if not in theory) feminist film theory can offer those who do not fall into these "categories." Thus, from this question ("Is the gaze male?"), and out of the tensions inherent in Mulvey's hypnotically absolutist approach, emerged the crucial issue as to whether and how the spectatorial agency not only of "women" as (an uneasy) category but of people of other categories of marginality – people of color, third-world subjects, disenfranchised social classes – might manifest itself.

It seems almost absurd at this point in history to explicate Mulvey's tirelessly chewed-over argument about the visual power endowed by patriarchy upon male spectators and their onscreen spectatorial surrogates. Although taking Mulvey's work as at least a distant starting point for academic discussions of contemporary feminist film theory has been *de rigueur* in most of the nearly forty years since the essay was written, critics now usually place more importance on what her work did not accomplish than on what it did. Many, even most, contemporary feminist film theorists have at one time or another positioned their own work in opposition to the Mulveyan pessimism about the power of the non-male (and nonwhite, and nonheterosexual) spectator in relation to classical cinema. Such positionings reflect the historical importance of Mulvey's creation of a vocabulary for describing gendered looking relations in cinema. I am often struck, however, by what I described earlier as warding-off gestures that surround invocations of Mulvey's early work, perhaps especially in analyses of Hitchcock and gender. These "corrections" to early gaze theory's narrow perspective on the female spectator have produced brilliant work, but the compulsion to distance one's critical practice from 1970s gaze theory is noteworthy as well. Mulvey's essay continues to define, if only as a counterexample, the terrain even as critics claim to have moved beyond it.

Mulvey's basic hypothesis is that classical cinema designates the "woman as image, man as bearer of the look."[5] According to Mulvey and those who share/d her views, this paradigm obtains in dominant cinema practices, with the exception of some films that manage to hijack the phallic instrument of the camera with specifically feminist political agendas in mind. According to Mulvey's Althusserian-Lacanian-Freudian theory (especially as further elaborated upon by Mary Ann Doane), the choices open to the female spectator are few. Either this spectator takes up a masochistic identification with the object of a punitive male gaze, or adopts kind of transvestite identification with the "active" male protagonist. Although women occasionally broke through and borrowed the cinematic "apparatus," this was an exception to way that narrative and "the look" were organized as "masculine" practices. If the premises of her argument derive from a Marxist reading of Freud and Lacan, in her essay we can also see the traces of Brecht's or even Adorno's uncompromising cultural politics, albeit without the note of Adorno's and Horkheimer's contempt for cinema as mass culture object. Mulvey describes mainstream cinema as showing little potential as a site where the voices (or "looks") of an oppressed class can be heard (exerted). Mulvey describes a cinematic apparatus, in Althusser's sense, that limits the on-screen woman's available cinematic roles to either an object of sadistic voyeurism or a glorified "phallus." The woman may play a role like that of the "final girl" Carol Clover has seen as central to the contemporary horror film, the figure who barely escapes the axe or the chainsaw or the meat hook with which deranged manhood wishes to take her apart. On the other hand, she may play the role of the rarefied impermeable phallic symbol, a condensation not unlike – indeed, often identical to – the fetishized commodity. According to this familiar argument, which is almost certain to make twenty-first-century students groan, the woman-as-fetish serves to reassure men that women's "castration," in the Freudian sense, presents no threat to their own intactness.

Mulvey's close reading highlights her focus on Hitchcock's films as prime deployers of these ideological traps:

> In *Vertigo* in particular, but also in *Marnie* and *Rear Window*, the look is central to the plot, oscillating between voyeurism and fetishistic fascination. As a twist, a further manipulation of the normal viewing process which in some sense reveals it, Hitchcock uses the process of identification normally associated with ideological correctness and the recognition of established morality and shows up its perverted side. Hitchcock has never concealed his interest in voyeurism, cinematic and non-cinematic. His heroes are exemplary of the symbolic order and the law – a policeman (*Vertigo*), a dominant male possessing money and power (*Marnie*).
>
> (23)

By saying that Hitchcock's "heroes" are exemplary of the "symbolic order and the law," and that as such they ("they" being, presumably, heterosexual male characters within the Hollywood cinematic apparatus) are structurally obligated to "view" women in cinema in dualistic terms, Mulvey emphatically sets up her own argument for the deconstruction of its various binaries. Hers is the language of manifestos. Mulvey herself was no doubt amazed by the powerful and long-lasting response to her strong ontological and epistemological claims about what cinema *is*, and what the gendered spectator can *know* or *see*.

Although the observation may not seem intuitively obvious, I think it is important to point out that Mulvey's radical approach in "Visual Pleasure" follows as it historically anticipates the logic of critical race theory. Both are grounded in a refusal to accept liberal compromise with entrenched ideological systems that presume that "equality" among subjects is guaranteed as inevitable by capitalist democracies, and that social reform will slowly fulfill this guarantee (whether it be more women directors who "control" the apparatus of production, more African-American professionals, or a queerer armed forces). That Mulvey's (or the essay's) form of radicalism, however one construes it, came to be regarded as reactionary and as an obstacle to change is ironic, though perhaps necessary in light of historical – and academic – pressures.

In her later essay, "Afterthoughts on 'Visual Pleasure and Narrative Cinema,'" Mulvey acknowledged the need to take a look at female spectatorship but located the female gaze and female identification with onscreen character between "the deep blue sea of passive femininity and the devil of regressive masculinity."[6] Again, this formulation was soon deconstructed as a binary that excluded other possibilities of looking in the cinema for women (including lesbian and racially infected "looks"). Whatever the force of this critique, self- or otherwise, Mulvey's work thus served the purpose of highlighting contradictions in the structures of powers in mainstream cinema so starkly that others were roused to respond. Her careful delineation of how the "male gaze" can be a tool of aggression and the way that the "female gaze" is circumscribed in classical cinema may only be regarded at this point in history as a useful polemic. But like any other form of oppression, this "male" power Mulvey describes must be taken seriously.

Mulvey's critique of *Rear Window* glosses over the nuances that Tania Modleski's extremely valuable book on Hitchcock, *The Women Who Knew Too Much*, would bring to the fore.[7] Read with such nuances in mind, *Rear Window* presents as a comedy as much as a suspense thriller. But Modleski, like Mulvey, does not forget that what is at stake is a dismembered woman's body. The film remains one where the woman's body as partial object, ever the potential target of violence, is continually in evidence, in the persons of Miss Torso, Thornhill's dismembered wife, and even Miss Lonelyhearts, reduced to a synecdoche. Mulvey's two-part argument holds that in all of those films, the "other" role women may play is to float by as glamorous fetishes symbolic of the way male "lack" is projected outward and concealed under the glorification of women. Thus, the woman can also become the kind of precious object that is Lisa – played as such by the most glamorous ingenue of her time, Grace Kelly – whose "perfection" actually irritates Jeffries. As such a "fetish" object, women (or the cinema's construction of womanliness) may hold limited power, unsatisfactory and dangerous as that "solution" may be.

While Mulvey was writing "Visual Pleasure," in 1973, Claire Johnston and Pam Cook were also pioneering new work on female spectatorship.[8] They marshaled the Marxist analytical framework in which textual (like economic and class) "contradiction" can be brought forth to address the problem of women's agency in their relationship to cinema. Even now, the rhetoric of finding "gaps and fissures" in cinematic texts that "open up space" to the agency of disempowered groups is habitual to feminist critics. (Indeed, one reason I am writing this essay is because my students often think that such concepts were alien to second-wave feminist theory.) In a review of three books by Cook and Johnston, E. Ann Kaplan observes that Cook and Johnston turn toward cultural studies, even as they continue to draw on other schools of thought:

> There was some early influence from Richard Hoggart and Raymond Williams, who in the early 60s saw the need to come to grips with mass culture. More recently, they have been influenced by Stuart Hall and the group developing new approaches to cultural studies at Birmingham University.... Johnston and Cook are not afraid to take concepts from writers representing divergent positions. Thus they make free use of the theories of Brecht, the auteur critics

(*Cahiers du cinéma*), the French structuralists (particularly Lévi-Strauss and Roland Barthes), historical materialism and Russian Formalism.[9]

Thus, even as Mulvey was approaching feminist film theory (and the study of Hitchcock) from a perspective taken largely from Lacan, Cook, Johnston, Kaplan, and others were discussing the model provided by Stuart Hall's rereading of Gramsci's concept of the "organic intellectual." The role of organic intellectual would minimize the feminist's position as representative and mouthpiece for "the people," while contributing a critique of hegemony to feminist conversations. But feminist film theorists also took upon themselves the task of, to put it frankly, subverting academia from within – with mixed results. Working within an academic context, it is almost impossible to avoid making authoritative claims and to producing a canon that takes on a certain rigidity over time. Under the conditions of capitalism (and in some other economic systems), academic work is commodified and reified, made into a *thing*. This canon becomes that which must be surpassed. In Johnston's and other feminist critics' work in the mid-1970s, strong emphasis fell on how contradictions (in a Marxist sense) in the ideological currents running through film could speak to this problem by enhancing women's revolutionary consciousness of class and gender positions in film. The endings of films were considered especially interesting, in that textual "closure" (one can see the influence of semiotics here) could work to distract the spectator from the openings for agency that had been glimpsed in the film, especially on melodramas aimed at women, to detect the internal contradictions in films that seem to represent women as powerless.

Doane's ambitious *The Desire to Desire* turns, reasonably enough, to the "woman's film" as a place where the female spectator's role is paramount and open to analysis; in so doing, it turns to Hitchcock, especially to *Suspicion* (1941) and *Rebecca* (1940). Doane's is philosophical work that takes the logic of arguments to the edge of their implications. But her location of lack of power in the cinematic realm within the psyche of the female spectator is in describing the way that women's desire and concomitant spectatorship are severely circumscribed. Doane does locate certain subversive qualities in the woman's film, especially in the paranoia of the female Gothic structure in *Suspicion* and *Rebecca* (in which the woman investigates her possibly unloving and/or homicidal husband):

> in their articulation of the uncanniness of the domestic, and especially in their investigation of the woman's relationship to the gaze, [these] gothic films not only reside within the genre of the woman's film, but offer a metacommentary on it as well. In their hyperbolization of certain signification strategies of the woman's film, they test the very limits of the filmic representation of female subjectivity for a female spectator.[10]

But rather than contributing to women's visual empowerment, the films produce a ghostly critical discourse that is hyperbolized and then absorbed. The strange disconnect – this seems to be the case in Mulvey's work as well – is that the critic herself is able to produce such a powerful commentary on these scenes of "projection."

Mulvey offended readers because she "offered" no opening for exploring the nuances of female, lesbian, and other disenfranchised groups' empowerment in mainstream cinema. As Mulvey said in a question and answer period at the 1999 Hitchcock Conference sponsored by New York University, she regarded and still regards Hollywood cinema as an apartheid cinema. There is some merit to the argument. Hollywood cinema has been bitterly racist, sexist, and homophobic, whether such was "intended" or not. In their brutal assessment of the ideological structures of classical cinema, however, theorists like Mulvey and Doane have come to be regarded as promulgating the very ideologies of exclusion they sought to critique. In "Visual Pleasure," Mulvey concedes that while Hitchcock's *Vertigo* (1958) foregrounds the problems of voyeurism and fetishistic romantic fantasy that are the perverse results of masculine insecurity, she finds that the film nevertheless activates and reinforces the very processes that it ostensibly foregrounds in the narrative. Ironically, arguments against her own reading of the film have sometimes used a similar logic.

As a critic, Mulvey encouraged women to develop their own forms of cinema, designed to forego the deeply seated habit of finding pleasure in a "masochistic" enterprise, and producing new forms of pleasure. This move to opt out of the pleasures offered by classical cinema – indeed, to "destroy" pleasure – certainly presents a grim picture of how women might effectively empower themselves as spectators and filmmakers. Mulvey herself turned to making antirealist films, which represented an attempt to strip cinema of its normative ideological structures. In this context, I would like to revisit briefly Jacobowitz's comments on cinematic realism in Hitchcock's films:

> [F]eminist theory radicalized criticism ... at the cost of reducing all realist films to the same formula, Students therefore resist the idea that viewer positions are not locked in place, that identification and point of view are complex and can be subverted intentionally to question the viewer's reliance on gender stereotypes (as in *Vertigo*), that realism in its more sophisticated forms demands an understanding of a complex language that was nurtured by the studio system and challenges the theoretical picture of classical realism solidified in the last thirty-five years.[11]

While it is certainly true that "realist" cinema is complex, and that Mulvey and Doane both reached pessimistic conclusions about those films' capacity to disempower the female viewer, the semiotic and psychoanalytic theory on which these studies relied spoke of identity as performative, coded, and mobile. In more recent years, even as notions of "identity" have been further complicated by post-structuralism, Foucauldianism, and the move toward "posthumanism," the question of "identification" with film characters still brings to the fore the vexed question of the range and specificity of identity itself, whose political history in the field of film and cultural studies is fraught with tension and paradox. The variables of identity are almost endless, and are linked more or less coherently to other such "identities" only under the pressures of history.

Over the past thirty-five years much has happened in feminist Hitchcock criticism to complicate those models of spectatorship. Hitchcock's classical realist films are almost all genre films (for Hitchcock, the "suspense" thriller, the female gothic, the spy film, and so forth), and are highly formulaic. But even as we continue to see greater and greater malleability in "available" spectatorial responses to the films, I am not ready to abandon the concept that classical Hollywood's recognizable formulae are shaped by the ideologies of their time (hegemonic and non-hegemonic), and that, as the editors of *Camera Obscura* put it, film is "a dynamic process of the production of meanings, inscribed within the larger context of social relations."[12] While some of this terminology may feel dated or constricted, the underlying ideas about how feminist film theory is to be carried out entailed flexibility and social context, as they do now in what most critics seem to consider a more informed way.

Jacobowitz herself advances the claim that in 1988, Tania Modleski engineered a radical turn away from the rhetoric of "classical" feminist film theory regarding the films of Alfred Hitchcock. I certainly agree with that assessment. Modleski's exploration of masculinity and identity in those films was revelatory. By introducing the vulnerabilities of the Hitchcockian male, in part by introducing male ambivalence toward "his" own fundamental bisexuality, Modleski radically challenges earlier emphases on the "power" of the male spectator within and without the Hitchcock narrative and point-of-view structure. Modleski locates a crucial juncture in Hitchcock's oeuvre in the narrative structure of *Rebecca*. She sees Hitchcock's own dismissal of the book as "novelletish" and "typical of a whole school of feminine literature at the period," and his rejection of the film as "not a Hitchcock film," symptomatic of a denial of what in fact is an obsession in Hitchcock's films: the bisexuality of the human subject. Although Modleski has been criticized as sticking too closely to the psychoanalytic bent of earlier feminist theorists, the importance of her identification of the "threat" of female bisexuality as a structural foundation of the films can hardly be overemphasized. Her penetrating analyses of *Blackmail* (1920), *Murder!* (1930), *Rebecca*,

Notorious (1946), *Rear Window*, *Vertigo*, and *Frenzy* (1972) made possible a completely different approach to Hitchcock, one based on the inner contradictions of the male-perceived boundarilessness of female sexuality.

Modleski's reading of *Vertigo* is especially gripping, in its systematic deconstruction of Scottie's "power and freedom" in the film, to invoke Scottie's description, to the unmasked Judy, of qualities in Gavin that he clearly envies. As that comment suggests, Scottie marches to the scenario of another man.. His "taste" in women is revealed to be utterly predictable, to the point where the cosmeticians who remake Judy to his ideal of Madeleine "know what [he] wants. The fascination and horror involved in what she sees as his ultimate identification with the woman who wandered the streets, Carlotta Valdes, locates, for me, that which is sublime and indelibly poignant in the film. Ultimately Modleski argues that "Hitchcock is neither utterly misogynist nor that his work is largely sympathetic to women and their plight in patriarchy, but that his work is characterized by a thoroughgoing ambivalence about femininity."[13] Her view of Hitchcock's insight into men's fears about and fascination with women's fundamental "bisexuality" helped put masculinity studies focusing on Hitchcock's films on the map.

An area of difficulty in her work which Modleski has confronted involves the use of the very term "bisexuality," which I described above as useful as a *figure* marking where the violent impulse and the vulnerabilities of some of Hitchcock's men may reside. Teresa de Lauretis, Lucretia Knapp, Rhona J. Berenstein, and Patricia White[14] all critique Modleski's psychoanalytic formulation of female pre-oedipal bisexuality, and its emphasis on the mother-daughter bond, in which the mother is the daughter's first love object, reluctantly but finally given up. From the lesbian perspective articulated by these authors, insistence on bisexuality and the pre-oedipal denies specificity to lesbian desire. *Rebecca* is a critical case of contention. Berenstein is particularly adamant that to treat Rebecca and Mrs. Danvers as mother figures is to ignore the (adult) lesbian allure of both Rebecca and Mrs. Danvers. In her responses to her critics Modleski gracefully concedes that "[t]he arrested development of our theories [remaining in the preoedipal paradigm] was itself a case of arrested development."[15] She next addresses another, very complex paradigm drawn from classical feminist readings of Hitchcock, which would maintain that one cannot simultaneously identify with and desire another woman (on-screen, for the moment). Berenstein strategically insists on that separation in order to posit a specific and adult lesbian sexuality that is not just part of the daughter's pre-oedipal state of undifferentiated sexual/identificatory absorption in a "mother." Still, I must agree with Modleski that multiple desires are clearly enacted here – that the second Mrs. de Winter (Joan Fontaine) is powerfully caught up in the sensual relics of the first Mrs. de Winter. Rebecca's ghostly bisexuality, which according to Mrs. Danver's account is largely play-acting when it comes to men, electrifies the characters and radiates from the screen when Mrs. Danvers shows off Rebecca's room, with its monogrammed sheets and undergarments, caressed by women's hands. That bisexual appeal is, I think, much more attractive and interesting than anything that goes on with the cranky Maxim de Winter, who, if he was not, should have been sleeping with Frank.

As gender-related studies of Hitchcock's films have proliferated in recent years, it is not always clear what might or might not be called a "feminist" reading of the films. Perhaps any work that takes to task the patriarchal character of the films or points to their anti-patriarchal gestures or tendencies might be called a "feminist" study. In my teaching I aim to introduce to my students the "Queer Hitchcock" so wonderfully described by the late Alexander Doty in his article of that name. But the value of a feminist voice per se in Hitchcock studies is made newly apparent by Patricia White's "Hitchcock and Hom(m) osexuality," in which she interrogates the indifference or erasure of feminine desire in some queer writing on Hitchcock, specifically Lee Edelman's "*Rear Window*'s Glasshole" and D. A. Miller's "Anal *Rope*." White marshals Luce Irigaray's neologism, "hom(m)osexuality," to signal how masculine sexuality may be played out through the bodies of women – putting the "homme" (man) back into "homosexuality" and eliding the lesbian presence White, Knapp, Berenstein, and others have worked to bring into the realm of the visible. According to White, Edelman's and Miller's "male-associated desire to escape the phallic regime, associated with anality, is a potentially radical one," but maintains that these analyses of *Rope* (1948) and *Rear Window* are, ironically, "disrupted by the differences women make" (White 8), and ultimately call on masculine authority. It is up to the reader to determine whether White's critique is accurate: my point here is that by putting lesbian and gay Hitchcock criticism at odds, White makes a risky gesture but takes precisely the kind of risk that keeps gender criticism robust.

I would like to return to a 1986 essay, which, after my initial skeptical assessment of its "epistemological" project, also became pivotal to my teaching and thinking about Hitchcock – Virginia Wright Wexman's presciently titled "The Critic as Consumer: Film Study in the University, *Vertigo*, and the Film Canon." Wexman approaches *Vertigo* from the perspectives of both the Hollywood industry and California history, focusing on the film's touristic representation of San Francisco, and the production history of the film, especially the way its female star was treated:

> In the case of Kim Novak, control over her image was exercised not just by Hitchcock but more importantly by industry mogul Harry Cohn, president of

Columbia Pictures, who arranged to have her constantly watched, forced her to live in her studio dressing room and eat only food prepared by the studio chef, and called her "the fat Polack." Like Judy, Novak was docile enough to accept this bullying for the most part, while occasionally fighting for a modicum of recognition of her own identity-managing, for instance, to keep her surname despite its ethnic overtones.[16]

Wexman details how Hitchcock's work with his star in the film "reflects his understanding of and collaboration with the practical and conflict-ridden nature of the American film industry's investment in such figures," and shows how the "allegorical" relationships depicted in the film (Gavin Elster as Hitchcock; Judy as Kim Novak) take material and historical form. Clearly here is an essay about Hitchcock and "feminist theory," but "The Critic as Consumer" shows how gender studies of film are caught up in various larger processes, having to do with race, capital, and nation. *Vertigo* functions as a travelogue, tried-and-true cinematic means for the middle-class spectator to gain direct access to exotic locales. The film is a touristic document ultimately "disseminating and domesticating the far-off," an example of how "cinema participates in th[e] rhetoric of tourism."[17]

Wexman's analysis seems more than ever deeply insightful as a reading of *Vertigo*'s industrial work, and it is complemented by new work on *Vertigo* that also places in ideological context the specificity of San Francisco as locale.[18] She goes on to sketch a political reading of the glimpses of history revealed by the film, drawing on the work of Fredric Jameson and Michael Rogin to formulate an approach to the problem of the film's fetishism: not so much the fetish of the necrophilia Hitchcock enjoyed dropping into conversations about *Vertigo*, but Scottie's fetishism of Madeleine's upper-class manner and aristocratic surroundings (to the detriment of Midge's middle-class sensibility), and the dangerous fetish of Carlotta Valdes's "otherness." Wexman notes, for example, that it is the "darkly ambiguous" Carlotta, rather than Madeleine, who appears in Scottie's desiring dream, and she reminds us of Hitchcock's statement about *Marnie*: "'The fetish idea. A man who wants to go to bed with a thief, just like other men have a yen for a Chinese woman or a colored woman.'"[19]

This discussion of race and class as "fetish" is where Wexman opens up a pointed critique of psychoanalytic feminist readings of Hitchcock's films:

> Given the widespread interest in psychoanalytic readings of Hitchcock's films, it is note-worthy that no critic has commented on the director's remarkable equation of fetishism with miscegenation here. And, more importantly, no one has observed the workings of a similar displacement of racial and class

issues into the sphere of sexuality functioning in the films themselves. Carlotta represents what ultimately terrorizes Scottie, and the fears Carlotta arouses in him are more culturally specific than either Hitchcock or his feminist critics are in a position to acknowledge. As *Vertigo* illustrates, the oppression of women in our culture is intimately related to particular political conditions, and the forms of its representation often exploit such associations.... Cinema scholars have now honored this venture as one of their top ten favorites. Such a valuation reflects not only on its object but also on those who sit in judgment.[20]

Looking back over the objections I raised in my first responses to Wexman's excellent discussion of *Vertigo*, I am most of all struck by how valuable opportunities for conversation got lost in methodological disputes. Despite whatever cynicism one may express about the political effectiveness of academic discourse, Carolotta's role as fetish object – as a *colonial* fetish object – is vital to understanding the film's political work. But I felt that Wexman underestimated the extent to which political "specificity" could be consistent with psychoanalytic feminist studies of Hitchcock's films. But just as Wexman was tying certain feminist theories of the era to the to the most rigid expressions of the methodologies they invoked, I was placing her in a similar position, both because I believed my objections to be "true," and probably as well, for the young scholar's the pleasure of entering into academic polemics. Wexman was certainly opening a desperately needed conversation on postcolonial readings of Hitchcock. Instead of focusing on that opening, I jumped on the epistemological impasse: Where did Wexman herself get the "power and the freedom" to produce such a reading? I took the answer to be that Wexman was claiming that because she did not adhere to psychoanalytic criticism, she did not have a professional stake in masking "the ideological workings of racism and xenophobia beneath a discourse of sexuality." This claim, according to her argument, allowed her an unrestricted vision of the film. From my perspective, it seemed that the psychoanalytic methodology of Hitchcock's feminist critics was being made to stand in for the putative class and race blindness of all of the newly and temporarily empowered academic (generally white) feminists, among whom Wexman was certainly positioned.

While perhaps symptomatic, my response continues to raise a question: Did feminist film critics need to deny the racism and xenophobia of films like *Vertigo* (or, perhaps, to ignore *Vertigo*'s radical critique of its own colonialist foundations) in order to protect academic positions? Even by 1986, it was already becoming clear that the academy, after some resistance, could absorb and deflect importance from most "contestatory" readings or approaches in the humanities, including those deriving from queer and critical race theory, as effectively as it could feminist psychoanalytic theory.

Mulvey's challenge to patriarchy did not go far enough: its consideration of gender was too narrow, and it did not directly address race or class. But did the work of the "gaze theorists," by describing the hobbles placed on the female spectator – even by positing something as undifferentiated as a "female spectator" – block the development of work on Hitchcock (as auteur or symptom, example or exemplar of Hollywood itself) that would "create spaces" for other, marginalized subjects?

The feminist gaze theorists' real error was, I think, to exclude their own consciousness and dual experience of Hitchcock's films from their theories of female spectatorship. They expressed a sense of being trapped in a "male gaze" and described very well the experience of that entrapment. The "agency" that flowed from this exclusion coincided with the entry of feminists into the academy. And so that contorted sense of agency was taken as an always-already hegemonic discourse by those who came afterward. The effort was made to balance this study of the Hitchcockian abuse of women with a woman-created cinema, but that, too, had its drawbacks, especially insofar as that cinema was so often (frequently inacurately) framed as avant-garde, prohibitive, elitist. Some are convinced that "classical" feminist film theory is a wall of hegemony that must be broken, and while I cannot claim to understand all the reason and emotion behind that, I share some of this view. But not its despair. Can we hope that through images and language we can understand one another?

Having grown up in rural Georgia during the 1950s and 1960s, I am a strong believer in what bell hooks describes as the "oppositional gaze."[21] The movie theater in McDonough, Georgia, where I learned to love film, seated white people in the orchestra and black people in the balcony. Most of the time these two spaces were filled with kids. A daughter of white sharecroppers, slave owners, hillbillies, and of the handful of Catholics (converts, weirdly enough) in Henry County, I was fully aware of this segregation. As Catholics we were thoroughly unpopular with the KKK but white enough to avoid assaults on our persons (though not on our land, itself stolen from the Creeks a century earlier). At the McDonough theater, where I never saw a nonwhite person buy candy or sodas, I remember once asking a black child if I had accidentally taken his place in line for the triple monster feature. He gave me a baleful look that I took to mean: "Are you kidding? We have a *separate* line." Even at that time, in my embarrassment at my idiocy, I realized that "white privilege" had allowed me the luxury of not understanding the mechanism by means of which white kids got down to the orchestra and black kids got to the balcony.

My experience leads me to feel that the straight white "look" can hardly be interrogated enough, and it is in this spirit that I also take the critiques of

gaze theory I have been thinking about in this essay. I can report of my earlier self that I was pleased to see that the kids in the balcony did not hesitate
to spit on the kids in the orchestra seats. I found this little "fuck you" appealing, and not irrelevant to Hitchcock. For there are so many Hitchcockian
"fuck-yous" to domination scattered unevenly through the films that were
fun to describe, but only for a time, as monolithic (Bellour, Mulvey). But it
is time to move on: to recognize that the fuck-yous to inflicted pain, constricted, terrified gazes, and bourgeois crap are expressed in endless acts of
defiance, which sometimes go as far as a murder we (yes, we) cannot help
sharing. Toby Miller and Noel King remind us that in *The 39 Steps* (1935),
"we meet a crofter's game and sexy wife (Peggy Ashcroft), who hides and
romances Hannay at great personal cost – retributive domestic violence."[22]
Although she does romance Hannay, hers is a desperate cry for understanding, and theirs a poignant representation of sudden communication and
mutual need across culture, gender, and class. And these gestures continue –
sometimes in a comic register, more frequently in a tragic or even violent one.
In another "silent" scene, Verloc in *Secret Agent* (1936) reads impending ret-
ribution in his wife's eyes and the knife in her hand. Bruno in *Strangers* pops
a brat's balloon, and stages an elaborate self-sacrifice to get back at Guy,
that closeted phony, played by the not-so-closeted Farley Granger. Judy in
Vertigo, who owns my heart, tore up the letter. Midge's moment elsewhere
in that film backfires: "Stupid! stupid! stupid!," she cries after she paints a
mock portrait of Carlotta to win Scottie back from madness. Alice White
in *Blackmail* sins by paint brush. Leonard in *North by Northwest* fires the
blank gun. Reasonably enough, swishy, beautiful Norman Bates killed the
mother who cheated on him, and the son who did the same to the mother.
Recall that Marion Crane's attempt to scratch her way out of her cage sank
her body into a swamp, along with the mad money. Patricia Hitchcock's
played murder in Senator-Daddy's parlor, but her glasses burned her when
Bruno looked. Marnie's Mama kept Billy's sweater, and made a pie for smug
little Jessie. Rebecca laughed and laughed, and Mrs. Danvers took down
Maxim, that aristocratic "trade-unionist," and Manderlay, built, by association, on colonial wealth. Perhaps best of all, speaking of ambiguously colonial subjects, who also happen to be trannies, Fane makes a grand, grand
exit in the last scene of *Murder!*.

These moments and so many more beyond them ask a set of questions: How do we respond to Hitchcock, to domination, to Hitchcock
and domination, which are ultimately the stakes of the feminist intervention in Hitchcock criticism? Although I am a credentialled film scholar and
although this volume is intended to help you, the reader, become one too, we
might want to follow his characters in their beautiful defiance, and to trust

their knowledge. They point us not to other filmmakers, or other academics, but, in their spectacular way, to the ordinary people around us whose acts of petty defiance in the midst of acquiescence they emblematize. For academics and students, my primary audience, they help me, at this post-feminist, feminist moment, assert truths both simple and complex for all of us: despite our own blindnesses, the competitiveness of our job markets, our differences and similarities, most of us want to learn more about not only how to think about Hitchcock's films but how Hitchcock's films, sometimes despite themselves, help us think differently, to interrogate our received ideas about the mechanisms of agency and exclusion The end point of the revolution Laura Mulvey began is to realize that the people who teach us to do so are all around us.

NOTES

1 Thomas Leitch and Leland Poague, eds., *A Blackwell's Companion to Alfred Hitchcock* (New York: Wiley-Blackwell, 2011), pp. 452–453.
2 For the classic statement of first- and second-wave feminist theory, see Ellen Du Bois's 1991 essay, "Feminism Old and New Wave," now available at http://www.uic.edu/orgs/cwluherstory/CWLUArchive/wave.html (accessed August 14, 2014).
3 Mary Ann Doane, "Heads in Hieroglyphic Bonnets," in *Film and Theory: an Anthology*, ed. Robert Stam and Toby Miller (Oxford: Blackwell), pp. 495–509.
4 *Screen* 16 (1975), pp. 6–18.
5 Laura Mulvey, "Visual Pleasure and Narrative Cinema," *Screen* (1975), vol. 16, no. 3: 6–18; reprinted in Laura Mulvey, *Visual and Other Pleasures* (Bloomington: Indiana University Press, 1989), pp. 14–26. Page numbers in my essay are taken from the latter edition.
6 "Afterthoughts on 'Visual Pleasure and Narrative Cinema' Inspired by King Vidor's *Duel in the Sun*," in *Visual and Other Pleasures*, pp. 31–40.
7 Tania Modleski, *The Women Who Knew Too Much: Hitchcock and Feminist Theory*, 2nd edition (London: Routledge, 2005) contains a long and very useful set of engagements with Hitchcock criticism of the period with which I am dealing here.
8 The most powerful, in my opinion, is Claire Johnston, "Women's Cinema as Counter-Cinema," in *Notes on Women's Cinema* (London: Society for Education in Film and Television, 1973), in Sue Thornham, ed., *Feminist Film Theory: A Reader* (Edinburgh: Edinburgh University Press, 1999), pp. 31–40.
9 E. Ann Kaplan, "Aspects of British Feminist Film Theory: A Critical Evaluation of Texts by Claire Johnston and Pam Cook," *Jump Cut*, no. 2 (1974), pp. 52–55, http://www.ejumpcut.org/archive/onlinessays/jc12-13folder/britfemtheory.html (accessed March 17, 2014).
10 Mary Ann Doane, "Paranoia and the Specular," in *The Desire to Desire: Women's Films of the 1940s* (Bloomington: University of Indiana Press, 1987), p. 125.
11 Jacobowitz, op. cit, pp. 452–453.

12   "(Re)Inventing *Camera Obscura*," pp. 303–304.

13   Tania Modleski, *The Women Who Knew Too Much: Hitchcock and Feminist Theory* (New York: Routledge, 1988, 2005), p. 3.

14   Teresa de Lauretis, *The Practice of Love Lesbian Sexuality and Perverse Desire* (Bloomington: Indiana University Press, 1994); Lucretia Knapp, "Queer *Marnie*," and Rhona Berenstein, "'I'm not the sort of person men marry': Monsters, Queers, and Hitchcock's *Rebecca*" both in Corey K. Creekmur and Alexander Doty, ed., *Out in Culture: Gay, Lesbian, and Queer Essays on Popular Culture* (Durham, NC, Duke University Press, 1995), pp. 239–261 and 262–281, respectively.

15   Modleski, *ibid.*

16   Virginia Wright Wexman, "Film Study in the University, *Vertigo*, and the Film Canon," *Film Quarterly*, 39 (1986), p. 35.

17   Ibid., p. 35.

18   Douglas A. Cunningham, ed., *The San Francisco of Alfred Hitchcock's Vertigo: Place, Pilgrimage, and Commemoration* (Lanham, MD: Scarecrow Press, 2012).

19   Wexman, p. 36, cites François Truffaut, *Hitchcock* (New York: Simon and Schuster, 1984), p. 227.

20   Wexman, pp. 36–37.

21   bell hooks, "The Oppositional Gaze," in *Black Looks: Race and Representation* (Boston: South End Press, 1992), pp. 115–131.

22   Toby Miller and Noel King, "Accidental Heroes and Gifted Amateurs," in *A Companion to Hitchcock*, p. 439.

7

DAVID GREVEN

Hitchcock and Queer Sexuality

In no film by Alfred Hitchcock does a "positive image" of queer sexual identity occur. Hitchcock has repeatedly come under fire for this dearth of positive representations of queer characters. Hitchcock's representation of women has also been controversial, but as Tania Modleski has insightfully shown, it is also more complex than the charge of misogyny would allow, more complicatedly a mixture of ambivalent attitudes.[1] Is the same thing true of his engagement with queerness?

In my view, yes, Hitchcock's career-long interest in queerness is analogously complicated. Indeed, queerness and femininity complement each other in his films: queerness provides the opportunity for a satirical upending of the normative social order, disrupting the social and attesting to the limitations of its fantasies of order and decorum, while the ambivalent sympathy for femininity allows Hitchcock to undermine the stability of the male protagonist, who must come to recognize the value and also the vulnerability of the woman he has placed in peril.

While several gay critics have charged Hitchcock with a pervasive homophobia – Manny Farber, John Hepworth, Vito Russo, D. A. Miller – many have found much that is resonant in Hitchcock's work as well, beginning with Robin Wood, whose early work *Hitchcock's Films* later emerged as an opportunity not only for a revisionist critical project but also a midlife coming-out story, and extending to Alexander Doty, Patricia White, Lucretia Knapp, and several others.[2] Moreover, Hitchcock has been embraced by High Queer Theory, as exemplified by Miller (again), Lee Edelman, Jonathan Goldberg, and Judith Halberstam.[3] Debates within this body of queer critical work have proven both contentious and stimulating, extending via Knapp to surprising opportunities for lesbian affinity in *Marnie*, and Patricia White's critique, in her study of lesbian representation in classical Hollywood, *Uninvited*, of Hitchcock's *Rebecca* (1940).[4]

Here, I begin an overview of the kinds of debates over homosexuality in Hitchcock that dominated Hitchcock criticism from the early

1950s to the late 1980s. The temporal borders of this critical period are significant. It was during the 1950s that both French and American critics began to champion the "auteur theory" and Hitchcock as exemplary of it, a serious artist of surpassing moral vision and consistent creative integrity whose films could be studied individually and as a whole for recurring themes, preoccupations, motifs, stylistic penchants, and philosophical stances. By the late 1980s and during the early 1990s, a sea change in gay and lesbian criticism occurred, as "queer" – once a term of abuse – emerged as not only a preferred term but a powerful theoretical lens. Queer theory consistently targeted identity and stable constructions of gendered and sexual subjectivity as not only illusory but also ideologically pernicious. Once queered and freed from their obligatory commitment to identity politics, Hitchcock's films come to seem more challengingly resistant to the structures of power of their time periods, the Cold War 1950s and 1960s in particular. This is not to suggest that a queer Hitchcock is free from ideological constraint or debate – far from it. But the reception of Hitchcock's work has transformed over the past two decades, with queer critics much more likely to find affinities in the suspense master's movies and to view them as sites of resistance to the overwhelming heterosexism of both Hollywood and American culture generally.

After tracing out this critical history and contextualizing its key debates, I consider two films that offer revealing glimpses into Hitchcock's mutually urgent and reinforcing preoccupations with both queerness and femininity – *Psycho* and especially *North by Northwest*. I turn to the latter in particular because Edelman has offered a powerful if vexing treatment of that film. The image of its homosexual henchman Leonard (Martin Landau) crushing, with his foot, the hero's helpless hand as he barely grasps an unforgiving crag on Mount Rushmore metonymically represents Edelman's argument: queers should take their opprobrium as an opportunity to represent back to straight culture its pernicious investment in "life" – futurity, reproductivity, progress – and hence offer a deathly resistance to heterosexual fulfillment, family, and fantasy. In crushing Roger O. Thornhill's/Cary Grant's hand, Leonard is also crushing the hopes of heterosexual union embodied by the woman, the secret agent Eve Kendall (Eva Marie Saint), whom Thornhill is attempting to save from imminent death with his *other* hand. But considering the ambiguous, highly charged tensions between Leonard and Eve, Hitchcock highlights the intermeshed social fates of women and queers and explores linkages between homophobia and misogyny, which Hitchcock himself, through his ambivalent but also hetero-suspicious attitudes, casts into startling relief.

From Homophobia to Queer Affinity: Hitchcock Criticism
from Auteur Theory to Queer Theory

In their famous book *Hitchcock: The First Forty-Four Films* (1957), Eric Rohmer and Claude Chabrol influentially read Hitchcock as an auteur, and his works as consistent expressions of the director's Catholic upbringing and sensibility. Discussing one important early Hitchcock film, the critics offered an answer to the questioning of its moral vision:

> In *Murder!* the homosexual kills when unmasked. Unlike the protagonists of *Rope,* or Bruno Anthony (Robert Walker) in *Strangers on a Train,* he considers himself abnormal and is aware that his vice is a defect. But he is also incapable of loving, and he is interested only in escaping the consequences of his crime. When Hitchcock gets around to probing the problem of homosexuality in the two other films, we will become aware that his condemnation of homosexuality is justly based on the impossibility of true homosexual love: since this love is only an imitation, it is condemned to nonreciprocity. Diana [the wrongfully imprisoned heroine of *Murder!*] loves the homosexual, since she allows herself to be convicted in his stead, but the homosexual doesn't love her, since he permits her to do so.[5]

Rohmer and Chabrol's reading of Hitchcock is also a reading of the figure of the homosexual. Without irony, they appropriate Genet's reading of homosexuality as "counterfeit love" and assign to Hitchcock their own wholly heterosexist biases. As Donald Spoto has repeatedly shown, Hitchcock was not homophobic in life, at least insofar as disliking gay people. Rather, Hitchcock was fascinated by homosexuals and curious about their behavior and lifestyles.[6] The deadened, corrupt, pernicious sexuality of the homosexual as Rohmer and Chabrol find it to be depicted in *Murder!* has more relevance to their biases and their desire to impose a strictly theological framework on Hitchcock's films than it does to the director's own figures of the homosexual. They miss out on the decadent, transgressive charm of queer Hitchcock figures such as Peter Lorre's characters in *The Man Who Knew Too Much* (1934) and *Secret Agent,* Joseph Cotten's suave Uncle Charlie in *Shadow of a Doubt,* and, especially, Robert Walker's "dear, degenerate Bruno," as Pauline Kael described him, in *Strangers on a Train.*

However biased Rohmer and Chabrol may have been, their work nevertheless made it possible to appreciate Hitchcock as an artist rather than a mere entertainer, thereby inspiring the first wave of auteurist Hitchcock criticism and influencing critics such as Andrew Sarris, whose popularization of the auteur theory would in turn prove hugely influential, and Robin Wood. Wood's *Hitchcock's Films,* published in 1965 and still one of the finest books written on the director, stemmed from both Wood's early rejection by *Sight and Sound* and his essay on *Psycho* published by *Cahiers du cinéma*. Influenced at Cambridge by the famous critics F. R. Leavis and A. P. Rossiter, Wood wrote finely honed, deeply well-informed, thorough close readings of a series of Hitchcock films. He was one of the first critics to champion *Vertigo* (calling it one of the four or five greatest works of the cinema), which he likened to Shakespeare and to Keats's poetry; he called *Psycho* "one of the key works of our age," and, likening it to *Macbeth*, read into it the enduring trauma of the Holocaust.[7]

Wood's work is relevant to this chapter not just because of its merits but also because of its importance as an evolving text in the history of queer film criticism. Wood published a new version of his 1965 work as *Hitchcock's Film Revisited* in 1989; in 2002, he published yet another version that now included a new preface of some length and a new chapter on *Marnie* entitled "Does Mark Save Marnie?" The *Revisited* essays remain an unprecedented moment of self-revisionist criticism; they are also significant as coming-out stories. During the 1970s, Wood divorced his wife and came out as a gay man, and the new material in *Revisited* 1989 reflected his immersion in Marxism, feminism, and psychoanalytic theory inflected by these critical perspectives. *Revisited* 2002 goes into considerable detail about the anguish of the closet and also his non-monogamous long-term relationship with the film critic Richard Lippe, with whom he began the film journal *CineACTION!*, which Lippe continues to coedit. (Wood died in 2009.)

Wood, especially in the *Revisited* phase, frequently discussed the homosexual/gay/lesbian elements in Hitchcock's work. While Wood considers the question of "Hitchcock's homophobia," he more generally found Hitchcock to be an artist whose work contributed to an anti-homophobic project. For Wood, the value in Hitchcock's work lies in its penchant for puncturing the myth of heterosexuality as inherently normative and desirable, with homosexuality cast in the role of inferior copy. In Wood's treatment, films like the bleak *Rope*, inspired by the real-life Leopold and Loeb murder case in which two elite young homosexual men killed a friend for the thrill of it, while not projecting a positive view of homosexuality, nevertheless offers a penetrating critique of a culture of homophobia and its effects, psychological and social, on gays and lesbians. My own reading of *Rope* follows Wood's, although I am not a partisan of Wood's "therapeutic" framework for reading Hitchcock's films, as I explain later in the chapter.

The question of Hitchcock's homophobia took on an especially urgent life in an essay that marked a crucial turning point for queer theory. D. A. Miller published "Anal *Rope*" in 1990, as the AIDS crisis was still raging in the United States without any effective treatment for it and homophobia was at its height. Miller's essay evinces an intense suspicion of structures of power, with Hitchcock emerging as the ultimate source of power over the classical film text. Miller theorizes that in *Rope* the anus functions as a zone of phobic repression. Hitchcock's refusal to make a film with any cuts (though, of course, several exist) aesthetically registers the director's fused fears of castration and sodomy, figured as the core, defining practice of gay male sexuality. *Rope* "braids" both the fear of castration and the negation of castration with the intention of restabilizing normative male heterosexuality. The film's obsessive interest in hiding the nature of the cut is directly linked to this homophobic endgame. "The most immediate reason for wanting to hide the cut, then, is that it is imagined to be a penetrable hole in the celluloid film body; and though there are countless obvious and ordinary reasons for wanting to hide the anus, it is hidden here as what remains and reminds of a cut."[8]

In his essay "*Rear Window's* Glasshole," Lee Edelman draws on Miller's formulations in order to counter Laura Mulvey's famous, endlessly debated essay "Visual Pleasure and Narrative Cinema," specifically her contention that classical Hollywood cinema is organized around and dominated by the male gaze. Edelman argues that it is the anus that cannot be acknowledged in Hollywood technologies of the visual – and therefore, that an issue of equal salience to the sexual spectacularization of female bodies is this phobic ban against the visualization of the anus and concomitant acknowledgment of its existence. Hitchcock's mastery of film techniques such as montage, Edelman posits, work to blind us to the presence of this nether domain, rendered unrepresentable.

Both arguments have proved controversial. Patricia White has critiqued the ease with which these gay male critics discuss Hitchcock films with an exclusive emphasis on issues of queer male sexuality, ignoring the roles of women in the films and larger feminist issues. Modleski takes Edelman to task for failing to consider the importance of misogyny in Hitchcock, especially the theme of domestic violence.[9] While I agree with Modleski, a great critic, I would add that homophobia is not opposed to misogyny in American culture, but that both flow from a dread of feminine "weakness," and that Modleski diminishes the importance of homophobia in order to heighten awareness of feminine vulnerability. Judith Halberstam's treatment of *The Birds* is relevant here, for she uses this film as a means of critiquing Freud's theorization of female paranoia in his 1911 "Psychoanalytic Notes Upon an Autobiographical Account of a Case of Paranoia." Halberstam opposes Freud's incorporation of female paranoia into a system of homosexual panic, which he then associates with male paranoia.[10] Like White and Modleski, Halberstam attempts to block the erasure of the feminine in male critical paradigms, straight and queer.

Lucretia Knapp's discussion of the relationship between the titular Hitchcock heroine Marnie (Tippi Hedren) and Lil Mainwaring (Diane Baker) was an early indication of the potentialities of recognizing a positive queer Hitchcock. Knapp emphasizes Lil's role to Marnie as "protector, comforter, and sympathizer."[11] In the source for Hitchcock's film, Winston Graham's novel *Marnie*, Lil is a gay man named Terry Holbrook, frequently described as "bitchy." The Lil of the film, prone to tart observations, seems instantaneously aware of Marnie's desirability. "Who's the dish?" asks dark-haired Lil as she wields the sexual gaze over blonde, remote Marnie. Lil, who alternately schemes against and aids the heroine, evokes the far more malevolent Mrs. Danvers (Judith Anderson) in *Rebecca* (1940) – a film of which *Marnie* is a disordered, or reorganized, remake – who successfully tricks the heroine into dressing up in the female de Winter ancestor's dress for the masquerade ball. While I concur with Knapp about the lesbian resonances here, I would point out that Marnie is as constitutionally opposed to same-gender friendships as she is to normative heterosexual relations. Marnie is a poignant, affecting, sympathetic character precisely because of her aloneness and her despair.

In his *Cold War Femme*, Robert J. Corber places Hitchcock within the context of Cold War America, using Jess Stearn's best-selling book *The Grapevine: A Report on the Secret World of the Lesbian* (1965) as an index to homophobic attitudes of the period.[12] The view that most lesbians looked and acted just like conventional straight women began to influence both societal understandings of lesbianism and attempts to contain its threat. The lesbian could no longer be typed as the "butch," nor could she simply be diagnosed through a sexological model that linked sexual and gender nonconformity. Hitchcock's *Marnie* again proves exemplary, featuring a blonde femme whose desire is ultimately "realigned" with normative heterosexuality in its institutionalized forms, especially marriage. More persuasively, Jonathan Goldberg has written about the queer potentialities of Hitchcock's *Strangers on a Train*, based on Patricia Highsmith's 1950 novel but also quite distinct from the source text in several key respects, chief among them that, in the novel, the presumably "normal" heterosexual protagonist Guy Haines does fulfill his side of the bargain and murder the "psycho" Charles Anthony Bruno's father, after Bruno murders Guy's inconvenient first wife, Miriam. In the film, Guy does not murder Bruno's father and, indeed, helps bring Bruno to justice for the murder of Miriam. In a striking (if also, in the end, brief) reading of the film, Goldberg brilliantly retools Rohmer and Chabrol's findings for queer purposes: "Rohmer and Chabrol open Hitchcock's work to a homosexuality without limits. Rather than a world of persecuted gays, Hitchcock would seem to offer queer films, displaying not so much a minoritarian logic as a queer universalism.... It's there, I think, that we can take our pleasure in Hitchcock."[13] As Goldberg remarks, he values *Strangers* "precisely for the ways in which its apparent distinction between Guy and Bruno houses insidious suggestions of identification between them that are perhaps even more provoking than Highsmith's outrages."[14]

The Feminine versus the Queer: *Psycho* and *North by Northwest*

Alexander Doty provided scholars with a helpful schema of Hitchcock's queer-themed characters and films: "If we use a definition of queer that includes all sex, gender, and sexuality non-normativity, the Hitchcock films with the most consistent critical and audience queer quotient have been (in chronological order) *The Lodger*, *Murder!* (1930), *Rebecca*, *Shadow of a Doubt*, *The Paradine Case*, *Rope*, *Strangers on a Train*, *Vertigo*, *North by Northwest*, *Psycho*, and *Marnie*."[15] While I cannot do justice to these films here, I want to discuss *Psycho* and *North by Northwest* as representing two major components of Hitchcock's queer themes: a fascination with the attractiveness of homosexuality and/or queerness, and a pattern that I call "the feminine versus the queer."

Hitchcock's films are marked by an unsettling attraction to the villain. In most cases, this villain is male and, also in most cases, suggestively queer. Both Thomas Elsaesser and Richard Allen have made brilliant cases for understanding Hitchcock's view of male homosexuality as a version of the Wildean dandy.[16] But the dandy is not the only model for queer nefarious-ness. Female characters such Mrs. Danvers in *Rebecca*, Mrs. Sebastian as well as her son Alex in *Notorious*, the duplicitous Mrs. Drayton in *The Man Who Knew Too Much* (1956), and Leonard in *North by Northwest* exceed and/or cannot be understood through this model. If we consider Hitchcock's uses of Anthony Perkins in his 1960 film *Psycho* as well as the distinc-tions between the director's version of the characters of Norman Bates and Marion Crane from that in the source material – Robert Bloch's novel by the same name – the queerness as well as proto-feminism of Hitchcock's cinema can be seen with greater clarity.

The Norman Bates of Hitchcock's film does not exactly fit the model of the dandy, but he is analogously presented as an artist figure, his stuffed birds artfully perched on walls signature works of art. Indeed, his ulti-mate art installation is the grisly mummified corpse of his mother, a cen-tral prop in a performance art that involves masquerade, ventriloquism, and tableau vivant combining life and death (the corpse of Mrs. Bates is positioned in various life-like poses: a specter at the window, a spectator before the blank screen of a bare wall in the basement). For a proprietor at a nearly unfrequented motel that time and progress have largely forgotten, Norman is also quite modishly dressed in black turtleneck and corduroy slacks when the private investigator Arbogast (Martin Balsam) stops by to question him about the missing Marion Crane (called Mary in the novel). Perkins was a matinee idol of the 1950s who played such roles as the son of a pacifist Quaker family who goes off to fight in the Civil War in *Friendly Persuasion* (William Wyler, 1956) and Jimmy Piersall, a real-life major league baseball player who struggled with mental illness in *Fear Strikes Out* (Richard Mulligan, 1957). Hitchcock seized on the quality of hidden depths beneath Perkins's all-American but gangly, sensitive persona. Hitchcock's goal, one achieved with utter success, would appear to have been to represent the 1950s style American male youth in all of his slightly feminized, troubled, winning awkwardness and then to take this image and deconstruct it, to reveal it as a mask for an inexpressible monstrousness, one that can only be conveyed through the nearly blinding cinematic effects used to depict the mother-possessed Norman in the final shots of the film. Norman, having been revealed as the impersonator of his dead mother, whom he murdered, sits in a prison holding cell, but it is "Mother's" words, her voice-over, that we hear as the camera steadily bores into his face. The image of Mother's face, a skull with an eerie grin, is superimposed, almost subliminally, on Norman's, and then this Mother-skull-Norman face blurs, through the use of the dissolve, into the shot of a car being dragged out of a swamp by a long metal chain. The overall effect, a mechanistic image of lifelessness and death, emerges from the annihilation of Norman's psyche, the destruction of Marion's life (her body in the trunk of the swamp-swallowed car), and the final emphasis on nonliving objects (the car, the chain, the swamp), all resonances intensified by Bernard Herrmann's terrifyingly bleak score. Alexander Doty aptly described the finale of *Psycho* as a "queer apocalypse."[17]

In Bloch's 1959 novel (which Hitchcock, with merciless shrewdness, bid for anonymously and managed to buy the rights to for less than $10,000), when Mary meets Norman during the dark rainy night on which she checks into the Bates Motel, she notices his "fat, bespectacled face" and "soft, hesitant voice."[18] Earlier, when Norman tensely talks to "Mother," she says regarding him, "You're a Mama's Boy. That's what they called you, and that's what you were. Were, are, and always will be. A big fat, overgrown Mamma's Boy!"[19] Although both Bloch (reworking the notorious Ed Gein case) and Hitchcock both deploy the by-then normalized Freudian view of homosexual males as narcissistically fixated on their mothers, the long, lanky, youthful body of Perkins's Norman, and his winsomely winning handsomeness, could not be more distinct from Bloch's original conception.

Even more telling differences occur in the big scene between Marion/ Mary and Norman. In Hitchcock, the two have a cold-sandwiches-and-milk supper in Norman's parlor behind the "officious," as he puts it, motel office; in Bloch, the two are actually in Norman's kitchen within the dread Bates house. Hitchcock frames the Bates house as the Gothic genre's Terrible House par excellence, a place unimaginable as a scene of conviviality, only to be entered clandestinely, as Lila Crane (Vera Miles), Marion's sister, does at the climax. Hitchcock frames, too, the dinner conversation between Marion and Norman as an extraordinary series of shared intimacies, parries, odd disclosures, defensive maneuvers, silencings, eruptions into violence, and seeming restorations of stability. It is one of his most important sequences, superbly realized by the actors, Joseph Stefano's brilliant script, and Hitchcock's tight shot–reverse shot cinematic plan. The glaring, ominous stuffed birds preside over all, especially in a striking low-angle, side-view shot of the seated Norman, waving up his arms in direct proximity to the stuffed owl, its wings extended, that bears down on him from above as if ready to strike at any moment.

In Bloch, however, the tête-à-tête between Mary and Norman lacks any sense of intimacy, especially on Mary's part. Rather, Mary reveals little of herself and brusquely informs Norman that his mother-centered, hermit's life is headed for disaster: "Mr. Bates, you'll pardon me for saying this but how do you intend to go on this way? You're a grown man. You certainly must realize that you can't be expected to act like a little boy all the rest of your life. I don't mean to be rude, but – "[20] In the film, Marion's remarks along these lines seem more genuinely motivated by compassion for Norman derived through her sense of parity between them and their situations, one enhanced by Norman's own extraordinary acuity into both of their situations as evinced by his famous speech about "private traps" within which we are all clamped. "We bite and claw, but only at the air, only at each other, and for all of it, we never budge an inch," Norman says in Stefano's script. Indeed, far from feeling compassion for Norman, Bloch's Mary gains in self-esteem after her exposure to him. "*He* was the lonely, wretched, and fearful one, really. In contrast, she felt seven feet tall." This surge of comparative pride leads her to provoke her host even more directly: "You aren't allowed to smoke. You aren't allowed to drink. You aren't allowed to see any girls. Just what *do* you do, besides run the motel and attend to your mother?"[21] Hitchcock/Stefano/Leigh's Marion is never this brusquely direct. Rather, she tentatively suggests to Norman that his overly ardent devotion to his mother has robbed him of a life. Perhaps her insights into Norman's predicament are what allow her to realize that her own actions have been irrational, that her theft of the $40,000 from her boss's odious client, the Texas oil man Tom Cassidy, stemmed from her desire to change her vacillating lover Sam Loomis's (John Gavin) mind about marriage. She excuses herself from dinner, having resolved to return to Phoenix and try to remove herself from her own "private trap."

What makes the horrific murder of Marion doubly horrible is that it represents so grotesque a literalization of the betrayal of bonds between this queer, lonely man and this lonely, desiring woman who momentarily broke bread, literal and emotional. While Norman takes down the painting of the biblical story of Susannah and the Elders (a scene of attempted rape) in order to peep at Marion as she undresses in Cabin One, it is also not clear what Norman sees when he looks at her – if he is enflamed with erotic desire or feels revulsion or, indeed, nothing at all. (He may be possessed by what Edelman in *No Future*, following Lacan, calls *sinthomosexuality*, a drive toward meaninglessness and antisociality, embodied for him in characters such as Robert Walker's Bruno Anthony and Martin Landau's Leonard.) That no clear erotic, sexual, and/or romantic drive impels his responses to her reinforces the queerness of his character, as does the arsenal of feminizing devices, as noted by Thomson, that Perkins, probably in collaboration with Hitchcock and Stefano, brought to his interpretation of the role. The sundering of bonds, or potential bonds, between queers and heterosexual women – a violent break that occurs in *Murder!, Secret Agent, Rebecca, Shadow of a Doubt, Notorious, Rope, The Paradine Case, Strangers on a Train,* and *North by Northwest* – throughout Hitchcock's oeuvre reaches its terrifying apotheosis in *Psycho*, as Norman Bates destroys the woman whose situation solicited his insights and who offered him insightful sympathy.

North by Northwest, as well as *Psycho*, offers as an opportunity to consider, once more, just what a queer understanding of Hitchcock's cinema yields. Made right after the devastating *Vertigo*, *North by Northwest*, while filled with dark themes, is ultimately a comedy that ends in heterosexual fulfillment. As noted, Edelman, in his provocative reading, focuses on the ethical dilemma represented by Leonard crushing Thornhill's hand with his shoe-clad foot. Edelman counterintuitively values Leonard as the embodiment of the queer death drive, "rescuing" Thornhill from Eve Kendall's promised heterosexual marriage. While I find Edelman's argument exciting and daring, I want to redirect our critical attention to the figure that Edelman spends the least time discussing, Eve Kendall. While queer members of the audience may identify with Leonard, or Vandamm, I believe that queer audience members are likelier to identify with Grant/Thornhill or with Saint/Eve for the simple reason that they are attractive, appealing characters, played by attractive, appealing stars, who are put into perilous situations. Heterosexuality may be excruciatingly constrictive when deployed as a universalizing sexual program for all audience members, but its relationship to film narrative – which is always heterosexualized and heterosexualizing in its conventional forms – is also standard, even cliché. Whatever our sexual orientation, we desire to see the romantic couple find fulfillment – or, we must radically break with this institutionalized response to narrative. An immersion in the narrative of *North by Northwest* is most typically going to involve identification with the leads and the romantic couple regardless of the sexual orientation of the viewer.

Stanley Cavell, in his well-known theory of the screwball comedy as the comedy of remarriage (many of which films starred Cary Grant), has famously read *North by Northwest* along these lines. For Cavell, the point of these films involves the man's transformation through the "assault" of the woman's emotional and sexual power, but more importantly the man must "educate" the woman.[22] Whether or not we should take Cavell as simply exposing the narrative designs of such films for what they are or himself imposing, and therefore callously, a rather insensitive, if not misogynistic, sensibility on the films, we do well to remember that, as Pauline Kael (not a feminist by any stretch) argued in her review of Jonathan Demme's *Something Wild* (a film with Hitchcockian overtones), the women of screwball "perform a rescue mission" on the male, waking him up out of his sexlessness and repression.[23] I want to suggest that the queerness of *North by Northwest* lies in Hitchcock's simultaneous denaturing of what heterosexual desire and romance mean, and his interest in depicting Thornhill as a man transformed into a complex human being through the development of his love for Eve. What sounds like a fairly typical sexual narrative is actually a queer experiment.

To begin with, when Thornhill meets Eve – a double agent, performing the role of Vandamm's mistress but really working with the U.S. government – on the train and has dinner with her in the dining car, the entire scene has a stylized, almost eerie languor that takes it outside of time (as if the world were now in slow motion) and social convention. In terms of the latter, Roger's predicament allows Eve/the woman a surprising amount of reciprocal agency, including the right to request, if not demand, sex. Moreover, these demands are silkily conveyed through verbal wit ("I don't particularly like the book I've started ... know what I mean?" she propositions Thornhill artfully over dinner on the train). When they are back in her compartment, Hitchcock provides his most striking version of a love scene that looks like a murder scene (we may recall Truffaut's *mot* that Hitchcock's love scenes look like murder scenes, his murder scenes like love scenes), as Thornhill, with his immense hairy hands, grasps Eve's neck as they make out against a wall.[24] In a brilliant effect, Hitchcock films the couple in this amorous intimacy from a posterior view as well, rendering the wall behind them invisible, as if their passion had obliterated any barrier but also to emphasize the covert access to their bodies and sensations and emotions we are granted as invisible voyeuristic viewers. Indeed, the invisibility of the wall behind them from this posterior view not only allegorizes our seeming invisibility as spectators but also, crucially, places us in Eve's position, making us, in effect, Eve, kissing and being kissed – and grasped and overpowered – by Grant/Thornhill. Hitchcock feminizes the viewer and puts all viewers, male or female, straight or gay, in the position of being ravished by Cary Grant.

In one of the most striking visual touches of the film, Hitchcock pans across a row of connected telephone booths in the Chicago train station once Thornhill and Eve have arrived there. Thornhill has ventured to Chicago intent on meeting the mysterious government agent "George Kaplan" whom he has been mistaken for by Vandamm. Ostensibly, Eve is on the phone because she is calling Kaplan – who does not actually exist, of course – at his hotel. The pan across the phone booths reveals that Leonard is talking in one of them and that Eve, several booths down, is talking to Leonard, who is giving her the address she needs. The address Leonard gives Eve and that she then gives to Thornhill takes him to the highway in the cornfield where he will encounter the infamous crop-dusting plane, the agent of death through which Vandamm will attempt to eradicate Thornhill once and for all. There is an extraordinary shot of Eve and Leonard both exiting their respective phone booths after their exchange of information – neither looks at the other, both stand stock still for a moment, and each goes their own way. Hitchcock's favored technique of "pure cinema" – his use of the visual, not the screenplay, to convey meaning – makes this shot of distant phone booths an affecting metaphor. Eve and Leonard are each characters who work for nefarious men – Vandamm, the Professor, on some level Thornhill as well – yet cannot work *together*, must work against one another while maintaining, for a time, the ruse of collaboration. Their silent voices (we see them speaking but cannot hear what they say); their physical distance from one another in the bland, conformist, commercial, industrialized row of anonymous phone booths; their physical distance and inability to recognize the other when they stand outside the phone booths: all work together to suggest something of these characters' subject positions within the social structures of the diegetic world. The woman and the homosexual male are alike adrift in a world of conformity, powerlessness, and subservience to questionable father figures, never able to recognize or acknowledge one another.

Interestingly, when Eve finds Thornhill and delivers the false information to him, Thornhill *is* able to recognize her – he detects that something is "wrong," that Eve is troubled. Whatever occurred between them in the train compartment has given him access of some kind to an understanding of her. There is an intimacy – which is also a shared vulnerability – that Thornhill develops with Eve, and she with him. For she is indeed troubled, and troubled because she knows she is giving him directions to his own death.

North by Northwest boldly builds on *Vertigo*. In a justly famous moment much discussed by feminist critics, *Vertigo* breaks with its male protagonist's point of view to give us Judy Barton's (Kim Novak) flashback, which establishes an identification with her that competes against the identification with the male protagonist, Scottie (James Stewart). In her flashback, we learn what really happened when Madeleine seemed to fall from the tower: Gavin Elster had murdered his real wife and thrown *her* body off the tower, and used Scottie as a hapless witness to Madeleine's suicide, Judy having pretended to be the real Madeleine, all part of Elster's diabolical ruse. *North by Northwest* goes even further in giving the woman much greater knowledge of and agency in the man's death plot. Eve's palpable discomfort, if not despair, in giving Thornhill the murderous information and Thornhill's recognition of her discomfort convey a sense of empathy between these unlikely would-be lovers that allows them both to see past the obstructions of the social order, its insistence on strictly maintained gender roles, even, perhaps, its insistence on heterosexual normalcy.

That the man must be stoic, taciturn, unfeeling, and certainly never feminized by feeling; that the woman must be artfully seductive, narcissistically obsessed with her own image in order to present an image to the man of her attractiveness that will then incite a reciprocal sexual hunger in him; that sexual difference must be maintained as the absolute code and plan for relationships between men and women, but also same-gender relationships as well, organized around the logic of compulsory heterosexuality in culture no less decisively than relations between those of the opposite sex: all of the binding social strictures organized around normative gender roles and sexual difference dissolve, if only momentarily, in the scene of partial, stalled, palpable empathy between Eve and Thornhill.

While a great deal more needs to be said about this film, we can revisit the moment in which Leonard exposes Eve as a double agent to Vandamm. Leonard effectively outs himself with the reference to his "woman's intuition," and then Vandamm comically chides Leonard for being jealous

("I'm really touched"). This exchange renders comedic the *real* trauma of sexual silence in the film, in this case the closeted homosexual's non-access to expressive desire. This scene offers an acute commentary on the disordered emotional bonds of the film. Leonard, probably in love with the rich, powerful, witty Vandamm but unable to express his love directly, engineers Eve's death as the only possible expression of this love. The homosexual male, himself entrapped in a culture of homophobia that borders on the murderous, can only mirror back this culture's worst aspects, specifically its misogynistic view of woman as whore, to which type Eve is forever likened, by Thornhill as well as the villains, and even by the Professor, in his callousness, as a threat to be destroyed, and in so doing he reveals this culture's investments in the closet, which makes it impossible for Leonard – or Eve – to speak.

The "anti-social" turn in queer theory, as it has been called by Judith Halberstam and others, finds a complement in Hitchcock's work, which teems with outsider characters who find no secure place in the world, sometimes no place at all.[25] Marnie is an especially poignant character in this regard, but her isolated position is representative of that of several Hitchcock personae. At the same time, a profound desire for connection also informs several key Hitchcock works: anti-relationality is not the full, certainly not the only, story in his films. Hitchcock's most characteristic maneuver in his films is to call into question the very normative standards that would allow for such a reading. To arrive at something like a queer understanding of Hitchcock, we must first consider the powerful motives for refusing the demands of the social order on the part of his characters and works, and, second, disentangle the questions of desire and the longing for intimacy from their conventional, if not altogether binding, associations with normative heterosexual desire.

NOTES

1 Tania Modleski, *The Women Who Knew Too Much: Hitchcock and Feminist Theory* (1988; New York: Routledge, 2005).
2 See Robin Wood, *Hitchcock's Films Revisited* (New York: Columbia University Press, 2002); Alexander Doty, "How Queer Is My *Psycho*," in *Flaming Classics: Queering the Film Canon* (New York: Routledge, 2000), pp. 155–189 and "Queer Hitchcock," *A Companion to Alfred Hitchcock*, eds. Thomas Leitch and Leland Poague (Malden, MA: Wiley-Blackwell, 2011), pp. 473–489; Patricia White, "Hitchcock and Hom(m)osexuality," in *Hitchcock: Past and Future*, eds. Richard Allen and S. Ishii-Gonzáles (London: Routledge, 2004), pp. 211–229; Lucretia Knapp, "The Queer Voice in *Marnie*," in *A Hitchcock Reader*, eds. Marshall Deutelbaum and Leland Poague, second edition (Chichester: Wiley-Blackwell, 2009), pp. 295–311.

3 See D. A. Miller, "Anal *Rope*," in *Inside/Out: Lesbian Theories, Gay Theories*, ed. Diana Fuss (New York: Routledge, 1991), pp. 119–141; Lee Edelman, *No Future: Queer Theory and the Death Drive* (Durham, NC: Duke University Press, 2004), especially pp. 70–102, 118–149, and "*Rear Window*'s Glasshole," in *Out Takes: Essays on Queer Theory and Film*, ed. Ellis Hanson (Durham, NC: Duke University Press, 1999), pp. 72–97; Jonathan Goldberg, *Strangers on a Train: A Queer Film Classic* (Vancouver: Arsenal Pulp Press, 2012); Judith Halberstam, "Reading Counterclockwise: Paranoid Gothic or Gothic Paranoia," in *Skin Shows: Gothic Horror and the Technology of Monsters* (Durham, NC: Duke University Press, 2000), pp. 107–137.

4 Patricia White, *Uninvited: Classical Hollywood Cinema and Lesbian Representability* (Bloomington: Indiana University Press, 1999).

5 Eric Rohmer and Claude Chabrol, *Hitchcock: The First Forty-Four Films*, trans. Stanley Hochman (1957; New York: F. Ungar Film Library, 1979), pp. 27–28.

6 See, for example, Spoto's discussion of Hitchcock's response to Ivor Novello's openly homosexual "boldness." Donald Spoto, *The Dark Side of Genius: The Life of Alfred Hitchcock* (Boston: Little, Brown, and Company, 1983), p. 86. Novello starred in the Hitchcock films *The Lodger* and *Downhill*, both of which have queer aspects.

7 Wood, *Hitchcock's Films Revisited*, p. 150.

8 Miller, "Anal *Rope*," p. 134, emphasis in the original.

9 Modleski's Afterword, "Resurrection of a Hitchcock Daughter," can be found in the 2005 reissue of *The Women Who Knew Too Much*, pp. 123–161.

10 Halberstam, "Reading Counterclockwise," *Skin Shows*, p. 136.

11 Knapp, "The Queer Voice in *Marnie*," p. 302.

12 Robert J. Corber, *Cold War Femme: Lesbianism, National Identity and Hollywood* (Durham, NC: Duke University Press, 2011).

13 Goldberg, *Strangers on a Train: A Queer Film Classic*, p. 72.

14 Ibid, p. 17.

15 Doty, "Queer Hitchcock," p. 477.

16 See Thomas Elsaesser, "The Dandy in Hitchcock," in *The Persistence of Hollywood* (New York: Routledge, 2012), pp. 175–182, and Richard Allen, *Hitchcock's Romantic Irony* (New York: Columbia University Press, 2007).

17 Doty argues on behalf of not only Norman's queerness but also of Marion Crane's sister Lila, who investigates the Bates house in the climax. Alexander Doty, *Flaming Classics: Queering the Film Canon* (New York: Routledge, 2000), p. 188.

18 Robert Bloch, *Psycho* (1959; New York: The Overlook Press, 2010), p. 29.

19 Ibid, p. 15.

20 Ibid, p. 35.

21 Ibid, p. 35.

22 Cavell, *Cavell on Film*, ed. William Rothman (New York: SUNY Press, 2005), pp. 49, 57.

23 Pauline Kael, *Hooked* (New York: Dutton, 1989), p. 228.

24 As Truffaut put it, "in Hitchcock's cinema, which is definitely more sexual than sensual, to make love and to die are one and the same." See Truffaut, *Hitchcock*, and Helen G. Scott, *Truffaut/Hitchcock* (1967; New York: Simon & Schuster, 1985), p. 346.

25 See J. Halberstam, "The Anti-Social Turn in Queer Studies," *Graduate Journal of Social Science* 5.2 (2008): 140–156. See Leo Bersani, *Homos* (Cambridge, MA: Harvard University Press, 1995); Lee Edelman, *No Future: Queer Theory and the Death Drive* (Durham, NC: Duke University Press, 2004); and for a counterresponse to the queer anti-relation thesis that critiques, in particular Edelman's disregard for nonwhite queer aesthetic productions, see José Esteban Muñoz, *Cruising Utopia: The Then and There of Queer Futurity* (New York: NYU Press, 2009).

8

STEPHEN TIFFT

Mrs. Bates's Smile: *Psycho* and Psychoanalysis

"Yes, that's the trouble with mothers: first you get to like them, then they die."
— Mariette, Lubitsch's *Trouble in Paradise*

"I must have one of those faces you just can't help believing."
— Norman Bates

Alfred Hitchcock ensured that any reading of *Psycho* (1960) must plunge into the psyche's murky depths by embedding within its nerve-jangling climax a learned psychoanalytic interpretation, fluently delivered by a police psychiatrist who claims to explain the bizarre spectacle we have just seen: Norman Bates dressed in his mother's clothing and sporting a grey wig, butcher's knife raised triumphantly as he rushes down into the fruit cellar to wreak vengeance on Lila Crane for discovering his family secret. Despite its authorial imprimatur, for many Dr. Richman's harangue, if anything, discredits psychoanalytic explanation of Norman. Hitchcock's own ambivalence about the scene emerges in his worry that the speech would be a "hat-grabber" for the audience,[1] even while the sequence's strikingly bland visual style, compared to the visual brilliance of most of the film – the nearly static camera passively following Richman's bombastic lecture in a drab office for more than five minutes – suggests that the director wished to express banality in the scene's very filming. Yet after the first take Hitchcock rose to shake actor Simon Oakland's hand and said, "Thank you very much, Mr. Oakland. You've just saved my picture"[2] – perhaps meaning that serious psychological intelligibility had thus been conferred on a potentially absurd plot, or simply hoping that Richman's account would strike censors as sufficiently clinical to mollify outraged viewers. Or Hitchcock may have intended to goad viewers to undertake a more searching scrutiny of Norman's psyche.

The ambiguous status of Richman's interpretation of Norman calls into question the efficacy of psychoanalytic interpretation itself. For skeptics of the pretence of explaining unconscious dynamics rationally, this reductive account seems a fraudulent exercise in sheer far-fetched and monolithic speculation. But for psychoanalytic critics impatient with the complacent normalizing of American ego psychology, Richman's account shows the need for a more nuanced and destabilizing understanding of subjectivity. This essay begins with the premise that because psychoanalytic thought centers on the dynamics rather than the content of mental life – its paradigms concerning, for example, Oedipal conflict, melancholy introjection, the interplay of sadistic and masochistic impulses, the nature of psychosis, and the intricacies of multiple identifications and split subjectivity – it sets in motion an intricate play of interpretive positions, opening out volatile permutations of identity and desire. Hitchcock was familiar with Freud's writing, but one may still be surprised by the astonishingly fertile responsiveness of the films to psychoanalytic theory – and by the films' capacity to illuminate and to press the theory in turn.

From such a perspective, Dr. Richman may be taken as a straw man. Yet despite the ridicule his account has kindled, virtually all readings of *Psycho* in fact rely on its principal ideas. His bare explanation of Norman's impersonation of his mother as simply a device to suppress awareness of his matricide and his account of the neatly binary structure of Norman's psyche – for example, construing his homicidal rage solely in terms of the jealousy of his "Mother-half" when Norman is aroused by women – are obviously too pat. But most viewers' basic assumptions – that Norman had a disturbed Oedipal attachment to his mother, which prompted him to kill her and her lover, dig up and embalm her body, and ventriloquize her voice and impersonate her physically, and above all that Mother had become an alternative identity unbeknownst to his conscious mind, and that he killed under the sway of this identity – are also Richman's central claims, and nothing in the film, least of all the final scene, really contradicts them.

In fact, Richman's culminating claim – "He tried to *be* his mother. And now, he is" – falls away in virtually every reading of the film, however committed to the notion that *Psycho* destabilizes gender and identity. Norman Bates's attempts to keep his mother alive may seem outlandish, but in interpretations of the film it is Norman himself who dies hardest. What would it mean to say that "Mrs. Bates" is an autonomous character in the film periodically, and in the end, permanently? – to take Richman to represent not solely in parodic but in weirdly acute ways the film's dare to be read psychoanalytically? In what follows, I try to convey the interplay of psychoanalytic perspectives in the criticism on *Psycho*, and to explore some of its more neglected terrain – particularly the nature and implications of

Norman's matricide and split subjectivity – in order to take seriously the most adventurous and extreme representations of subjectivity in *Psycho*.

The very stuff of narrative had been moving inward in Hitchcock's films of the period preceding *Psycho*: increasingly his protagonists are beset less by external forces than by those of their own unconscious. As Hitchcock's films became more psychologically searching, their vertiginous findings came to threaten the norms of classical narrative. For its first forty-five minutes, *Psycho* looks like such a narrative, if a bleak one: structured around a romance reduced, in part by Sam's straitened circumstances, to fleeting and sordid sexual encounters, the plot pivots on Marion's attempt to put her affair on a more respectable footing by stealing $40,000 from her boss and fleeing to her lover. The film thus appears to be a story of the dangers of illicit desire, ramifying guilt – and eventual expiation and renewal, prompted by the extraordinary conversation over supper after her arrival at the Bates Motel, which elicits from Norman an unnerving vision of life with mad, abusive Mother:

> No; people never run away from anything ... I think that we're all in our private traps, clamped in them, and none of us can ever get out. We scratch and claw, but only at the air, only at each other. And for all of it, we never budge an inch.

To mark Marion's decision to return and face the consequences of her transgression, prior to her murder, the shower scene, despite its autoerotic elements, was staged as a return to moral health: "when she stepped into the tub it was as if she were stepping into the baptismal waters. The spray beating down on her was purifying the corruption from her mind, purging the evil from her soul."[3] Yet the shower scene, famed for its representation of physical and perceptual violation (of the spectator as well as Marion), is perhaps most subversive in "kill[ing] the star in the first third of the film," and thus shattering its thematic basis, grounded thus far in Marion's transgression.[4] Even Hitchcock's camera seems bewildered by her death: from a close-up of her face as she lies dead in the bathroom, it tracks and pans along the floor and into the bedroom, tilting to scrutinize the folded newspaper concealing the stolen money, but all this has suddenly become meaningless – so the camera moves on to frame the Bates house. Though our narrative sense may try fitfully to attach itself to the efforts of Sam and Marion's sister Lila to save her or at least to resolve her murder, ultimately the arbitrary nature of her killing empties Marion's plot of any further significance. Viewers may lament the lack of human interest at this stage of the plot, but Hitchcock was interested only in what threatens to become inhuman interest, so to speak – only in Norman. It thus appears as though the film is ruptured, its two halves related only by the arbitrary trauma of the murder.

In the ensuing interpretive void, structural psychoanalytic accounts have offered the most fruitful means for making sense of the film as a whole and for affording access to precisely *Psycho*'s most radical, disorienting features. Within such readings, the psychology of characters serves primarily to illuminate the psychodynamics that animate the ideas and affects of the film on a structural level. Thus, for Laura Mulvey, after the murder the film diverges from the individual moral project of containing Marion's illicit sexuality within patriarchal norms by becoming what Mulvey calls "a death-drive movie": she applies to the film's psychical energies Freud's concept of a drive or set of instincts that, in contrast to the life instincts or libido, strive to reduce tension to the zero-point, and that, when directed inward, tend toward the dissolution and self-destruction of the individual, and when directed outward, toward aggressive and destructive instincts against others.[5] Troubling both the aims and the nature of the living, the idea of the death drive is inimical to the aspirations of classical narrative. Similarly Raymond Bellour, arguing that the "structural perversion" of the film's ruptured narrative corresponds to forms of psychical perversion (notably voyeurism and fetishism) represented within the film, sees Marion's neurosis (her thwarted, illicit affair and subsequent crime) and Norman's psychosis as a means for Hitchcock to stage a reflection on the relationship of neurosis to psychosis both in sexuality more generally and in the structure of cinema itself.[6] Bellour traces the complicity, from the film's opening sequence, of Hitchcock's camera – and hence of the spectator's gaze – with Norman's later voyeurism, culminating in the viewer's eroticized relation to Norman's sadistic, homicidal desire in the murder scene.

For Bellour – as for Mulvey, Christian Metz, and other film theorists – the viewer's voyeurism in *Psycho* reflects a more general structural feature of cinema as a practice and an ideological institution. Such theories construe the cinematic spectator's act of looking in terms of the ineluctably split subjectivity analyzed by the psychoanalyst Jacques Lacan, for whom the subject necessarily is self-alienated by its entry into language. The eroticized looking of voyeurism must be understood in film theory in context of this constitutive lack of being; as Kaja Silverman writes, the cinematic image – preeminently the eroticized female body – "functions as a fetish within dominant cinema ... to represent that [imaginary] phenomenal plenitude which is lost to the male subject with his entry into language."[7] The shower scene has drawn so much attention in part because of its intriguing complication of these theoretical ideas: despite the male cast of cinematic voyeurism and the murderous displacement of rape represented in the shower scene,

Silverman and others argue that the spectator's perspective is not confined to the sadistic gaze of Norman (or Mother), but shifts between the perspectives of the victimizer and the victimized in a sustained disruption or dismembering of the viewer's positioning that subjects the viewer to a version of Norman's schizophrenia.[8] William Rothman probes Hitchcock's evocation of an uncanny force of terror beyond character in the sequence, showing how visual elements (the showerhead, the indistinct knife-bearing figure glimpsed through the shower curtain) associated initially with particular subjects – Norman, Mother, Hitchcock, the viewer – assume a kind of alien intentionality. For him the shower scene induces not merely the terror of eroticized violence and moral complicity but something inhuman and abyssal in the subject – not only in Norman but in, or exceeding, ourselves.[9] Such a sense will find its culmination in the final scene of the film.

Any account of Norman Bates must address the psychical structure of his relationship with Mother and the causes of his split personality, not merely to revivify a psychoanalytic account of character but to open up structural analysis of the film to a new array of psychical patterns, dynamics, and issues. Given the intensity and derangement of his relationship with his mother, speculation must begin with Norman's charged relation to the Oedipus complex, pivotal within psychoanalytic theory to the structuring of subjectivity and the genesis of psychopathology. On Freud's account, the Oedipus complex, at its peak from about three to five years of age, begins to dissolve as the child's ego replaces object-cathexes with identifications (thus a son heeds the father's prohibition and cedes his incestuous desires for the mother, identifying with the father and eventually finding substitute object-cathexes); the "authority of the father or the parents is introjected into the ego" as the nucleus of the superego.[10] Surmounting the Oedipus complex ideally does not merely repress but abolish the complex; failing this, it will return with pathogenic effect.

Norman "was already dangerously disturbed," reports Richman, "ever since his father died" – at age five, Norman tells Marion – and, Richman implies, evidently suffered the aborting of the complex's resolution. Norman's extravagant identification with his mother might lead one to suspect an incipient Oedipal desire for his father, so that in Mother are condensed Norman's unresolved wishes toward both parents. Conversely, we might read an identification with his father – though hardly in the sublimated, normative form resulting from the dissolution of the Oedipus complex – in Norman's voicing, through Mother, of vehement prohibitions against sexual license: along with its eroticized, sadistic elements, the killing of Marion is on one level a killing of desire. Most luridly, Norman might be understood to act out a partial and ambivalent identification with his father in wreaking homicidal vengeance on his mother and her adulterous lover, a vengeance repeated by displacement in his misogynist violence against Marion and her predecessors. This line of thought would not merely substitute father for mother as the covert object of Norman's ambivalently incestuous desire and erratic identification. Rather, a traumatic miscarriage of his Oedipus complex – when object-cathexes are sliding unstably into identifications and both parents are still at play in the shifting permutations of love and hate – would generate such violent ambivalence and volatile gender identifications and realignments as mark Norman's psychotic state. Thus his relation to Mother neither rules out nor gives way to his covert trafficking with the imago of his deceased father, but both parallels and merges with it. For Slavoj Žižek, under the psychosis following from the foreclosure of what Lacan calls the Name-of-the-Father, what one might ordinarily read as the draconian prohibitive authority of a father appears instead as an archaic maternal function:

> [T]he father is absent, the paternal function (the function of pacifying law, the Name-of-the-Father) is suspended and that vacuum is filled by the 'irrational' maternal superego, arbitrary, wicked, blocking 'normal' sexual relationship (only possible under the sign of the paternal metaphor).[11]

Without the rationalizing effect of the Oedipus complex and the normal functioning of the symbolic order, "Norman is entrapped into the mother's desire not yet submitted to the paternal Law … his desire is alienated in the maternal Other, at the mercy of its cruel caprice."[12] Ordinarily Norman might resent such aggression passively, but the traumatic violence that inaugurated his psychosis – matricide – can be understood in Lacanian terms as a "passage to the act," the conversion of a violent idea to a real enactment. For Lacan, the passage to the act is "a flight from the Other" and "an exit from the symbolic network … entail[ing] a [momentary] dissolution of the subject" and a rupture in subject-object relations which may amount to psychosis.[13]

Norman's "passage to the act" of matricide may be understood to have inaugurated the most striking feature of his psychosis – his split personality. Richman explains this merely as a mechanism of denial, occluding Norman's mother's death and his own murder of her – a simplistic account providing no way to understand the tortuous dynamics by which he alternately impersonates and interacts psychically with Mother. Freud's account of the structure of melancholia, in which a survivor, unable to accept the loss of a precious object, "introjects" or internalizes it, yields a more precise understanding of Norman's radical evasion of grief; and although melancholia is not in itself a psychotic state, its aberrant response to loss, with the vicissitudes of the lost object, sheds light on his split identity. For Freud, the most far-reaching aspect of his theory of melancholia was its account of the process by which an object-cathexis is replaced by an identification with the lost object. Thus in melancholia not only is the lost object internally preserved, but the melancholic's identification with it produces a doubled internal subjectivity, through which the attachments and conflicts of the subject and the lost object can be continued in a kind of hidden colloquy: a situation that Norman appears to have projected hallucinatorily into the external world, in a psychotic exacerbation of melancholia. Moreover, the melancholic's irrational self-reproaches and delusional expectation of punishment may be understood as the basis of Mother's hectoring, derisive abuse of Norman: Freud notes that the melancholic's self-reproaches often seem to apply more aptly to the lost object, but are instead mirrored back against the melancholic's ego. Thus Norman suffers "an impoverishment of his ego on a grand scale," a sense of inferiority that can even result in "an overcoming of the instinct which compels every living thing to cling to life," inciting a suicidal impulse weirdly displayed by his allowing or inviting Mother to reverse the matricide by, in effect, killing him, or his identity, at the end of *Psycho*.[14]

If melancholy introjection thus provides one model for Norman's split personality, Freud's concept of the "splitting of the ego" extends this account to encompass Norman's psychotic disavowal of reality. Freud conceived of disavowal as a defense mechanism consisting in a refusal even to register the reality of a traumatic perception, an idea developed at length in his theory of fetishism, which derives from the fetishist's disavowal of castration: the fetish-object serves as a means to deny the absence of the phallus by taking its place, yet also to memorialize it through the unaccountable intensity with which the fetish is valued. But simultaneous with this disavowal of a traumatic perception, fetishists also display, with a separate portion of their ego, a recognition of the trauma. In his late work, Freud returned to this phenomenon as the basis of his theory of a splitting of the ego itself, which occurs more dramatically in psychosis: when an irresistibly imperious wish is frustrated by reality, the "ego creates, autocratically, a new external and internal world [by hallucination] … in accordance with the id's wishful impulses," inducing a perceptual conflict in which "the ego [may] avoid a rupture in any direction … by effecting a cleavage or division of itself."[15] A portion of the ego continues to recognize external reality, but in the splitting of the ego, there is no compromise such as that of the neurotic symptom: the two portions of the ego simply sustain their contradictory perceptions and commitments in unacknowledged parallel.

In his hallucinatory deformation of reality, what Norman disavows most obviously is the reality of his mother's death at his own hands. The other half of his psychical split, the normal attitude "which takes account of reality,"[16] emerges not so much in his reasonable accounts of Mother to Marion – part of his hallucinatory construction – as when the disavowal is shaken and his calm falters, as in his difficulty saying "bathroom" to her (site of Mother's former and impending murders), or in his stuttering, panicky efforts to turn aside Arbogast's requests to see Mother. Above all, the murderous fury Mother visits on Arbogast expresses a desperate anxiety lest Mother's secret be exposed – perhaps not so much to Arbogast as to Norman himself. That the secret's violent protection is carried out by Mother herself suggests the profundity of the psychical split.

Norman's hallucinatory denial of his mother's death seems to lack the defining force of the paradigmatic object of disavowal, the threat of castration. But in disavowing his matricide, he does in effect disavow that threat, construed as a fantasy articulating the father's prohibition against incest: in his mother's affair, the lover functions for him as, in effect, the father who excludes the son from his own monopoly on the mother; thus by killing this surrogate father as well as his mother, Norman might be understood to obliterate this exclusion while keeping Mother to himself in hallucination thereafter. Freud describes disavowal as a "refus[al] to accept any prohibition" and psychosis as "the expression of a rebellion on the part of the id against the external world."[17] While Richman construes Norman's matricide as the jealous vengeance of a (paternal) superego and his psychotic hallucination as a mechanism of flight, if Norman's "passage to the act" were a rebellion on behalf of the id, it would rather express incestuous urges. To see the matricide not as a punishment but as the carrying out of an ungovernable wish is to imagine it as his attempt to win back his incestuous exclusivity with Mother, fleeing *with* her from reality; and to conceive the sexual drive as inseparable, for Norman, from the death drive, directed outward or inward by turns – which really amounts to the same thing, given his internal split.

Linked with death, this moment of what Lacan calls *jouissance* cannot be acknowledged by Norman's consciousness, and so it can and must be perpetuated: as Nicolas Abraham and Maria Torok put it, "To have a fantasy of incorporation [their term for introjection] is to have no other choice but to perpetuate a clandestine pleasure by transforming it, after it has been lost, into an *intrapsychic secret*."[18] This secret seems to be shared, however, with Mother, not exactly an intrapsychic figure, but one whom Norman, even in his moments of relative normalcy, regards as real and autonomous. The strange autonomy of Mother as an undead character eludes the theoretical models we have examined thus far, which do not address such psychotic extremity as Norman's split identity. The work of Abraham and Torok on "encryption" affords an intriguing perspective on these dynamics: "Inexpressible mourning erects a secret tomb inside the subject. Reconstituted from the memories of words, scenes, and affects, the objectal correlative of the loss is buried alive in the crypt as a full-fledged person, complete with its own topography," along with the traumas that prompted the fantasy of incorporation ("Mourning *or* Melancholia," 130). Their notion of the phantasmatic object's being encrypted intact evokes the autonomy of Mother as half of Norman's split personality; its emphasis on the encrypted "person's" speech recalls the way in which Mother's language, when we overhear it, is remarkably distinctive, quite different from Norman's in its rhythms, locutions, tones, even in its nutty sense of humor (which contrasts so strikingly with Norman's understated, shambling wryness: "I will not hide in the fruit cellar! Ha-hah! You think I'm fruity, huh?"). A crypt is formed in the wake of "an idyll, experienced with a valued object and yet for some reason unspeakable," followed by its traumatic loss.[19] (Thus Norman's agitated proclamation to Sam: "I had a very happy childhood. My mother and I were *more* than happy.") Abraham and Torok's concept of encryption prompts us to look for the source of the unspeakable in his mother, opening up the startling prospect of a Mrs. Bates complicit in the incestuous – even if only emotional – intimacy that we would ascribe to Norman's unconscious urges:

> No crypt arises without a shared secret's having already split the subject's topography …. Crypts are constructed only when the shameful secret is the love object's doing and when that object also functions for the subject as an ego ideal. It is therefore the *object's* secret that needs to be kept, *his* shame covered up. ("Mourning *or* Melancholia, 131)

It is not Mother that is encrypted, but the mother of the shameful secret; Mother is a front who displays the moral rigor of an ego ideal. Since the encrypted object "is the genuine subject of the [patient's] acts" ("Mourning *or* Melancholia," 134), Abraham and Torok complement Freud's formulation of the way in which the melancholic displays "the ego in the guise of the object" by proposing the reverse: "*the 'object,' in its turn, carries the ego as its mask*.… This one is an imaginary and covert identification, a crypto-fantasy" ("Lost Object," 141). Such "endocryptic identification" suggests not only the extreme but also the reversible splitting we find in *Psycho*: not only does Norman identify with his encrypted maternal object, but "Mother" apparently identifies with him. This dizzying sense of reversibility emerges not only in the film's final scene but in earlier conversations we overhear in which Mother "ventriloquizes" Norman. Yet if this personality is truly split and dual, if Mother is an autonomous subject, what is encrypted for Mother? Not the Norman with whom Marion dines, nor the reasoning Norman who carries a protesting Mother down to the fruit-cellar, but the Norman of the shameful secret of matricide and deathly *jouissance*, the murderous Norman who eludes her consciousness. Thus she is able to see everyday Norman as pathetically servile, as lacking "guts." It is Mrs. Bates who now lacks guts, thanks to Norman's taxidermic art; but for Mother, the gutless Norman serves as the ego, carried as her mask.

For this double personality, precariously balanced on disavowal and encryption, grounded in an alternative, hallucinatory reality vulnerable to daily incursions from the external world, the exposure in the fruit-cellar – where Norman, dressed as Mother, has to face her corpse in the presence of Lila and Sam, who subdues him and divests him of wig and dress – is catastrophic. Abraham and Torok in effect describe the result:

> Faced with the danger of seeing the crypt crumble, the whole of the ego becomes one with the crypt, showing the concealed object of love in its own guise. Threatened with the imminent loss of its internal support – the kernel of its being – the ego will fuse with the included object.
>
> ("Mourning *or* Melancholia," 136)

For Norman, this fusion amounts to a sort of suicide: publicly forced to choose between being Norman and being Mother, he gives himself over to her – an immolation lucidly imagined within Freud's model for the operation of primary masochism, whose originally self-directed energies are normally turned outward in aggression or sadism (such as Norman was about to visit on Lila), but under certain circumstances may be turned inward again in redoubled impulses of self-destructiveness.

But however tenable the idea that the figure who is taken off to jail now "is" Mother, or "Mrs. Bates," Norma Bates yet floats uncannily free of the unwigged figure on the cellar stairs. In her subtle argument about Mother as a specter, a figure of irrepressible return, Shirl Yang points out that at this moment of crisis, amid the screams of Lila and the shriek of Herrmann's violins, Hitchcock has dubbed into the sound-track a woman's voice crying, "I am Norma Bates!" – a voice that cannot come from any of the characters present, including Norman, whose face we see. This uncanny device in a sense confirms the autonomy of "Mrs. Bates": it might be seen as the voice-over of Norman's encrypted subject, breaking free of the crypt and of him. For Yang, however, it clearly escapes and confounds the logic of the narrative: "[T]he moment in which Norman and Norma come un-synched is one in which any possibility for closure collapses."[20] The banal moment of resolution in the D.A.'s office is thus challenged by the scene that precedes it and is further eclipsed in the final scene, in which Mother – or, since Norman is putatively no longer with us, "Mrs. Bates" – meditates on the fall of her son (a scene as cinematically thrilling, as starkly beautiful, as the penultimate scene is plain). On one level, "Mrs. Bates's" interior monologue confirms the basics of Richman's account, but most observers agree that this scene exceeds moral balance and narrative closure – even, Silverman suggests, the symbolic order within which subjectivity is articulated. Yet its travesty of moral reason (if we grant "Mrs. Bates" her existence and her self-exculpating speech at all, it would seem sheer physicalist sophistry to assign the murders clearly to Norman) instigates a brilliant trumping of the founding impulse of Hitchcock's genre. For beyond the unmasking in the fruit-cellar, beyond Richman's settling of accounts, Hitchcock uses "Mrs. Bates's" interior monologue to reopen, in a radically new way, the question of the "whodunnit."

This culminating question of *Psycho* – who *did* do it? that is, who or what is this subject? – challenges us to rethink identity as such, as Hitchcock's cinematography suggests: most of the scene consists of an extremely slow track-in to scrutinize "Mrs. Bates," sitting against a bare wall, always slightly off-center in the beautifully spare composition of the shot – and ever more unsettlingly inscrutable, the closer we get to her. Many rigorous analyses of the film simply take it as a given that the figure before us in the cell is Norman (however deranged). Yet since, for psychoanalysis, the subject is not a given but a construct, the identity "Norman" is as phantasmatic as "Mrs. Bates." Thus there is no reason to privilege the former, and the scene whose singular contention is that Norman is only one of two subjects residing in the same body merits serious attention.

In a sense, the scene offers an established convention of film narrative: the interior monologue, in voice-over, of a character who situates herself within the film's events. The voice has been cleared of any trace of Norman, and "Mrs. Bates" is characterized surprisingly vividly in her sly special pleading, her ruthlessness in sacrificing Norman, her canny, contentious relation to authority, her mysterious sense of humor. It would be easier, however, to accept the voice-over as the consciousness of this character if the body were absent. The graphic bonus of this inassimilable body, the claim of impossible embodiment, has productively unsettled readings of the film's ending: Linda Williams finds the idea that Norman now "is" Mother – the overcoming of one identity by another – less shocking than the spectacle of a young male body with an older female voice, fascinating for "the slippage between masculine and feminine poles of an identity."[21] Yet the questionable idea that the body we see is a "pole" constituting masculine identity suggests that Williams's fascination is inseparable from the eclipse of Norman's identity by whatever subjectivity the voice here claims. For Michel Chion, the impossibility of embodiment, the fundamental preoccupation of *Psycho*, disables a virtually Eucharistic grounding not only for gender but for identity in general. Although the film has tantalized the viewer with the realization of such embodiment from our first hearing Mother off-screen, at the promised climax, he argues, her monologue has a quality "characteristic of spirit possession or ventriloquism."[22]

I have stressed Mother's relative autonomy as a subject to stimulate our speculative understanding of the trauma that instigated the structure of Norman's split personality. The stakes of arguing that "Mrs. Bates" emerges as an independent figure at the end – that she can't be taken for granted as a figment of Norman, but supplants (or even "kills") him – are somewhat different. For faced with this character in no-longer-Norman's body, we are made to contemplate subjectivity itself in a profoundly alien aspect, which is missed precisely to the degree that we see this figure simply as the psychotic mass-murderer Norman Bates (a reading available as early as the fruit-cellar). Žižek explores this alien subjectivity as a Lacanian allegory. In *Psycho*, he argues, Hitchcock's tendency to subvert the viewer's identification with the subjects of his films is taken to its extreme: we are "forc[ed] ... to *identify with the abyss beyond identification*," to "confront an 'absolute Otherness' which precludes any identification."[23] His most impressive stroke of reading in support of his claim that the film approaches the "subject beyond subjectivization" concerns a desperately unnerving point-of-view shot during the murder of Arbogast, when Hitchcock cuts from an overhead shot of Mother coming out to stab the detective to a medium close-up following him as he topples down the stairs, from the perspective of the pursuing slasher: the psychotic, sickening indeterminacy of the consciousness vacated by Norman (*Bold Gaze*, 251–252). In this point-of-view shot the viewer is suddenly slid into a position that is both subjective and nonsubjective, alien and empty and horrifying all at once.

Žižek reads the approach to the "subject beyond subjectivity" here and throughout the film as amounting, in Lacanian terms, to the return or incursion of the Real into the symbolic order, a momentary rupture in the signifying systems through which we apprehend our world. The encounter with the Real, or "Thing," is represented in the final scene in the figure whom I have been calling "Mrs. Bates," but this reading is complicated to the degree that a distinctive subjectivity – seemingly proffered by the face staring at the viewer in the cell, in contrast to the empty point of view in the murder scene – is made to carry the burden of the allegorical concept. Thus

Žižek empties out any residue of personality in the image, and reads it in thoroughly abstract terms:

> [T]he unapproachable Thing which resists subjectivization, this point of failure of every identification, is ultimately *the subject itself* .... the ultimate "secret" of *Psycho* ... epitomized by Norman's gaze into the camera ... is that this Beyond is in itself hollow ... there is no depth of "soul" in it (Norman's gaze is utterly "soulless," like the gaze of monsters and the living dead) – as such, this Beyond *coincides with gaze itself.*
>
> (*Bold Gaze*, 245, 257)

The challenge to our notions of subjectivity in the shot is unmistakable; but why has this eerie alternative personality ("Mrs. Bates") suddenly reverted to being simply "Norman"? Perhaps Žižek needs to invoke a more recognizable version of a subject than the enigma in the cell to throw into relief the way in which the subject, as such, is emptied out by the gaps and divisions theorized by Lacan. Granting the theoretical cogency of this account of the subject in general, it is nonetheless disconcerting that Žižek's analysis requires such distancing from the particular subject in the image he begins with – in contrast to his intense engagement with the image of Arbogast's fall down the staircase. Something of the specificity of the climax of *Psycho* slips away from Žižek's account.

A more specific uncanniness in this image, having to do with the peculiar nature of "Mrs. Bates," emerges in her little joke, and with it her smile. Hitchcock said that he made the film with "quite a sense of amusement," that for him it was "a *fun* picture,"[24] and numerous critics (perhaps expressing indirectly their discomfiture with its problems of meaning) have referred to it as a joke: absurdist, sick, sadistic, gallows, or lavatory. Yet "Mrs. Bates's" joke feels different from any of these registers. Following up a perhaps accurate yet still paranoid line of thought that "they're probably watching me," she looks down at a fly on her hand (or no-longer-Norman's hand) and thinks, "I'm not even going to swat that fly. I hope they are watching ... They'll see and they'll know, and they'll say, 'Why she wouldn't even harm a fly.' " During this voice-over she begins to smile in a macabre way, and at the end, continuing to smile eerily, she looks up from under lowering brows directly at the camera. The smile confirms that it is a joke – that her sparing the fly is a pretence – but its force is enigmatic: Does she tacitly concede that she is lethally violent? That she is grimly satisfied to put one over on the authorities by blaming Norman? It is impossible to specify her intended meaning, except insofar as it must concern a gap between a sincere assertion that she wouldn't harm a fly and some, to her, redounding irony in that idea. The difficulty of – yet provocation for – reading this moment is compounded when she looks at the camera: for now we know that she knows that we are seeing her joke, and she virtually challenges us to interpret it. This joke needs no further punchline; it is a rhetorical gesture directed at the viewer, and the smile inescapably an index of personality – of thought and emotional attitude and interlocution. "Mrs. Bates," whoever or whatever she is, is a subject, though of a peculiar sort – not solely "*the subject itself*" as a hollow gaze.

This is not to humanize "Mrs. Bates," an alien presence and a tough customer, a persona that recedes even in asserting itself. It is this that makes her smile so uncanny, so creepily enjoyable. Still edging away from engaging this phenomenon, Žižek sees not a smile but a "mocking expression," which he reads as a gesture on Hitchcock's part, evoking his "modernist allegory" of the film's "own process of enunciation" ("In His Bold Gaze," 234, 218). Elsewhere, however, he speaks of a Lacanian concept that gives us better access to the valence of this moment: the concept (echoing the Marxian idea of the surplus value of a commodity) of "surplus enjoyment (*plus-de-jouir*,)" an exceeding of intelligible pleasure that has the paradoxical power to convert pleasure objects into their opposite, and vice versa – a reversible affective excess that captivates the viewer at this moment, leaving him or her both intrigued and appalled (*Looking Awry*, 12). "Surplus enjoyment" produces a nostalgia for a natural state in which one knew how to feel about an object of desire; but such a sense of loss no sooner flickers in these final moments of *Psycho* than it is mocked, as the lost stability and humanness of personality, which "Mrs. Bates" both elicits and defies, and as other images of loss that Hitchcock leaves us with: the mortal loss of the *vanitas* image of Mother's grinning skull that is superimposed over that smile for a fraction of a second, venerable Christian emblem of the afterlife, here a ghastly prospect – and, over "The End" in the final image of the film, the dredging-up-backwards of Marion's car, its trunk bearing the lost money and lost protagonist that no longer make the slightest difference to us.

We are close here to Žižek's ideas of a hollowness beyond signification; but if this culminating scene of *Psycho* is hauntingly uncanny, it is not through simply arriving at ideas that may even mollify one in their emptiness and relaxation of stakes. Such theorizing may well leave a feeling of nestling into the death drive. Yet the stakes of Žižek's argument can only be shown by preserving the experience of confrontation with the image of the subject in its alien immediacy, without which the effect is to identify with non-identity, rather than to expose a crucial slippage within the movement of identification itself. In the figure of "Mrs. Bates," it is as if the death drive itself comes back to life, without being discernibly less deathly: uncanny precisely in the uncertainty Freud describes, as to whether one is confronting a phenomenon

Figure 8.1. Mrs. Bates's smile. *Psycho* (1960).

of life or of death, or some horrifying indistinction between them – as if, Norman gone, the film itself has taken over hallucination, coinciding with it. As a subjective presence, "Mrs. Bates" seems to claim a kind of undead subjectivity for the place of the Real – as if the Real were "looking" at us even though it does not look, does not mean; challenging us with an intimation not only that all signification is exceeded by an inert and empty beyond – for to say this is to offer the nescience, the voiding of innervation, of the death drive, which Freud posited as the consummation devoutly wished by every organism – but that even "there" in that empty Beyond, we cannot rest, cannot do without a haunting by the undead phantasm of subjectivity. It is not really subjectivity, however; has no ineffable depth, as Žižek rightly insists; nor is it, after all, a "place," either. Christopher Pye describes the Real as a movement or slippage of the subject out of the signifying frame, sliding away from its inscription there only as a figure of self-annulment.[25] Such a receding figure may be glimpsed in "Mrs. Bates's" smile (Figure 8.1): holding out a ghastly promise as a simulacrum of subjectivity, a kind of object for our enjoyment, her smile dies on the lips – the lips that were never really hers, and are no-longer-Norman's. "Mrs. Bates's" smile is the index of a personality that slips away, in its uncanny animating intelligence, even as it is mouthed by a body voided of its animating subjectivity, yet still undead.

NOTES

1 "The Making of *Psycho*," in *Psycho*, dir. Alfred Hitchcock (1960; Universal City, CA: Universal Studios, 2000), DVD.

2 Stephen Rebello, *Alfred Hitchcock and the Making of "Psycho"* (New York: Dembner, 1990), p. 128.

3 Janet Leigh's account of Hitchcock's direction, in Leigh, with Christopher Nickens, *"Psycho": Behind the Scenes of the Classic Thriller* (New York: Crown, 1995), p. 70.

4 Hitchcock, quoted by François Truffaut in *Hitchcock* (New York: Simon and Schuster, 1967), p. 207.

5 Laura Mulvey, "Alfred Hitchcock's *Psycho* (1960)," in her volume *Death 24x a Second: Stillness and the Moving Image* (London: Reaktion Books, 2006), pp. 86–92.

6 See Bellour's influential analysis of *Psycho* in his *The Analysis of Film*, ed. Constance Penley (Bloomington: Indiana University Press, 2000).

7 Kaja Silverman, *The Acoustic Mirror: The Female Voice in Psychoanalysis and Cinema* (Bloomington: Indiana University Press, 1988), pp. 38–39.

8 Kaja Silverman, *The Subject of Semiotics* (New York: Oxford University Press, 1983), p. 211.

9 William Rothman, *Hitchcock: The Murderous Gaze*, 2nd ed. (Albany: SUNY Press, 2012), pp. 300–307.

10 See Sigmund Freud, "The Dissolution of the Oedipus Complex," *The Standard Edition of the Complete Psychological Works of Sigmund Freud*, tr. James Strachey, vol. XIX (London: Hogarth, 1961), pp. 171–179.

11 Slavoj Žižek, *Looking Awry: An Introduction to Jacques Lacan through Popular Culture* (Cambridge, MA: MIT Press, 1992), p. 99.

12 Slavoj Žižek, "'In His Bold Gaze My Ruin Is Writ Large,'" in Žižek, ed., *Everything You Always Wanted to Know about Lacan (But Were Afraid to Ask Hitchcock)* (London and New York: Verso, 1992), pp. 228–229.

13 Dylan Evans, *An Introductory Dictionary of Lacanian Psychoanalysis* (London and New York: Routledge, 1996), pp. 136–137.

14 Freud, "Mourning and Melancholia," *Standard Edition*, vol. XIV, p. 246.

15 Freud, "Neurosis and Psychosis," *Standard Edition*, vol. XIX, pp. 150–151, 152–153.

16 Freud, "An Outline of Psychoanalysis," *Standard Edition*, vol. XXIII, p. 202.

17 "Splitting of the Ego in the Process of Defence," *Standard Edition*, vol. XXIII, p. 275; "The Loss of Reality in Neurosis and Psychosis," *Standard Edition*, vol. XIX, p. 185.

18 "Mourning *or* Melancholia: Introjection *versus* Incorporation," in Nicolas Abraham and Maria Torok, *The Shell and the Kernel: Renewals of Psychoanalysis*, vol. 1, ed. Nicholas T. Rand (Chicago: The University of Chicago Press, 1994), p. 131.

19 "'The Lost Object – Me': Notes on Endocryptic Identification," in Abraham and Torok, p. 141.

20 Shirl G. Yang, *Spectral Hitchcock* (B.A. Thesis, Williams College, 2013), p. 16.

21 Linda Williams, "Discipline and Fun: *Psycho* and Postmodern Cinema," in Robert Kolker, ed., *Alfred Hitchcock's* Psycho: *A Casebook* (Oxford, New York: Oxford University Press, 2004), p. 180. Linda Williams, "Discipline and Fun: *Psycho* and Postmodern Cinema," in *Reinventing Film Studies*, ed. Christine Gledhill and Linda Williams (London: Arnold, 2000), p. 362.

22 Michel Chion, "The Impossible Embodiment," in Žižek, ed., *Everything*, p. 204.

23 "In His Bold Gaze," pp. 226, 234.

24 Quoted by Robin Wood, *Hitchcock's Films Revisited*, revised ed. (New York: Columbia University Press, 2002), p. 142.

25 Christopher Pye, *The Regal Phantasm: Shakespeare and the Politics of Spectacle* (London and New York: Routledge, 1990), p. 91.

PART III

Hitchcock's American Films: Some Case Studies in Form and Content

9

ALAN NADEL

Expedient Exaggeration and the Scale of Cold War Farce in *North by Northwest*

North by Northwest (1959) contains a stunning and also frustrating God's-eye-view of Roger Thornhill fleeing the UN building, immediately after he has been photographed standing, with a bloody knife in his hand, over the corpse of Lester Townsend. In a compilation of confusions typical of bedroom farce, Thornhill has by this relatively early point in the film been misrecognized, misunderstood, or disbelieved by almost everyone he has encountered, from the thugs working for Vandamm, the head of an international espionage ring, to the Glen Cove police, to the staff at the Plaza Hotel, to his own mother. In the tradition of classic farce, the film generates momentum from the mounting frustration produced by the collision between what perception confirms and memory denies. Thornhill remembers being kidnapped, being force-fed a bottle of bourbon at the Townsend estate, and being forced to drive an automobile with near-fatal consequences. The ostensive Mrs. Townsend, when questioned by the police the next day, confirms Thornhill's memory of the Townsend estate, but insists he was an intoxicated dinner guest who left early, in the same way that Vandamm, as the ostensive Mr. Townsend, had insisted the night before that Thornhill "remember" he is CIA operative George Kaplan.

Comedy and Madness

As many have noted – associating it with black humor or, following Stanley Cavell, a comedy of remarriage – *North by Northwest* has a strong comic component.[1] None of these discussions, however, points out that formally *North by Northwest* is, more specifically, a *farce*.

Dating from antiquity, farce – one of the most enduring forms of comic drama – relies on misconceptions, mistaken identities, and the mayhem endemic to a world that seems to have lost its mind, for which reason, honesty, or morality provides no antidotes. Rather, farce functions much like the Derridian pharmakon, its own internal logic mandating supplemental toxins as the only remedy for a toxified reality. "One might argue," John Dennis Hurrell says,

> that farce, with its temporary reversal of the well-ordered and morally directed world, is a kind of assertion of man's continual capacity for setting his house in order through the ingenious use of his capacity to make practical, rather than ethical decisions.[2]

But the situation of farce is that those "practical" decisions are made while dealing with a world that seems to have gone mad. The central character in a farce, therefore, resembles Hamlet when he utters the phrase to which *North by Northwest*'s title alludes: "I am but mad north-north-west. When the wind is southerly I know a hawk from a hand-saw" (II, ii). Doubting the sanity of the world into which he has been plunged by a ghost appearing to be his father, Hamlet forestalls making an ethical decision by making the practical decision to feign madness, lest he be deceived by a case of mistaken identity. ("The spirit that I have seen/ May be a devil," he states, "and the devil hath power/ T'assume a pleasing shape" [II, ii].)[3]

That the devil in *North by Northwest* has the power to assume a pleasing shape is certainly exemplified in casting the handsome and suave James Mason to play the role of the demonic Vandamm. His calm self-assurance sets the perfect pitch for the absolutely farcical opening episode of the film, in which, true to the ethos of farce, everyone is a victim: advertising executive Roger Thornhill, during a business meeting in a cocktail lounge at the Plaza, attempts to signal the bellboy so that he may send a telegram. He makes the signal, however, at exactly the moment that the boy is paging a "George Kaplan." This leads two thugs to mistake Thornhill for Kaplan and therefore to kidnap him. They take him to the Glen Cove estate of Lester Townsend. There Vandamm, whom we later learn heads an espionage ring, demands to know what "Kaplan" knows about Vandamm's operation; but he makes that demand of Thornhill, who knows nothing about Vandamm's operation or about Kaplan's. Were Thornhill aware of Kaplan's operation, he would know that Kaplan's identity was created because the CIA didn't know enough about Vandamm's operation. In other words, when Thornhill tells Vandamm that he doesn't know anything, this is more or less true, whether he is speaking for himself or for Kaplan, but a premise of farce is that the conditions that circumscribe speech render truth unreliable. The fiction of Kaplan, we later learn, must be maintained (even posthumously) because, as the Professor who directs the CIA's unit following Vandamm explains, "we don't know enough about [Vandamm's] operation." But when Vandamm hears this truth from the man he presumes to be Kaplan, he is certain the utterance is fictitious.

If these events exemplify farce, more generally farce could be viewed as the quintessential Hitchcock genre, especially in the way that (in Eric Bentley's words) "farce brings together the direct and wild fantasies and the everyday and drab realities."[4] After all, almost all of Hitchcock's films involve in some way the wrong man mistaken for the right one, not just as an initiating plot mechanism but repeatedly, and by everyone. It is not just that Hannay in *The 39 Steps* is taken for a murderer or a politician or, by the Scottish farmer, for the seducer of his wife, but that Hannay also misperceives others. With nearly fatal consequences, for example, he takes the Professor for the man who will exonerate him rather than a villain who would kill him. Charlie, in *Shadow of a Doubt*, mistakes her uncle Charlie for her savior, and initially he makes the same mistake about his niece. *Notorious* is an encyclopedia of misconceptions and mistaken identities organized around Devlin's and Alicia's misperceptions of one another, misperceptions echoed equally by the CIA and by Alicia's husband, Alex, as well as by Alex's overt household (himself, his mother, his servants) and his covert household (the spy ring). In fact, it would be hard to find a Hitchcock film that did not have moments of classic farce. What, after all, is the trouble with Harry all about?

In *North by Northwest,* however, farce is more sustained and more integral to the film's thematics than in any other Hitchcock work. For Hitchcock is using farce not just to reflect the human condition (at least for the creatures of Hitchcock's world) but also to construct a sustained commentary on the historically specific circumstances of the Cold War.

National and International Farce

Much of *North by Northwest* criticism understandably underscores the film's Americanness. Specifically, Thornhill/Grant, Steven Cohan has shown, represents an examination of the American character in crisis.[5] The poster for the film, Cohan points out, which shows a man in free fall, provides a disoriented exemplar of the mid-century professional class, as much dislodged from the film's diegesis as is the character Thornhill from his customary routines or the actor Grant from the masculine image that his screen persona had come to signify. In this context, I want to suggest that Thornhill's adventure also undermines the fundamental meaning of allegiance that the concept of the double – be it the double agent, the Communist cell member, or the closeted homosexual – constantly worries within the cultural scheme of Cold War binaries.

Foregrounding the regulatory systems of the 1950s, Robert Corber reads Thornhill's engagement with the CIA, through the persona of George

Kaplan, as the process whereby Thornhill serves his country. He does so by learning to regulate his unruly and disorganized character in a manner consistent with what Corber calls "the Cold War settlement," which politicized the regulation of private life as much as it sexualized the political identity of American citizens. "When Thornhill agrees to impersonate Kaplan," Corber accurately points out, "he demonstrates his maturity as an American citizen."[6]

The Cold War, as Corber demonstrates, explains a great deal about Thornhill. Thornhill and *North by Northwest*, this essay argues, also says a great deal about the Cold War, which projected a politically bifurcated world as a courtship narrative, in which the Soviets, figured both as seductresses and as rival suitors, reflected an inescapable duality in ostensibly monolithic blocs.[7] Framed by the trope of courtship, every state was always already potential partner and potential rival for other couplings.

Nothing exemplifies better the failed attempt to mask the dualities of Cold War international rivalries than the UN Charter, written in 1945.[8] "The Organization is based on the principle of the sovereign equality of all its Members," the Charter emphatically states, in the spirit of which the Charter empowers the General Assembly to admit states that comply with UN principles and exclude those that do not, the chief criterion for acceptance being that the states be "peace-loving" (Article 4, item 1). Therefore, UN members pledge themselves to "effective collective measures for the prevention and removal of the threats to peace." At the same time, the members also accept the UN's role in the "*suppression* of acts of aggression or breaches of the peace" (emphasis added). Thus, while all members "shall settle their international disputes by peaceful means in such a manner that international peace and security, and justice, are not endangered" (Article 2, item 2), the member states must also agree "to make available to the Security Council, on its call and in accordance with a special agreement or agreements, armed forces, assistance and facilities, including right of passage, necessary for the purpose of maintaining international peace and security" (Article 43, item 1), for the Security Council may decide to "take such action by air, sea, or land forces as may be necessary to maintain or restore international peace and security" (Article 42).

If the decision to "take such action" is, in theory, equally binding on equal members, all equally pledged to international peace, the manner of compliance is determined by a body structured to preserve the *inequality* of its members. Of all member states, only fifteen serve on the Security Council; of those fifteen, only five are permanent. Even among the privileged permanent members, a structural inequality enables one member to veto decisions made not just by the majority of Security Council members, who had been elected by a majority of the member states, but also decisions made by a majority or supermajority of the four other permanent Security Council members. In the interest of achieving a world peace based on the equality of nations, the equal states must submit to an inequitable distribution of power, so that if all sovereign states are equal, a la the UN Charter, some states, a la *Animal Farm*, are more equal than others.

International Farce and Expedient Exaggeration

In light of this background it may be apt that the backdrop for the only successful murder in *North by Northwest* – ultimately the only successful covert activity in the film of any sort – is the site constructed to maintain world peace. "In a film in which international relations are seen as conducted in terms of the blackjack manifestations of rival cliques of spies," George Wilson notes, "the usual symbolism of the United Nations appears more than ordinarily bizarre."[9] In the macabre and, I think, intentionally political structure of the film, Hitchcock makes this political irony – the murder of Townsend at the UN – the logical extension of the bedroom farce at the Plaza where, for Thornhill, the farcical energy of all the initial mistakes, misconceptions, and misrepresentations had a short time earlier culminated in overt laughter. Having gotten access to Kaplan's room, Thornhill, in front of his skeptical mother, interviews the chamber maid and the valet, each of whom confirm – in scenes echoing Shakespeare's *A Comedy of Errors* – that he is indeed George Kaplan although he has no knowledge of being Kaplan. Then the phone rings, and Thornhill answers it, in effect confirming to his callers what he continues to deny to his mother. Who else but Kaplan, the callers rightfully reason, would answer the phone in Kaplan's hotel room? Thornhill has thus identified and located Kaplan for the callers, and they head up from the hotel lobby to complete their homicidal mission, while Thornhill, like the man in a French farce unjustly pursued by an angry cuckold, flees before the circumstances that incorrectly prove his guilt actually result in his death.

Because split-second timing is the essential lubricant of well-made farce, Thornhill and his mother enter the crowded descending elevator exactly one second after the potential assailants exit the adjacent ascending one, allowing the two thugs to join Thornhill and his mother. When Thornhill signals his mother that these are his pursuers, she asks, loudly, "You gentlemen aren't really trying to kill my son, are you?" The villains disguise their discomfort with laughter that, starting out nervously, grows stronger and becomes contagious, leaving Thornhill the awkwardly unamused butt of a joke, illustrating that, as Bermel points out, farce "has two main laughter-releasing mechanisms: characters who are only partially engaging, and improbable situations in which they are caught up."[10] The scene in the elevator thus intersects two forms of hysteria – the hilarity of farce and the immobility of fear – such that the laughter proves a release valve for the incipient violence, and comedy trumps terror.

Or rather, as we find out in the next scene, simply defers it. The Plaza episode illustrates that farce, as Eric Bentley notes, "is a conception that bristles with menace" (248), a bristling that virtually spills out of the Plaza's bedroom and into the United Nations Secretariat. Once again the confusion of mistaken identity and the anxiety of escalating danger play out when Thornhill, meeting the real Lester Townsend at the UN, replicates the previous night's scene in Townsend's Glen Cove estate, where Vandamm, playing the role of Townsend, refuses to believe that Thornhill is actually Thornhill. Now Thornhill, playing George Kaplan, similarly refuses to believe that Townsend is Townsend. Thornhill's misconception, however, gets an innocent man killed; Thornhill succeeds, in other words, where Vandamm had failed. The moment is pure farce: Thornhill went to the UN because the police exonerated the fake Townsend from the attempted murder of Thornhill, which precipitates the murder of the real Townsend by the command of the fake Townsend, who had attempted to kill George Kaplan, whom he thought was the fake Roger Thornhill. But Thornhill, by being blamed for the murder of the real Townsend, in effect exonerates the fake Townsend once more.

At the UN the hilarity in the Plaza elevator is replaced by the violence it has forestalled. By transferring its energy from the hotel to the UN, the film graphs the potential violence of bedroom farce to the actual violence of international espionage. In so doing, Hitchcock brokers an unholy marriage, one suggesting that the Cold War is not only a courtship narrative but one in which even the most innocent ad men cannot keep the blood off of their hands, the whole thing – the myth of nationalism and the myth of internationalism, the covertness of covert action or its overt objectives, the relentless auctioning of allegiance and the transparency of puppet states, the arbitrary relationship between legitimacy and demonization, the fundamental distinction between hot and cold wars – is pure farce writ grotesquely large.

The God's-eye-view shot of Thornhill fleeing the UN, which reduces him to an ant, *reveals* his utter unimportance from the perspective of the UN's global politics, underwritten throughout the Cold War by an array of actions, often involving UN soldiers (Figure 9.1).

The UN member states, moreover, were simultaneously engaged in multilayered competitions with one another: armed conflicts, as in Korea;

Figure 9.1. The God's-eye-view shot of Thornhill fleeing the UN.
North by Northwest (1959).

counterinsurgency, as in Vietnam; armed intervention, as in Hungary; as well as covert operations by the United States, the Soviet Union, and numerous cohorts and subsidiary states throughout Africa and Latin America. In addition, an intelligence war, commencing with the multinational scramble for postwar German secrets and scientists, remained unabated for more than forty years, organized primarily along the polarities of the Cold War axes.

Expedient Exaggeration

The idea that the UN was operating at cross purposes is implied by the stunning Saul Bass opening credit sequence that presents a series of vertical lines, intersected not horizontally but skewed by 30 degrees from the horizontal axis (Figure 9.2), suggesting the film is more about misalignment than alignment, especially in that the credits follow the skewed lines rather than parallel the implicit horizontal border.

As these credits appear, the green background transforms into a large glass office building, with a façade that resembles that of the UN. As in the shot of Thornhill fleeing the UN, we are high up, in this instance not looking directly down but rather from an angle that gives us a distorted reflection of the traffic of daily life below, the life belonging to individual citizens rather than to an abstract notion of global citizenship. That is the ground-level traffic we will see in the final credit shot and the opening action to which it segues:

Figure 9.2. The skewed credits that open the film.
North by Northwest.

Roger Thornhill is rushing out of an elevator of a busy midtown office building while dictating to his secretary. Even though they are only a few blocks from the Plaza, she urges him to take a cab, and he secures one by telling the people who are about to enter it that he is with a sick woman. Inside the cab, his secretary chides him, "You knew you were lying." "In the world of advertising," he responds, "there's no such thing as a lie. There's only expedient exaggeration." Thornhill's quip not only identifies a convention of farce but also connects it to important issues of scale implied by the cut from the lofty skyscraper to the quotidian, anonymous rush of city pedestrians. The sequence's simultaneous transition from the stars named in the credits to the ordinary characters they play in the story similarly signals two registers of scale important to the film. In addition, Thornhill's quip associates him with the character he is about to become, the CIA's expedient exaggeration, George Kaplan.

"Expedient exaggeration" is also a good way to describe the UN's mandate to secure world peace. "The UN's later embrace of anti-colonialism" Mark Mazower explains, "has tended to obscure the awkward fact that like the League it was the product of empire and indeed, at least at the outset, regarded by those with colonies to keep as a more than adequate mechanism."[11] Nationalism, furthermore, requires expedients because nations need informing myths to unify a large and multifarious population. One has only to consider the quotations from Chairman Mao, Stalin's revisionist history, or the proliferation of adult Westerns on American television in the

1950s to recognize the zeal with which the Cold War employed the principle of expedient exaggeration. Perhaps nothing more grotesquely literalizes this aspect of American mytho-historical hagiography than the heads carved into Mount Rushmore.

Vandamm, who proves to be in many ways Thornhill's kindred spirit, articulates Thornhill's proclivity toward expedient exaggeration when, at the auction in the middle of the film, he accuses Thornhill of "overplaying" his part. This is another way, among several, in which Vandamm doubles Thornhill. Like Vandamm (an anagrammatic echo of "ad man"), Thornhill sells ideas, and like him, Thornhill is a-moral. Late in the film, Thornhill arranges for the murder of Kaplan, the man he is impersonating, in order to keep secret the identity of another operative. In order to keep secret his identity as an international operative, Vandamm, similarly, had arranged for the murder of Lester Townsend, the man whom *he* impersonated.

But the most obvious doubling is that Vandamm and Thornhill are Eve's lovers, both lovers who, unaware of her double identity, put her in mortal danger. Unlike the Professor, who lured Eve into becoming a double agent with an appeal to principle, Vandamm seduced her, as did Thornhill, with charm, no doubt in part owing in the case of each man, as played by Grant and Mason, to an ersatz accent that converted a signifier of British national-ity into a geographically unspecifiable cosmopolitanism – exactly the work that the UN Charter performed of masking nationalism through vague, con-tradictory allusions to globalism.

Cold War Stars

Because stars, as this attention to accents illustrates, import to a film an array of associations beyond the film's narrative and the roles the actors play in it, the star is larger than his or her character, at time even arguably larger than the film itself. Hitchcock's use of stars thus constitutes one of many important issues of scale at work in *North by Northwest*, a film in which stars abound. These include not just Grant, Mason, and Eva Marie Saint (who at age thirty-four had already been nominated for two Emmys and won several film awards in the United States and abroad, including an Oscar) but also Leo G. Carroll, who had become a minor star on American television. In the doubling that proliferates in *North by Northwest*, these four stars in the end compete for screen space with four of American histo-ry's greatest stars, the Mount Rushmore Presidents.

Carroll also doubles Grant and Mason in that he too was a British actor who developed a distinctive manner of speaking. This similarity clues us to the overlooked fact that the Professor is as much a rival for Eve as are Thornhill and Vandamm. On one level, the film thus presents three British actors, Grant, Mason, and Carroll, vying to play the American Adam to Eva's Eve. Furthermore, the character Carroll plays is as perplexing as those of his male rivals. Although connections between *North by Northwest* and *The 39 Steps* have been pointed out,[12] no one has underscored the fact that in *The 39 Steps* "The Professor" names one of the most heinously cold-blooded villains in Hitchcock's canon. Most probably, this allusion is downplayed because in *North by Northwest* the Professor is on "our" side in the Cold War, and therefore we tend to assume, as did Eve (and as did Hannay in *The 39 Steps*), that the Professor's work is virtuous.

Just as Carroll's stardom is overshadowed by the leading actors, so too is the Professor's role. Dispassionately, he facilitates attempts to kill both Thornhill and Eve (and with equal dispassion has Vandamm's close associate, Leonard, shot). This typifies, however, the way the CIA actually worked, as it was not populated with flashy, debonair operatives, figures like Cary Grant (Grant turned down the role of James Bond before it was offered to Sean Connery) but with inconspicuous bureaucrats like Leo G. Carroll.[13] Equally inconspicuous was the way the CIA operated, through involvement with numerous American businesses, agencies, and organizations that fronted for it, including, infamously, the National Student Association.[14] In regard to foreign policy, the CIA worked covertly, often – and strategically – in direct contradiction to explicit U.S. policy. For example, John Foster Dulles, Secretary of State under President Eisenhower, made it appear that the United States was not involved in the internal affairs of other countries, while the CIA, run by his brother, Allen Dulles, orchestrated many regime changes throughout the 1950s. When these regimes fell, the United States, with John as its spokesman, played the benign albeit enthusiastic observer.[15] Officially, in other words, the United States abided by the UN Charter, while operating in blatant disregard for it.

If the "slow dissolve from Grant's face to the face of Mount Rushmore" denotes for William Rothman that "Grant is an authentic American hero" (244), I think it is because Rothman has fallen for Hitchcock's trick.[16] Grant, like all the rivals for Eva's Eve, is only disguised as American. In the dissolve Rothman praises, Hitchcock establishes the authenticity not of Grant but of George Kaplan, the ghost of George Kerby from the 1937 film, *Topper*, who launched the Grant star persona on one of the greatest trajectories in American film history. Like Mount Rushmore, Grant is an allusion to an illusion, a blank space revealed, as so many have noted, by the "O" at the center of Roger Thornhill's logo; Thornhill himself says it stands for nothing.

The "O" also turns his name to "ROT," thereby evoking the usual negative connotations associated with ad men. Cavell, truncating the quote from Shakespeare, also points out that Thornhill's trademark suggests "Hamlet's sense that something is rotten." The full line reads, "something is rotten in the state of Denmark" (*Hamlet* I, iv) a comment not on Hamlet but on the state. In other words, reading Thornhill's monogram through the film's allusions to *Hamlet* suggests that the state is rotten. Should it be any surprise, therefore, that the name in *The 39 Steps* identifying Hitchcock's quintessential villain now has been given to a CIA unit head?

The mélange of contradictory identities and the tricks they play with the loyalties of the characters and the assumptions of the audience make clear that George Wilson is correct when he says that, in *North by Northwest*, "the field of action is filled with a parade of performers who bear a problematic relation to their roles" (1169). But not so much because, as Wilson contends, they constitute a meta-commentary on the art of filmmaking, but rather because they compete generically under the global auspices of the UN and the duplicity it both masks and signifies.

The commonality of the principals consolidates at the auction scene, the only time when all four share the same space. Hitchcock shoots the scene as a relentless array of courtship triangles emulating the Cold War competition for partners among the member nations, ostensibly united by their common goals and interests. Grant and Mason, both in grey suits, white shirts, and grey ties square off against each other in perfect profile, with Eve directly between them (Figure 9.3).

This love triangle is preceded by a series of other triangulations, including one between Eve, Vandamm, and his homosexual secretary, Leonard, and one between Vandamm, Thornhill, and the Professor. The most important triangle for the purposes of this discussion, however, is between Vandamm, the visual track (where Eve is the figure of his affection), and the audio track (where the figurine as the object of his desire). The figurine identifies Vandamm with the UN's world of international espionage, as it contains the microfilm, whose secrets render microscopic Thornhill's personal affections or well-being, in the same way that the God's-eye-view shot from the top of the UN did.

The Scale of the Cold War

These shots and the political perspectives they represent contribute to the film's organization around issues of scale: Our attention is twice called to Eve's tiny razor, and Thornhill locked in the upper birth of Eve's train compartment compares himself to a sardine (Figure 9.4).

Figure 9.3. Grant and Mason, in grey suits, square off against each other, with
Eve directly between them.
North by Northwest.

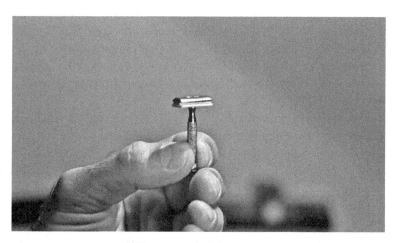

Figure 9.4. Eve's tiny razor.
North by Northwest.

When Thornhill is deposited on the road cutting through the expanse
of northern Indiana cornfields, long shots emphasize the disproportion
between his stature and the vast, flat landscape, and the refrigerator in the
back of the pickup truck Thornhill steals seems disproportionate to its con-
veyance. Even the early shots when Thornhill and then Vandamm first enter
Townsend's library suggest that something about the scale is slightly off, in
that they show Thornhill's and then Vandamm's full body, a portion of the

Figure 9.5. Thornhill's full body, and an expanse of the wall above, instead of the
conventional shot from the knees up.
North by Northwest.

floor, and a significant expanse of the wall above, instead of the more conventional Hollywood shot from the knees up (Figure 9.5).

In the film, Hitchcock's "conflation of cinematic subjects" (the "small"
and the "big"), Jonathan Auerbach and Lisa Gitelman insightfully note,
"corrupts the spectator's intuitive sense of scale" (745). This corruption is an
issue because intimacy is a dynamic of scale, in that closeness renders large, as
it does a tiny razor, what from another perspective might seem very small, in
the same way that a man on the street would from the top of the UN building.
Thus, its capacity for the close-up has, virtually since its inception, rendered
cinema an intimate medium. "With the close-up," Béla Balázs wrote in 1924,
"the new territory of this new art opens up."[17]

In the two-dimensional space of the cinematic medium, moreover, size
and distance share a common code, such that being larger makes things
closer. Thus the national and international agendae that loom large at the
UN render the lives of particular citizens, distant, that is, microscopic,
like Thornhill in the God's-eye-view shot with which I started. In terms
of national issues, in other words, intimacy is symbolic and romance is
metonymic. Love of country is, by definition, only possible as a member
of an impersonal mass, while love of an individual requires making that
individual distinct from and larger than the general populace. Politics and
(hot or cold) warfare subordinate the individual to the greater good, the
"big picture," while romance turns the big picture into a backdrop for

the expediently exaggerated desires of a few privileged individuals. The romantic couple represents metonymically all the true lovers in the population, while the nation represents symbolically a love greater than individual desires. As Rick says to Ilsa on an airfield of French-occupied North Africa, at the moment in *Casablanca* when nationalism – American and French – trumps romance, "it doesn't take much to see that the problems of three little people don't amount to a hill of beans in this crazy world." They will always have Paris, in other words, only if the Germans do not.

On the chart of scale relations I have just sketched, with nationalism at one end and romance on the other, farce becomes a radical extreme: the intimacy of romance exaggerated to grotesque proportions, in that farce requires a population of individuals with such inflated drives that everything *but* the problems of three little people amounts to a hill of beans. Thus by putting farce and espionage in conflict, Hitchcock forces us to view the same characters through opposite ends of a telescope, rendering them alternatively too distant and too intimate.

This too is the way we regard stars. On screen, they are not just characters but also everything that draws audiences to them, independent of the characters they are portraying. Just as the optics of the telescope, operating in two directions, allow antithetical interpretations of scale, stars both fill the roles of their characters and also exceed them. Stars bring to films a priori intimacy with their audience; stardom creates both an aura of grandness and a concomitant sense of closeness, each effect dependent on the close-up. "With the formation of a star system heavily dependent upon the maintenance of the aura," Mary Ann Doane reminds us, "the close-up became an important means of establishing the recognizability of each star."[18] In terms of the issues of scale at work in *North by Northwest*, stars make large the people who, from the international perspective of the UN, would be otherwise reduced to anonymous dots. The fate of Eve and Roger is minuscule, compared to that of the tiny microfilm. Thus the parallel characters, Thornhill and Vandamm, underscored by the star personae of Grant and Mason, replicate the competition between national and romantic objects by internalizing them. In this sense, we can see Vandamm's conflict as his having to decide through which end of the telescope he should view Eve. Although he eventually decides to regard her as distant and small – his final plan is to throw her into the ocean – his hesitancy leads to his undoing. The same holds true in reverse for Thornhill, who, despite all the demands that his stardom be invested in a nationalist ethos, cannot resist seeing Eve as the inflated object of his personal beloved gaze.

These issues of scale, intimacy, romance, and nationalism are powerfully represented in the scene at the auction which pits the auras of the two stars against one another. Importantly, in that scene, the figurine is larger, in terms of national security, than anything except the even smaller microfilm it contains. The brilliant and very peculiar framing in the scene makes vivid the interpersonal and international conflicts at stake in these issues of scale, while underscoring that both issues are characterized by courtship narratives. In numerous shots we see only the very top of Eve's blonde head at the very bottom of a frame that features the heads and upper torsos of Thornhill, Vandamm, and Leonard. Such framing is usually considered verboten, especially in the Classical Hollywood style that attempts to present characters as whole and to obscure the viewer's cognizance of the frame. The appearance of a cut-off head top at the bottom of the screen would almost certainly indicate an error, something accidentally overlooked when the daily rushes were reviewed. But because the top of Eve's head appears in several shots – nineteen discrete shots in a ninety-second sequence – Hitchcock is clearly using the stylistic transgression as a motif. As the shots change, moreover, the blond head top shifts back and forth along the bottom of the frame, such that the audio auction for large espionage secrets competes with a parallel "auction" over Eve (Figure 9.6).

The men, oriented and reoriented above Eve's head, also trope (or are troped by) the final chase over the heads on Mt. Rushmore, again, albeit inversely, for possession of the two "objects" at the auction, the statue and Eve. If the shot from the top of the UN makes Thornhill look microscopic, the shots on Mount Rushmore make the national icons look grotesque, suggesting that in this second struggle the significance of the two key objects has been radically redefined by a world of pervasive personal duality: the two Kaplans, the two Townsends, and the double agent, Eve. The dual scales at work in the film – and in any concept of nations united internationally – are perhaps best represented by the sequence Hitchcock was not allowed to film: "What I wanted to do," Hitchcock told Arthur Knight, "and was prevented from doing, was to have Cary Grant slide down Lincoln's nose and hide in the nostril. Then, I wanted Grant to have a sneezing fit," thus evoking an unavoidable contrast between Lincoln's monumental, immobile nose and Thornhill's tiny, animate one, that is, between the small spontaneity of human agency and the overwhelming rigidity of national symbolism.[19]

Again, as Farce

This takes me to one more parallel. Like the UN episode, the sequence immediately following, at the CIA headquarters, concludes with a God's-eye-view shot, this one also used to mark Thornhill's insignificance on the stage of global politics. The Professor's staff has figured out the events

Figure 9.6. As the shots change, Eve's blond head-top shifts back and forth
along the bottom border of the frame.
North by Northwest.

culminating in Townsend's murder, their farcical quality acknowledged by
one assistant when he says, "So horribly sad … somehow I feel like laughing." The Professor then concludes they should do nothing to save Thornhill,
and Hitchcock cuts to a God's-eye-view shot of entire board table, while
another assistant, the only woman in the group, announces: "Goodbye Mr.
Thornhill, wherever you are."[20]

The concluding God's-eye-view shots of these two successive episodes suggests that the CIA, like the UN, plays God. The shot from the UN visually
deprives Thornhill of all identity, making his life worthless, and the shot at

the CIA, through the sound track, weds him to a false identity that makes his life expendable. In two successive scenes, first the visual and then the audio register render Thornhill negligible, as devoid of meaning as the "O" in his logo. Viewed from on high, Kaplan is just another U.S. front and the farcical hotel bedroom his puppet state. Thornhill, therefore, will serve as well as any interchangeable figurehead upon whom the United States has conferred bogus identity, just as in the end he will climb over a monumental set of American figureheads, scrambling for a small figurine, with even smaller figures on microfilm, in order to return his identity to the human scale of the bedroom farce, the marriage plot, the courtship narrative, shorn of its Cold War alignments and misalignments, consummated in the small upper berth of a sleeping compartment of a train thrusting itself into a dark tunnel.

Hitchcock, has acknowledged – as has just about everyone else – the symbolic consummation projected by the final shot. Hitchcock's joke on the censors is writ awfully large: only a full frontal carving of Lincoln, all the way to the base of Mount Rushmore, could produce a phallus as huge as the Twentieth Century Limited. At the same time, the tunnel also returns Thornhill to the dark hole, that zero at the center of his constructed logo, which Robert Stam identifies with the arbitrariness of Hitchcock's plot devices:

> The espionage of *North-by-Northwest* forms a Hitchcockian McGuffin ...
> The purpose of the spies, like those of the CIA, remains obscure, hollow like
> the 'O' in Roger Thornhill's name that "stands for nothing."[21]

But perhaps more accurately the *microfilm* is the film's McGuffin and espionage its theme, the central intelligence whose agency is thematized by all the intersecting narratives: the Oedipal story (a quintessential espionage narrative), the romance story, the advertising/propaganda story, and the international rivalry story. Espionage is a subversive activity, one relying on untrustworthy allegiance, divided loyalties, and malleable identities. Those critics who argue that Thornhill actually is Kaplan are right, perhaps, to the extent that this is a Cold War film. Its unity comes not from disdain of historical specificity but from engagement with it. In this regard, Hitchcock seems to be citing Marx, who wrote: "Hegel remarks somewhere that all great events and characters of world history occur, so to speak, twice. He forgot to add: the first time as tragedy, the second as farce."[22]

NOTES

1 See, among others, Marian Keane, "The Designs of Authorship: An Essay on *North by Northwest*," *Wide Angle* 4 (1980), pp. 44–52; Robin Wood, *Hitchcock's Films Revisited*, 2nd edition (New York: Columbia University Press, 2002), p. 101; Stanley Cavell, "*North by Northwest*," *Critical Inquiry* 7 (1981),

pp. 762–763; Robert Allen, *Hitchcock's Romantic Irony* (New York: Columbia University Press, 2007), pp. 59–60.

2 John Dennis Hurrell, "A Note on Farce," *Quarterly Review of Speech* 45 (1959), p. 210.

3 Cavell devotes much time to the *Hamlet* reference in the film only to conclude that Hitchcock is announcing that he wishes to compete with Shakespeare's most famous play and that it is a play. Cavell fails to consider that *Hamlet* is a famous play *about* something, about a student thrust into a world of murder and intrigue about which he has no understanding and for which no preparation. His ability to respond is relentlessly complicated by his inability to distinguish illusion from reality, and by the necessity to assume a false identity with real consequences.

4 Eric Bentley, *The Life of the Drama* (New York: Atheneum, 1964), p. 241.

5 Steven Cohan, *Masked Men: Masculinity and the Movies in the Fifties* (Bloomington: University of Indiana Press, 1997), p. 1 and ff.

6 Robert Corber, *In the Name of National Security: Hitchcock, Homophobia and the Political Construction of Gender in Postwar America* (Durham, NC: Duke University Press, 1996), p. 201.

7 See Alan Nadel, *Containment Culture: American Narratives, Postmodernism and the Atomic Age* (Durham, NC: Duke University Press, 1995), pp. 13–37.

8 Stephen Schlesinger, *Act of Creation: The Founding of the United Nations* (New York, Basic Books, 2004), contains a copy of the *United Nations Charter*. All *Charter* material is quoted from that copy, pp. 295–321.

9 George Wilson, "The Maddest McGuffin: Some Notes on *North by Northwest*," *MLN* 94 (1979), p. 1163.

10 Albert Bermel, *Farce: A History from Aristophanes to Woody Allen* (Carbondale: Southern Illinois University Press, 1990), p. 22.

11 Mark Mazower, *No Enchanted Palace: The End of Empire and the Ideological Origins of the United Nations* (Princeton, NJ: Princeton University Press, 2009), p. 17.

12 See among others, Cavell, pp. 767–768, and Donald Spoto, *The Art of Alfred Hitchcock: Fifty Years of His Motion Pictures*, Centennial Edition (New York: Random House, 1976, 1992), pp. 342–344.

13 See Joseph Trento, *The Secret History of the CIA* (New York: Basic Books, 2005), and Tim Weiner, *Legacy of Ashes: The History of the CIA* (New York: Random House, 2008); this is also the general impression conveyed by Allen Dulles's *Craft of Intelligence: America's Legendary Spy Master on the Fundamentals of Intelligence Gathering for a Free World* (New Haven, CT: Globe Pequot Press, 2006).

14 Hugh Wilford details the range of organizations and public figures knowingly funded by and/or cooperative with the CIA in its covert propaganda agenda, including William Paley and Gloria Steinem: see *The Mighty Wurlitzer: How the CIA Played America* (Cambridge, MA: Harvard University Press, 2008).

15 Stephen Kinzer has documented the impact of the Dulles brothers in formulating and disguising U.S. interventionism; see *The Brothers: John Foster Dulles, Allen Dulles and their Secret World War* (New York: Times Books, 2013).

16 William Rothman, *The "I" of the Camera: Essays in Film Criticism, History and Aesthetics*, 2nd ed. (Cambridge: Cambridge University Press, 2004), p. 244.

17 Béla Balázs, *Visible Man, in Béla Balázs: Early Film Theory*, tr. Rodney Livingstone (New York and Oxford: Berghahn Books, 2010), p. 38.

18 Doane, *Femmes Fatales: Feminism, Film Theory, Psychoanalysis* (New York: Routledge, 1991).

19 *Alfred Hitchcock: Interviews*, ed. Sidney Gottlieb (Jackson: University Press of Mississippi, 2003), p. 199.

20 Like the comment in the scene about laughing, this remark, paraphrasing comedian Jimmy Durante (whose trademark signoff was "Good Night, Mrs. Calabash, wherever you are") serves as a piece of meta-commentary signaling the film's farcical mode.

21 Robert Stam, "Hitchcock and Buñuel: Desire and the Law," *Studies in the Literary Imagination* 16 (1983), p. 21.

22 Karl Marx, *The Eighteenth Brumaire of Louis Bonaparte* (New York: International, 1994), p. 1.

10

MURRAY POMERANCE

Looking Up: Class, England, and America in *The Man Who Knew Too Much*

A duke who has served a prison sentence is still a duke, whereas a man about town, if once disgraced, ceases to be "about town" for evermore.
– George Orwell, "Raffles and Miss Blandish"

When Alfred Hitchcock told François Truffaut that the first version of *The Man Who Knew Too Much* (1934) had been made "by a talented amateur" and the second (1956) by a "professional," he elided that the earlier was an English and the later an American film, both made by a kind of "mid-Atlantic man" at work in "one of the newer industries, advertising, public relations ... motion pictures, the whole world of brokerage, persuasion, savantry and shows that has grown up beyond the ancient divisions of landowning, money-lending and the production of dry goods."[1] The 1934 film, shot at Gaumont British studios in Borehamwood under the tutelage of Michael Balcon and the Left-leaning Ivor Montagu, was thoroughly British. The 1956 remake came in the heyday of Hitchcock's fecund period at Paramount, produced by Herbert Coleman and intensively supported, from the earliest days of its conception, by the filmmaker's close friend, agent, business partner, and confidant Lew Wasserman.[2] By this time Hitchcock had for more than fifteen years resided in, and grown comfortable with the culture of, California (on both sides of the Tehachapi), and indeed during preproduction was driven down by his designer Henry Bumstead to swear citizenship to the United States. Even in Los Angeles, however, Hitchcock remained an Eastender.

It was hardly strange, in Hollywood or elsewhere in the diaspora, for Englishmen to associate together and treasure memories (however mottled) of home.[3] We are told by Patrick McGilligan that a coterie of English transplants to Hollywood kept company with Hitchcock at the time of the breakout of World War II, including Cedric Hardwicke, Vivien Leigh, Laurence Olivier, Herbert Marshall, Charles Laughton, Errol Flynn, and Ronald Colman. Most were established in Hollywood by the end of the 1930s. A small group, including Reginald Gardiner, Boris Karloff, Victor Saville,

Robert Stevenson, and Charles Bennett, met along with Hitchcock at the offices of Cecil B. DeMille and operated "as a virtual cell of British intelligence, with the goal of nudging America toward involvement in the war" at a time when the American public was still fiercely divided about military engagement against Hitler.[4] Later on, Hitchcock "adopted a jaundiced view of his London years. He felt unappreciated in his home country, and thought that cinema would never be taken seriously by the British. 'No well-bred English person would be seen going into a cinema; it simply wasn't done,' Hitchcock said to an interviewer. 'Outside England there is a much more universal concept of life'."[5]

It was in June 1938 that Hitchcock arrived in the United States *en famille* (having stopped briefly the year before); he would return to England but sail back less than a year later, handily signed to a contract with David O. Selznick by the intrepid and gracious agent Kay Brown (Katharine Brown Barrett, 1905–1992), a charming and intelligent entrepreneur who understood Hitchcock immediately, entertained him at her Long Island retreat, and arranged for the introductions that would open American doors to his canny, curious, and always laboring creative mind. To make *Rebecca* (released in Los Angeles March 27, 1940), and later to join Gregory Ratoff, Victor Fleming, John Cromwell, William Wellman, George Cukor and other directorial "collaborators," Selznick had imported Hitchcock with grandiose plans and high hopes. That their partnership would turn out less than holy, leading to only a vituperatively argumentative relationship on *Spellbound* (1945) and Hitchcock straining on his leash with *The Paradine Case* (1947), hardly diminishes the blazing excitement and anticipation of Hitchcock's earliest American moments, as Leonard Leff has shown.[6] Nor did the blunt confrontation between thoroughly American Selznick's social aggressiveness and Hitchcock's tongue-in-cheek British reserve dampen Hitchcock's creative forces on their first picture together. What Selznick now had in his stable was the stupendously famous British Master of Suspense whose *The Lady Vanishes* (1938), *Sabotage* (1936), *The Secret Agent* (1936), *The 39 Steps* (1935), and *The Man Who Knew Too Much* (1934) had galvanized British and European viewership.

It was *The Man Who Knew Too Much*, Dan Aulier writes, that "built the foundation for Hitchcock's extraordinary success throughout the rest of the decade" notwithstanding the dismaying fact that "mismanagement" of this property at Gaumont by Charles Moss Woolf, leading to its being exhibited as a second rather than as a first feature, compromised profits detectably.[7] Preparing the film, Hitchcock solidified a partnership with the actor-writer Charles Bennett, whose 1928 play *Blackmail* (written for Tallulah Bankhead) had made some success on the West End and was subsequently adapted by the filmmaker for the screen. On his own initiative (he recognized the character's popularity), Bennett had written a story based on Bulldog Drummond, the rights to which name and persona were owned by John Maxwell at British International Pictures (later Elstree Studios).[8] "Bulldog Drummond's Baby" recounted the kidnapping of the celebrated detective's child by arch-criminals conspiring toward a political assassination. Hitchcock at the time was employed at B.I.P., where he made *The Ring* (1927), *The Farmer's Wife* and *Champagne* (both 1928), *The Manxman* (1929), *Blackmail, Murder!* (1930), *The Skin Game* (1931), *Rich and Strange*, and *Number 17* (1932), before coming into disagreement with Maxwell and moving over to Michael Balcon's Gaumont British. When he brought along Bennett's Drummond story property, he could not also transport the central character, so the piece was rewritten for a family of tourists. Both versions of the film that sprung from this writing retained the touring family as central.

In his brief analysis of the film, Ken Mogg's suggestion of sources in Howard Hawks's *Scarface* (1932) – most poignantly the death of Tony Camonte's sister as paralleled by the dramatic death of "Nurse" Agnes (Cicely Oates) – points to Hitchcock's early and intensive fascination with distant, unseen America and Hollywood, recalling his childhood habit of memorizing street maps and railway timetables from far-off places (44, see also Spoto, 20). Thus, the film was a British production already dreaming America. What riddles *The Man Who Knew Too Much* (as it does *The Skin Game*) is a saturated consciousness of class division and vested interest in British society. Bennett may have thought Hitchcock failed to share his passionate concern about the poor and destitute, but the film remains an astute portrait of the distinction between working-class hungers and a society that still favored the upper class,[9] a society riddled by "the perpetual uneasiness between man and man" yet fostering, as George Orwell wrote, "the temptation to believe that it can be shouted out of existence with a few scoutmasterish bellows of good will."[10]

Stephen DeRosa, who has written extensively about Hitchcock's collaboration with John Michael Hayes, commented about the author of the first *Man Who Knew Too Much* – whose work Hayes was instructed by Hitchcock *not* to read as he wrote the 1956 version (personal conversation) – that his "true genius lay in story construction, and his scenarios were built on many devices now regarded as 'Hitchcockian': the 'MacGuffin', the double-chase, the charming villain and the use of exotic locales woven dramatically into the plot. With Bennett, Hitchcock's cinematic vision came into clear focus."[11] Bennett told "BBC Omnibus" in 1986, "I think more work was done on the script in the evening over cocktails than any other time."[12] Hitchcock's feeling about Bennett, however, at least by the point *Jamaica Inn* (1939) was in preproduction, was that, "the world's finest stooge" (McGilligan, 160), he would be "ideal for him on the story construction" but that later on "[I] would have to have a dialogue writer" (McGilligan, 218). As Bennett was "basically a carpenter, whose foundations and framing required sanding and ornamentation," other writers had to "join the pool" adding nuance to the film, including "the Cambridge-educated playwright A. R. (Arthur Richard) Rawlinson and the actor-writer Edwin Greenwood," as well as "the well-known satirist D. B. 'Bevan' Wyndham-Lewis," who did "spot-writing" (160). Hitchcock's pal (and "kindred spirit" [McGilligan, 157]) Angus MacPhail arranged for Emlyn Williams to contribute to the dialogue for the 1934 film as well; for the later version, many early ideas for scripting came from MacPhail, but the dialogue – snippy and endlessly revealing – was written, as with *Rear Window* (1954), *The Trouble with Harry* (1955), and *To Catch a Thief* (1955), by the urbane yet somewhat withdrawn Hayes. "Hitchcock and Hayes began making the necessary alterations and revisions to the treatment, along with Angus MacPhail, whom Hitchcock kept on salary. 'Hitch had to have somebody to talk things over with and keep notes,' remembered Hayes. 'But it was left up to me to finally write it' " (DeRosa, 171).

While the fundamental, skeletal stories of both versions of *The Man Who Knew Too Much* are similar, involving the temporary breakup of a family through a kidnapping designed to camouflage a political murder, there are differences worth noting if one is interested in Hitchcock's sociological vision and his change of perspective once established in the United States. A central issue underpinning this variance is the knowledgeable expectation of the audience for whom the narrative is intended. Hitchcock and Bennett, born and bred to the English class system, understood it both subtly and "naturally," and – as one will in England once one has come to understand its culture – saw class everywhere, in the grossest and finest ramifications. But another angle was needed for the Americans, progressivists at heart, who always sought ways of moving onward and upward and whose experience of class difference, if it had been highlighted and exacerbated during the Great Depression – "men and boys hopping freights and pitching camp outside towns that didn't want them; the Joad family on its biblical trek through town and desert, Hooverville and sanitary camp: this is not travel but a way of standing still or running in place"[13] – came, during the consumerist frenzy of the 1950s, to represent only a murky vision of social hell anathema to their increasingly desperate middle-class hopes and dreams. "Precisely the uncompromising optimism of Americans makes every inevitable failure to accomplish what can only be dreamed an unredeemable torment," writes Leslie Fiedler.[14]

The first *Man Who Knew* begins with a strange gesture: an unidentified hand turning through Swiss travel brochures, especially St. Moritz. I will shortly return to this curious hand. Instantly we move to the ski slopes of the town, the highest such ones in Europe in the historically oldest of ski towns, not to mention an enduring haven for the exceedingly rich who, since the middle of the nineteenth century, have regaled themselves with the brisk pleasures of being here in winter. It is winter now, the snowy vista is pristine. A huge crowd has lined up to watch a jumping competition, and we see one contestant flying through the air toward a magnificent landing. In the crowd stands young Betty Lawrence (Nova Pilbeam) with her dachshund. Excited by the hubbub, the dog jumps away, onto the ski run. She follows to grab him up, threatening to block the jumper's finish. The man must now take a fall to avoid hitting her. Lifted up by a little crowd of well-wishers – including a grinning little fellow in a fur-lined coat (Peter Lorre) – and in jolly good spirits, the man manifests himself as Louis Bernard (Pierre Fresnay), a kind of "uncle" to Betty and family chum of her parents:

> LOUIS: That was my last chance. Oh! Your fault, horrible woman!
> BETTY: It wasn't. It was a silly little dog.
> LOUIS: I might have been killed, you know. Do you realize that my last day here might have been my last day on earth?
> BOB: Your last day here?
> LOUIS: Mn hmm.
> BOB: You're not leaving tonight are you, Louis?
> LOUIS: I'm afraid, yes. By the last train.
> BETTY: Oh, Uncle Louis!
> LOUIS: Why do you call me uncle?
> BETTY: Well, you're just like an uncle, aren't you?

This is all nothing but affectionate, even slightly seductive, play. Louis's attraction to the girl is blocked because of his "familial" status if not her outright youth; in more ways than one she is a "horrible" woman and could have "killed" him. Yet, too, he is an accomplished skier – jumping skis make turning virtually impossible and can be used only by those who know the slopes – and knows how to fall: has done so, no doubt, many times over, in far more precarious circumstances. Betty hasn't nearly killed him at all, but to say she almost has ices the cake. The dark subtext of this conversation will become real as within hours Louis is killed in fact and the story swings into motion.

We move to a nearby spot where Bob's wife Jill (Edna Best) is competing at skeet shooting against Ramon (Frank Vosper), an unctuous and preening but exceptionally talented marksman. Young Betty cannot keep still watching this, and her nervous squealing distracts her mother, forcing her to lose concentration and the contest. Much later in the film this exceptionally awkward, even irritating moment will be doubly reprised: the intrusive vocalization and Jill's missed aim will be reset at the Royal Albert Hall, where, losing her own self-control at the climax of Arthur Benjamin's "Storm Clouds" cantata, she will cause this shooter – as it turns out, a professional assassin – to miss *his* aim; and Jill's failed marksmanship will redeem itself when with one shot she pegs Ramon, who threatens Betty on a dismal East London rooftop. The film, writes William Rothman, "has no male figure who is Jill's equal and does not acknowledge the implications of this imbalance."[15]

After the sharpshooting contest, a revealing moment ends the scene. Hanging back with Ramon as the others move into the hotel, Bob fixes the shooter with the trace of a smile: "You have defeated my wife. You are a dirty dog." This is a call to courtly propriety, enunciating rights accruing to a man's class position. The implication – complex, perhaps, for American sensibilities but patently clear to English viewers – is that Ramon would have shown far better etiquette by invisibly contriving to miss his own shot and let the lady win – although Jill's fortitude in the finale moment that I mentioned earlier clearly absolves her of the need for protection and gentility (but only in retrospect). Further, the breach has subtly enough taken the form of an insult, if not to Bob's integrity per se then at least to the dignity of his family and estate. In earlier times, he is saying more or less outright, he could have openly called Ramon out with the sort of epithet he here uses only to playfully mock.

More than a dithering tourist, Bob Lawrence is a man of some position whose keen senses inform him when he has received a blow to his dignity. As we do not explicitly discover him on an estate (where we do discover the characters in *The Skin Game*), Bob's is perhaps some of "the new wealth of the financiers [that] was added to the old wealth of the great families of landowners."[16] Further, Ramon is not the gentleman he might appear to be in St. Moritz, this notorious idyll of gentlemen; and, accompanied almost always by the overly expressive and overdressed Abbott (Lorre), he seems fake: neither Abbott nor Ramon have come here for the snow. They are up to something else, something unpleasant, something – as James Mason's Vandamm will echo much later in *North by Northwest* (1959) – "not very sporting at all." Abbott and Ramon are beneath their poses, utilizing the swank atmosphere for practical reasons without being at home there. It is Abbott's hand, I think, flipping through the Swiss travel brochures in the opening credit sequence. The Lawrences and their adopted friend Louis do not need brochures to find St. Moritz, one of their homes away from home.

In this they reflect the up-and-coming Alfred Hitchcock who had taken his bride Alma there for their honeymoon:

> St. Moritz – the resort where millionaires entertain at ski lodges and live in deluxe hotels year round – was Hitchcock's first choice for his experience of the good life, and to this place he and Alma returned, whenever they could, for the observance of their wedding anniversary.... The two hundred miles of ski and bobsled and toboggan runs in the vicinity engaged the honeymooners' attention only as spectators; never given to sport (much less to anything involving even the slightest risk), Hitchcock contented himself with sleigh rides.[17]

In the hotel's nightclub, to the swing of a perfectly banal orchestra, Louis has been flirting with Jill on the dance floor while Bob sits bored with daydreaming Betty (whom he could, if he wanted, give a dance), and plays at being jealous of Jill's new "beau," Louis the perfect playboy: suave, underspoken, handsome, twinkling, maybe a little too easy with other men's women. Bob has discovered Jill's knitting and he attaches the loose thread surreptitiously to the back of Louis's jacket so that within moments the dance floor is a tangle of wool. ("The thread of life," Durgnat quotes Hitchcock). Suddenly a bullet comes through a window and pierces Louis's chest. As he collapses into Jill's arms, he presses a key into her hand and begs her to tell Bob to search his room for a brush. Bob finds what he is looking for, and a secret message stuffed inside, but Ramon notices this and kidnaps Betty (in a sleigh!). Now Bob and Jill must work to find her (without showing too much muscle or the vitiating expenditure of energy).

A brief note about settings, especially Bernard's Swiss hotel room and the Lawrence flat in London (possibly Bloomsbury), whither the action retreats swiftly upon Betty's disappearance. Both spaces, designed for Hitchcock (an inveterate designer himself, therefore sensitive to spatial issues) by the great Alfred Junge, are notably capacious and elegant: the hotel room has high ceilings, molded walls, and a huge bathroom (of the old-fashioned type) with its own exit to the corridor. The Lawrence home is plushly, not ornately, furnished – the modernist style – and comes equipped with a service staff who can materialize drinks on a silver tray. At the Wapping rooming house where the film concludes, we will see a marked contrast. The area is a working-class labyrinth bordering the Thames, where characters of a distinctly lower breed – an aggressive dentist; Abbott and his lowly crowd – huddle and creep in the crepuscular gloom of a "maritime pomp" limned by Iain Sinclair: "brothels, grog shops, provisioners – the bustle and fret of a crowd in perpetual motion; oysters at midnight, drunks to be fleeced or pressed, news from abroad, the bartering of exotic animals."[18] As to the

East End in general (Hitchcock's home turf), "its huge docks were a chaos, shockingly organized, with no proper relations between employers, foremen and the dockers themselves.... There were thousands of casual dock labourers who, after standing about in the rain, might be lucky enough to earn about three shilling and sixpence, under a dollar, a day, and if they were married might be living in one room" (Priestley, 73). Here Abbott, who introduced himself in ostentatious fur, dies in a cheap corduroy jacket. At the attempted assassination itself, the Royal Albert Hall, long a bastion of high art and righteous British sentiment, is invaded by the tuxedoed but finally slovenly Ramon; it is merely his work site, not the ethereal temple its middle-class patrons take it to be.

A great deal of this material was taken straight from, or reflected concerns and observations of social-class indicators that were already articulated in, Bennett's "Bulldog Drummond's Baby."[19] To give just a brief list, we find "a clay pigeon shooting competition located at a continental luxury hotel"; a hotel manager "who casts suspicion on" our hero by inquiring why he "had been in Bernard's room after the murder"; and "a Scotland Yard inspector [telling Drummond (to become Lawrence)] that it is his duty to turn over all evidence to the Department" – telling him fruitlessly, that is, since, like a toff, accustomed to control, Drummond/Lawrence is focused on protecting his family. Also notable in the original story as evidence of class or class relationship is Phyllis Drummond's (Jill Lawrence's) skill as an "expert marksman" – something only the rich would have time for as a pure diversion.

The Bulldog Drummond novels by "Sapper" (H. C. McNeile) are largely tongue-in-cheek about class identification, one notable indicator of Bulldog's high status presented in *The Female of the Species* (1928) as the narrator tells us how the sleuth came into his acquaintance. What we learn of this narrator is that he inhabits a London club where he fears a certain glutton will have eaten the best parts of the Stilton, but then, up at a country house for a "peaceful" rest – "that world, the entire world of nannies, *cottages ornées* in Devonshire, honeysuckle iron balustrades, sailor suits, hoops and sticks, lolly Eton collars, deb parties, introductions to rich old men, clubs, cliques, horn-handled cigar cutters – in short, the ancient, ineradicable anxiety of class in England" (Wolfe, 45) – meets the sort of man who is quite habituated to such places and to having butlers and servants and a chauffeur with whom he can place bets on the horses:

"Do you think it quite wise to encourage the servants to bet?" I enquired a little pointedly as we started.

"Encourage, old lad?" he boomed. "They don't want any encouragement. You'd have to keep 'em off it with a field-gun."[20]

Metaphors are realities. Drummond invokes the field gun because he knows how to use one; he's been hunting. He is a member of that class.

In the American version, all of the material spaces and relational nuances I have pointed to earlier are transformed so as to appeal to an audience deeply committed to the principles of meritocracy – that we are all in essence the same, that hard work is required and requited in life, with those who work the hardest meriting and receiving the greatest rewards. What differences can be detected between people's conditions and life chances, then, are deserved. The English working and middle classes may value labor for its own sake, as redemptive or socially engaging, and they may think it helpful in somewhat ameliorating their circumstances; but they do not, as a rule, hold to the principle that assiduousness will help them get ahead; getting ahead – at least prior to the Beatles and the age of the new entertainment aristocracy – was not in the cards. This American linkage of success to striving is perfectly in tune with the production and personal reality Hitchcock encountered in David O. Selznick, a genius who had climbed his way into Hollywood power in part through marriage to Louis B. Mayer's daughter. Selznick "had urged Hitchcock to remake *The Man Who Knew Too Much* in the mid-1940s, but plans never went beyond preliminary story discussions," Stephen DeRosa writes. "By the mid-1950s, however, Hitchcock was sufficiently confident that a remake would not be a 'run for cover,' but that he instead could genuinely do something more with the story" (155–156). Here, Louis Bernard (Daniel Gélin) is not already a friend of the central McKenna family (James Stewart, Doris Day, Christopher Olsen), but adopts them when the somewhat eager and energetic young son Hank seems to commit a social gaffe on a bus. The family repairs to a clean but hardly sumptuous suite at the Mamounia, a hotel "for tourists of good taste," as Bernard puts it, and prepares to join him for dinner at a restaurant decorated in the ornate Moroccan style. Donning their evening wear, Ben and Jo are caught up in their middle-class identities. Jo gave up a stage career to be with Ben, but international fame did not elevate her class standing. She must put her talents to employment, in this case at the behest of her (producer) husband, who uses her voice to save the kidnapped Hank's life; in the mirror situation, Jill acted of her own accord, using her marksmanship craftily but also independently. Jo makes capital of her talent, while Jill merely plays with hers, even at the vital moment when the play briefly turns serious. Ben and Jo McKenna move in society through the vehicles of Jo's fame and Ben's medical credentials – "Herbie Taylor's ulcers; Alida Markle's asthma" – and must demonstrate the propriety of their position in every circumstance. Tonight, for example, as though attending a gala celebration rather than merely going out to a restaurant, they are dressed to the nines, the doctor in an austere and overly dignified dark navy suit and his wife in a "green print silk organdy sleeveless party dress with wide shoulder straps," a stole in "matching material," a "green leather contour belt" and "Miss Day's own rings" that would attract attention anywhere (Wardrobe). Their neighbors and eventual dining partners, the Draytons, are far more modest and unpresuming; they appear here to epitomize the lower stratum of the British middle class, and have made themselves clean and presentable but not in any way special, noticeable, or elevated.

After the murder of Bernard in the Marrakech marketplace, and Ben and Jo's removal to London, we find ourselves watching the self-conscious Americans in confrontation with British class interests. As collaborators in the political assassination, Drayton and his wife (Bernard Miles, Brenda de Banzie) turn out to be working-class menials, while Buchanan (Ralph Truman), his assistant Woburn (Noel Willman), and other agents of Scotland Yard or the police are semiprofessional working people who never lose sight of the dignitaries and "betters" over their heads. One epitome of the British servile class is the house manager of the Royal Albert Hall (Richard Wattis), whose extreme deftness and articulateness work to affiliate Jo McKenna with the wounded prime minister in such a way that she is happily invited into the embassy where, we will discover, little Hank has been tucked away. While Ben's nature is to address all persons with a kind of no-nonsense directness, he is blithely out of touch with class relations and cannot tell the difference between Ambrose Chapel the taxidermist (a benign replacement for the 1934 dentist, here established in Camden Town, "well known for its 'rural lanes, hedgeside roads and lovely fields' where Londoners sought 'quietude and fresh air'"[21]) and the dignified entrepreneur Val Parnell (Alan Mowbray), his wife's old producer friend who visits at the Savoy with his chorus of show business women. Even if we look at the McKenna suite in this hotel, a kind of equivalent of the Lawrence abode since it is the protagonists' home base in London, we find a rather cramped space, jam-packed with welcoming bouquets but entirely lacking the aura of class we saw earlier. This is the sort of room people like the McKennas would call "high class."

The speech patterns in the two films give even clearer indication both of class identity and of the filmmaker's varying concerns with it. Acoustically, the dominant theme of the British film is Bob and Jill's patter. They slur their words, swallowing or retaining syllables as often as not, in "the drawl of the fashionable Mid-Victorian 'swells,' who were suggesting to their listeners that they were doing them a favour by talking to them at all. It is the speech of lazy condescension, and all too often it has been the voice of official

Britain. The feminine equivalent, I would say, is a high-pitched staccato, impossible to modulate, rather like a hard stare turned into speech."[22] "The flippancy of Bob's manner," Charles Barr opines, "doesn't mean the 1934 film is lightweight. His, and the film's, playfulness ... [can be seen] as being a means of playing out, and then dealing with, matters of serious import."[23] In the ski sequence, for example, as Abbott brushes himself off, Bob mutters that the dog has been "knocking 'em cold":

> ABBOTT: Knocking them cold? What does it mean?
> BOB (MUMBLING): Just an expression, you know.
> NURSE (TO ABBOTT): Lucky if *you* didn't catch your death of cold.

Peter Lorre's Abbott, we are being informed, is a model of the foreigner from the south, attempting through cultivated delicacy and extreme mannerism to suggest sincere membership in the St. Moritz community when, obviously, he is overdressed and totally unaccustomed to dealing with the climate. He couldn't possibly "catch his death" of cold by falling into a snowdrift, yet the play in the nurse's anxious concern matches the verbal play between Louis and Betty as to Louis being "killed" taking that fall. Abbott, too, is arranging for Louis's death: arranging to have Louis knocked "cold." The 1956 version gives a widely varying display of speech patterns, from Ben McKenna's persistent drawl and incessant laboring to get a word in edgewise to his wife's artful but trained elocution; Mrs. Drayton's school-teacher imitation of the Queen; Drayton's regional dialect; and the (educated) Assassin's (Reginald Nalder) extraordinarily fluid Parisian French. Mixed among these are the voluble eloquence of the Albert Hall Manager, Val Parnell's cultivated London drawl, Buchanan's clipped and lofty managerial tone, and Woburn's stammering obedience.

In each film the centerpiece is a disappearing child. Betty Lawrence irritates accidentally, by expressing herself to an extremity and inadvertently producing a disruption in the surrounding action. She is too excited to keep a grip on her dog so he jumps away and she must now go off to save him, thus causing Louis to upset himself. She cannot keep her excitement in check while watching her mother shoot. When her father tells her to "Shut up, darling," he is meaning she should stop producing sound. But the feeling we have with the McKennas is that they have wanted Hank to shut up for some time yet have not found a way to tell him. This because it is not the sound he makes that disturbs their pleasure dream; it is his striving to fit in with them. He persists in using big words – the subject of considerable witticism in the early part of the bus scene; big, in the sense of inappropriate culturally for a kid his age. He is a prodigy. He is an adult in child's clothing. And this misfit is a perduring irritation. Hank cannot stop shining: seated with Lucy Drayton in the market, he glows like a fire. On the bus he radiates energy and confidence while his parents try to sink into private experience. At the embassy, even as Hank whistles to accompany his mother's crooning down below, we see and hear his unbridled expressivism, a powerful release of evocative energy. The whistling here and the whistling of the train in *The 39 Steps* and the factory in *Blackmail* are of a piece: pent-up embodiment in release.

A striking evocation of the McKennas' middle-class aspirations comes in the finale. Through the series of short scenes at the Savoy that have comically punctuated the drama of the search for Hank through London, the boy has been "visiting friends," according to Ben and Jo, this explanation required because Parnell and his maenads have been vocal in their eagerness to meet him and see which parent he resembles. What is interesting about the interaction in these scenes, however, is that the McKennas feel obliged in the face of these "old friends" to conceal the fact that their son has been taken from them. At the very end of the film, they bring him in front of this little audience in order, as it were, to gain proper approval as parents – a portrait of the American middle class in its obsession for proprietorship. The child is valued property, evidence of achievement – hence Jo's pestering Ben in the Marrakech market to "achieve" another; he is valuable evidence; and he is not to be lost. In all of Bob and Jill's exasperation and torment during Betty's absence from them, there is never an indication that the kidnapping might reflect *on them*. Hank, however, had to be returned, but also put on display. "I'm sorry we were gone so long but we had to go over and pick up Hank," is the punch line, meaning, "We knew all along where he was."

The joke is not that they are saying something that is not true. It is that they are saying something they very deeply believe *ought* to be true, and in front of the critical English audience always to be taken as existing on the historically and culturally higher plane to which every red-blooded American ought endlessly to aspire.

Acknowledgments

With gratitude to John Bennett, Adam Brown, Bill Krohn, Ken Mogg, Hugh Ritchie, and Daniel Sacco.

NOTES

1 Tom Wolfe, "The Mid-Atlantic Man," in *The Pump House Gang* (New York: Farrar, Straus & Giroux, 1968), p. 47.
2 And with important participation by the agent Herman Citron, who represented Doris Day, Jay Livingstone, and Ray Evans. The company called Filwite, which

appears in credits as the producing entity, was made up of Hitchcock, Wasserman, and James Stewart, who through its legal entity divided the above-the-line profits of the picture (neither Hitchcock nor Stewart took a salary per se).

3 At least one reporter informs us that in his Scotts Valley retreat (purchased in 1954), Hitchcock made a habit of eating Dover sole and steak and kidney pies that had been flown over from England (Marion Dale Pokriots, "Alfred Hitchcock found contentment in SV," Scotts Valley Historical Society, online at www.svchamber.org/svhistory/history/hitchcock.htm. Accessed December 5, 2013).

4 Patrick McGilligan, *Alfred Hitchcock: A Life in Darkness and Light* (New York: It Books, 2003), p.256.

5 Dan Aulier, "Classic British Movies: 1934–1939," in Ken Mogg et al., *The Alfred Hitchcock Story* (London: Titan, 1999), p. 43.

6 Leonard Leff, *Hitchcock & Selznick: The Rich and Strange Collaboration of Alfred Hitchcock and David O. Selznick in Hollywood* (New York: Weidenfeld & Nicolson, 1987).

7 Ken Mogg, *The Alfred Hitchcock Story* (London: Titan, 1999), p. 40.

8 Under the pen name "Sapper," H. C. McNeile had written a substantial number of novels, short stories, and stage plays about Drummond starting in 1920. In the West End, the character had been played by Gerald Du Maurier, a man well known to Hitchcock and a much celebrated actor, the original Captain Hook, as well as father of Daphne Du Maurier, whose "Rebecca" and "The Birds" were both adapted by Hitchcock quite famously. In 1922, Hugh "Bulldog" Drummond was played on-screen by Carlyle Blackwell in an Oscar Apfel film; subsequently, until 1969, in twenty-two more films starring, among others, Ronald Colman, Ralph Richardson, and Ray Milland.

9 "What you might believe to be Hitch's characterization of social class was probably my father's characterization, torqued by the creative tension between these film partners," John Bennett confided to me. "For example, my father was greatly concerned for the empowerment of women, including the post WWI homeless women of London.... On the other hand, Hitchcock had his own sadistic and misogynistic issues which twisted my father's redemptive motif toward audience suspense at the expense of women's anxiety" (Personal communication, December 7 and 10, 2013). Interestingly, Ken Mogg thinks "that Hitchcock responded strongly to Bennett's sympathy for the underdog," noting Hitchcock's desire in the 1930s to film *We the Accused*, "a classic depiction of sympathy of the fugitive from society" (Personal communication).

10 George Orwell, *The Road to Wigan Pier* (London: Penguin, 1937, 2001), p. 147.

11 Stephen DeRosa, *Writing with Hitchcock: The Collaboration of Alfred Hitchcock and John Michael Hayes* (New York: Faber and Faber, 2001), p. 55.

12 Charles Bennett, "First-Class Constructionist: Interview with Patrick McGilligan," in McGilligan, ed., *Backstory: Interviews with Screenwriters of Hollywood's Golden Age* (Berkeley: University of California Press, 1986), pp. 17–48.

13 Morris Dickstein, *Dancing in the Dark: A Cultural History of the Great Depression* (New York: W. W. Norton, 2009), p. 359.

14 Leslie Fiedler, "Looking Backward: America from Europe," in *An End to Innocence* (Boston: Beacon Press, 1952), p. 124.

15 William Rothman, *Hitchcock – The Murderous Gaze*, second edition (Albany: State University of New York Press, 2012), p. 115.

16 J. B. Priestley, *The Edwardians* (London: Sphere, 1972), pp. 56–57.

17 Donald Spoto, *The Dark Side of Genius: The Life of Alfred Hitchcock* (New York: Ballantine, 1983), p. 104.

18 Iain Sinclair, *Lights Out for the Territory: 9 Excursions in the Secret History of London* (London: Penguin, 2003), p. 322.

19 I am extremely grateful to the Estate of Charles Bennett and especially to Mr. John Bennett, who gave generously of his time in summarizing the content of this story for me; the quotations that follow are from his notes.

20 "Sapper" (H. C. McNeile), *The Female of the Species* (London: House of Stratus, 1928, 2001), p. 4.

21 Peter Ackroyd, *London: The Biography* (London: Vintage, 2001), p. 409.

22 Priestley, p. 98.

23 Charles Barr, *English Hitchcock* (Moffat: Cameron and Hollis, 1999), p. 138.

11

BRIGITTE PEUCKER

Blood, Paint, or Red?: The Color Bleed in Hitchcock

Especially in the 1960s, when Hitchcock is known to have consciously competed with European art cinema, color in his films derives its effect from the sliding value of red among blood, paint, and mere color. In such moments, a modernist, anti-mimetic move vies with Hitchcock's primarily realist goals. Yet this oscillation and other floating uses of color are already in evidence in his films of the 1950s, suggesting that Hitchcock's interest in the modernist use of color began earlier and that painting may have been its source. This chapter begins by exploring the duplicity primarily of the color red in the Hitchcock film, commenting on its realistic, its metaphorical, and its abstract uses. Then, drawing on the multiple meanings of "bleeding," it explores the collapse of ontological registers in Hitchcock, another aspect of the oscillation between realism and modernism. Here, too, it anchors its argument in the color red.

The question "blood, paint, or red?" does not originate with modernism: it is a trope of illusionism in its various forms, resuscitated in the nineteenth century by a literary interest in the implications of realism. In Edgar Allen Poe's *The Oval Portrait*, blood and paint are fused in an astonishing parable – and critique – of realism in painting. Poe's tale is familiar: it describes a painting that, in the manner of a vampire, absorbs the lifeblood of the woman who sits for it. As the portrait becomes more lifelike, the woman grows more pale. Obsessed with her image on canvas, her artist husband is blind to the real body before him. When the woman dies at the moment of the painting's completion, it is implied that her blood, which gives the painting its quality of life-likeness, is now used up. An inversion of the Pygmalion story, *The Oval Portrait* has much in common with Balzac's *The Hidden Masterpiece*, which likewise concerns the realist impulse to bring the painted body to life. In his attempt to create a life-like portrait, Balzac's artist Frenhofer succeeds in representing only "an enchanting foot, a living foot," while the rest of his painting is "a mass of confused color, crossed by a multitude of painted lines, making a sort of painted wall."[1] Although Frenhofer's painting is primarily abstract – it cannot contain color within line – the illusionistic foot seems so real that, were the "wall" of color and line to be removed, a living woman would be revealed.

Balzac's story famously makes its way into film via Jacques Rivette's loose adaptation, *La belle noiseuse* (1991), and while we never see the pertinent painting in this film, we do see a splash of red on a canvas. Whether this color signifies blood or paint is not fully resolved by Rivette. The relation is an oscillating one: no doubt Rivette had in mind Godard's notorious asser-tion concerning blood in *Pierrot le Fou* (1965) to the effect that it was not blood at all, just "red."[2] If Rivette pays tribute to Balzac's interest in the connection of paint to corporeality (the degree zero of realism would be to paint with nature itself, to paint with blood), it is only obliquely, as color. As Gilles Deleuze points out, Godard's formula–"it's not blood, it's red"– is "*the* formula of colourism."[3] Color's production of a rich affective response in the spectator is a commonplace of art theory from its beginnings, and its importance to what Deleuze calls the affection-image – the capacity of film to generate, via color, close-up, and other techniques, this emotional response – is in keeping with this tradition.

Modernism or Realism?

For Stanley Cavell it is black-and-white photography that signals drama, and color that renders films unrealistic and painterly. But while Hitchcock's work emerged from the monochromatic hues of Expressionist cinema, he preferred to shoot in color. *Psycho* (1960), he contended, was shot in black-and-white to render its violence more acceptable to the censors. (There were financial constraints, as well.) In black-and-white, Hitchcock claimed, blood looks less like blood. But *Psycho*'s nauseated viewers attested to its realism: the shower scene depicts blood graphically, realistically – photographically, as Cavell would say.[4] At the same time, however, the film presents Marion's body in a modernist mode, pictorially speaking: both camera work and editing strat-egies render the body abstract. This oscillation of registers in Hitchcock – between realism and modernist abstraction – is not confined to the films shot in black-and-white. Color promotes similar effects: there are moments when the color red figures blood, and those in which it remains virtually un-imaged, mere paint. Filling the frame, red may signal the distorted vision of the spectator; on the other hand, it may simply cloak the image in a color wash. Such a moment occurs at the end of *Spellbound* (1945), for example, as the film frame is unexpectedly suffused with red, a surprising effect amid the black-and-white of the film's other images.

We'll begin with *Torn Curtain* (1966), whose color system is intricate and owes a great deal to its Cold War, Russian-zone setting. Critics claim that the film's use of color – colors designed to imitate those of grayed early Agfa films, colors suited to the gray tones of East Germany – contributes to its realism.[5] But the artifice of its color design is also amply in evidence. For Paul Newman's Michael Armstrong and Julie Andrews's Sara, the way back to West Germany and safety is via hellfire. This is imaged on the stage of a ballet performance to Tchaikovsky's *Francesca da Rimini*, a composition noted for the swirling musical chromaticism by which it suggests the flames of hell to the ear. In the ballet scene aural and visual cues – chromatic both – combine in a moment of masterful cinematic synaesthesia, confirming this stage as an aesthetic space par excellence. The film's strategy, then, is in keeping with Eisenstein's dictum that "the problem of the true synchronicity of sound and image ... can only be resolved by color."[6] When Armstrong is spotted by the sharp eye of a vengeful diva, the flames on stage suggest to him the ruse of yelling "fire" to create the chaos necessary for escape.

But the color red is featured throughout *Torn Curtain*, not just in the fire on stage. It is the color of communism, of course, and according to Richard Allen, it is one of Hitchcock's "warning" colors in situations of danger.[7] Red may also be prominent because the production's designer was Hein Heckroth, a German painter who emigrated to England, where he became Powell and Pressburger's designer, winning an Academy Award for art design in *The Red Shoes* (1948). Trained as a painter, in *Torn Curtain* Heckroth seems a practitioner of what an artist friend called "the Côrot effect." Côrot, he claimed, used at least a dab of red in every picture he painted, often simply as a color effect, un-imaged. Woven into the gray-green tones of the film's fabric, in *Torn Curtain* red is used realistically when, for instance, it is the color of blood on a shirt and on a coat. The Russian flag is red, as is the mercury of an oversized thermometer, but so are a car, Julie Andrews' robe, and a prominent stripe behind the diva as she descends from a plane. And, not surprisingly, the banisters in Hitchcock's dangerous staircase setting have red stripes as well.

Sometimes red signifies in *Torn Curtain*, but sometimes it only works expressively – a red stool has no particular function except to add a touch of color, and to serve as a reminder, perhaps, of affect elsewhere. Further – as though to discourage reading color as a system – red is not always coded negatively. A man with red hair, Armstrong has been told, will help him escape. The flames of hell "burning " onstage are red and orange – yet two different stage doors, paths to freedom – are red as well. During the film's credit sequence, fire and red smoke fill its left side – this is undulating color, nearly un-imaged. And might the name of the bookstore in this film – it is

Elmo's Bookstore – have been chosen to suggest St. Elmo's fire? Yet of course St. Elmo's fire is *not* fire, it is a weather effect, and its color is blue. It is a false lead, in other words, a red herring. But perhaps Elmo's Bookstore prefigures the false flames that appear on stage later in the film. In a variety of ways, then, red in this film oscillates between signifying and non-signifying functions. Red promotes affect, yes, but sometimes it is simply like a spot of paint on a canvas. In such instances, its function is aesthetic.

Another Cold War spy story, *Topaz* (1969) treats the color red in similar ways. It begins in Moscow's Red Square – here color functions in the linguistic dimension of the film – where red flags and red-bedecked military uniforms are quite naturally featured. Red signifies politically. But with the cut to Copenhagen that quickly follows, the film moves to a setting in which the color red also predominates – a great deal *more* red is in the frame than is naturalistic. A street scene features children in red leggings and coats, and in a group touring the Royal Copenhagen porcelain factory there is almost no one who is not wearing some item of red clothing. Here red no longer signifies politically, if at all. Could this be a lesson for the spectator? If the color red has another function, then it is the cultural one of providing a foil for the escaping Russian family whose clothing has the neutral – dull – tones prevalent in the Soviet Union. Nevertheless, the daughter of the Russian spy-turned-traitor has a red wallet – and red hair – and thus participates in another color system involving red, one that has more to do with female sexuality than with politics.

We would expect the color red to reenter the political sphere when the film's narrative moves to New York, where Cuban Communists are visiting, and to Cuba itself, not surprisingly, since *Topaz* replays the Cuban missile crisis of 1962. To an extent this is the case. In New York a red neon light flashes "Bar-Grill" in the hotel where the Cubans are holed up, and the Cuban documents stolen by an American spy are contained in a red leather briefcase. And Rico Parra – the fictional Cuban military leader of the film (the film includes archival footage of Fidel Castro, as well) – has flaming red hair. Yet in these examples red functions more affectively than metaphorically. Later, in Cuba, the dripping of red blood from her hand (a common motif in Hitchcock) will serve to incriminate a peasant woman as a spy for the United States, while the blood on Rico Parra's hand is a stain that marks him as the murderer of the woman he loves, head of an organization that collaborates with the United States. The motif of the bleeding hand is repeated when, in Paris, a prominent French politician commits suicide after having been recognized as a spy for the Soviet Union. But it does not serve as a metaphor here, unlike the use of red to signify the budding sexuality of the young Russian girl.

Red often functions as part of a complementary pair in Hitchcock, in an oppositional color system. The dissonance promoted by complementary colors has a central role to play – especially the opposition of red and green, which, as I argue, is not only cued by narrative concerns. Of course in *The Birds* (1963), Tippi Hedren's more refined Melanie wears green while Suzanne Pleshette's voluptuous Annie is repeatedly associated with red, a pattern already present in *Vertigo* (1958), where the greens associated with the ethereal Madeleine are noticeably opposed to the reds that adorn the earthy Judy. Yet the color opposition featured in *Vertigo* is part of a more complex juxtaposition: both Madeleine and Judy are played by the same actress, their difference produced through artifice and intensified by the disturbed imagination of James Stewart's Scottie. Judy becomes Madeleine under the direction of Gavin Elster, resumes her life as Judy after his goal is attained, then becomes Madeleine once more at the behest of Scottie. Only the film's conclusion brings an end to this oscillation between the two personae, an oscillation that is color-coded. One is tempted to read the final collapse of the two women into one in death as already implicit in the complementary colors with which they are associated.

Green in *Vertigo* is associated with the spectral, ghostly quality of Madeleine/Judy as a kind of revenant, inverting this color's culturally conditioned associations with verdant life. Green lighting contributes to the macabre sequence in which Madeleine is "resurrected," with the flashing green neon sign outside Judy's hotel playing a central role. As so often in Hitchcock, narrative oppositions are expressed both metaphorically and linguistically. The green foliage of the redwood trees marks them as vegetative, hence presumably life bringing, but the narrative emphasis on their age inverts this connection. Since the redwood shares the vampire's horrifying inability to die, its vegetation is in some sense unnatural. These gigantic trees take their name from the red hue of their wood. As in the collapse of red and green in Madeleine/Judy, the redwoods contain and collapse these complementary colors. A confusion concerning categories is in evidence in *The Trouble with Harry* (1955), too, where the unnatural tint of the autumn leaves suggests that Harry's blood lends them their vivid color – not literally, of course, but figuratively, metonymically. The green color we expect foliage to be is absent and its red complement has taken its place. Hence the natural space seems artificial – even if the living leaf seems "painted" with a natural substance.

It is a commonplace to point out that the emphasis on red and green is where the obsession with doubling enters the color design of Hitchcock's films, substituting for the opposition of black-and-white in the earlier films. Gus van Sant makes use of this insight in his remake of *Psycho* as a color film: in van Sant's film Marion's lingerie is sometimes red-orange, sometimes green. But this oppositional color system does not only serve to emphasize the narrative juxtaposition of pairs of women in *Vertigo* and *The Birds*; sometimes it seems to exist for its own sake alone. Even in Hitchcock's first color film, *Rope* (1948), the complementary pair red and green – and their oscillation – is figured in the flashing lights of the neon sign that gains visual prominence during the course of the film. At *Rope*'s conclusion, after darkness has fallen, their cacophonous flashing – red and green, on and off – intensifies the uncontainable tension in the apartment. But while flashing signs have the function of expressing narrative tension and unsettling the spectator even in Hitchcock's early black-and-white films such as *The Lodger* (1927) and *Blackmail* (1929), in *Rope* the sign's colors lend this effect a special interest. Never fully in view, the sign's cryptic letters are not readily decipherable in the film and thus contribute to the abstract quality both of their presence here and of their alternation. Of primary interest, then, is the alternation – the oscillation between red and green that continues mechanically, automatically, cut off only by the end of the film.

The pairing – or juxtaposition – of red and green continues to play a significant role in *Frenzy* (1972), where expectations concerning their deployment are again undermined. Here, too, there is an aspect of color coding: Rusk the tie murderer is shown to be wearing a green tie when he strangles Brenda, who is likewise dressed in green. In a macabre turn, after committing murder, Rusk picks up the green apple – the "frugal lunch" in which he has interrupted Brenda – and begins to eat it. Here color is one of the ways in which the film suggests that it is the green-clad Brenda he is consuming – and once again green – the color of nature – signifies the unnatural. (Much is made of the fact that Brenda's husband Blaney – the much maligned "wrong man" who is nevertheless not totally innocent – has green eyes.) Later, after Rusk has disposed of Babs's body – stored in a sack of potatoes – he drinks wine and eats bread in an act of perverse communion. It certainly signifies that the murderer is a "greengrocer" – another verbal cue – who disposes of his corpses in Kent, "the garden of England." Finally, after yet another murder, Rusk is apprehended while wearing a red tie as a red lamp illuminates the female corpse on his bed. And while the shade of Rusk's tie hardly warrants consideration as a complement to the green that signifies the unnatural, in this film virtually every female character has hair in a shade of red. Brenda is a redhead, as is her secretary, Miss Barling; Babs Milligan has red hair, as does the inspector's wife. And so, for that matter, does the murderer's mother, who appears at his apartment window, leaning over a window box filled with red geraniums – and who is visiting from Kent. Surely so many redheaded women point away from a naturalistic color design and toward something more. No doubt the commonplace concerning the intensified sexuality of redheads is in play in *Frenzy*, and in this sense it is the red hair of the female victims that dooms them to a grave in the mother's green "garden." Yet a more abstract relation may be at issue.

Color-coded associations between food and women are already in evidence in *The Trouble with Harry*. We recall that the redheaded Jennifer Rogers is connected to the strawberries that are her favorite thing, and that Miss Gravely with her newly made-up face is spoken of as a "jar of preserves" – no doubt strawberry as well – that needs opening. By way of color, then, they are associated with the unnaturally orange and red landscape that is the landscape of death. Similar associations take a vicious, psychotic turn in *Frenzy*. Whereas consumption in Hitchcock's black comedy is restricted to sexual innuendo, fondly expressed, in this late film consumption substitutes for consummation – now only possible metonymically. The "eating of the apple" is literalized in *Frenzy*, substituting for the sexual act the phrase connotes. Eating is the act that links sex to murder, producing corpses to be replanted in the garden – the red-haired women, connected with fruit, are replanted in the green surroundings. Unstable opposites, green and red collapse into one another in death, much as in *Vertigo*. In this context, the complementary relation of red and green would seem to suggest a primal collapse of beginnings and ends, beyond the pleasure principle.

The color red has a psychologically charged and duplicitous role to play in *Marnie* (1964) as well. Marnie's mental illness is registered in the domain of sight, with the film linking her trauma to the blood of an inaugural crime scene. Again red is the color of intense affect, and warning chords provide a recurrent aural accompaniment to Marnie's reactions. Red gladiolas in her mother's house trigger her first "attack." Marnie's response is the same during the dream sequence there, and red ink spilled on her white blouse has a similar effect. At the races, a jockey's silks with red polka dots on a white background triggers it again. A second dream in the Rutland house connects the color with the traumatic event expressed in her fear of red: "No, Mama, don't cry … don't hurt my Mama!" And during an association game with Sean Connery's Mark as amateur psychoanalyst, the cue "red" provokes Marnie to shout "white! white!" Finally, a riding habit will set off the chain of events that leads to Marnie's mercy killing of her horse. Red is the color of affect, and it is also the color of blood, the substance for which the red in this film so obviously substitutes. The code would appear to be a simple one, the associations the film provides readily decipherable.

Interestingly, however, Marnie "sees red" only metaphorically: while something red is the object of her look, it is her image that is suffused with that color in virtually each instance, with red flashing light extending to fill the film frame. If the suffusion of the film frame suggests a permeability between the image and its material support, does this bleeding in the frame signal a "reality" they have in common – the color red as blood – or does it signal artifice – the color red simply as color? In some sense, the red film frame disturbs the spectator's vision, transferring the character's symptom to us. However, like a wash over realist images, it also cloaks representation in pure color.

The thunderstorm experienced in Mark's office is the exception to the rule that Marnie's image and the film frame turn red during her "attacks." In this sequence red light flashes in the window, not on Marnie, although the light immobilizes her against the door as she begs, in a child's voice, "stop the colors!" In a film whose system of metaphors is so carefully contrived, why is Marnie's image not suffused with red during her experience of the storm, as in all other instances? At one level, this variation undermines the notion of a closed color system. But perhaps it is because Mark's effort to "stop the colors" leads to an embrace, and the camera moves in to a tight close-up of their mouths, hers wearing surprisingly red lipstick, her red mouth seeming to substitute for the omitted suffusion. As we recall, the origin of Marnie's trauma lies in the murder she committed as a five-year-old, when she killed a sailor both in defense of her mother and – it is suggested – in disgust at his kiss. Mark's kiss both taps into and covers over the repressed memory, while the fleshiness of the couple's mouths in extreme close-up seems to stand in for a more private encounter – for the female body's interior spaces. As Marnie and Mark leave her mother's house at the film's conclusion, its red brick walls are prominent in the frame. Covered with raindrops from yet another thunderstorm, they look for all the world like drops of blood. At the level of metaphor, the mother's house is rendered body – it is yet another representation of a female interior, bleeding.

Lest we think that *all* images suggestive of the body are red in this film, however, we have only to recall the yellow purse in its opening frames: while its shape suggests intimate parts of the female anatomy, its color is jarring, unrealistic, out of synch with the subdued palette of the sequence. Here the bright yellow of the purse counteracts its anatomical shape, drawing attention to its color *as* color. A similar example occurs in one of the film's final scenes. Here there is an alternation between Marnie's dream-like memories of the killing and the diegetic present. Her memories are set off from the film's "present" by means of color: they have the sepia tones of old photographs – until crimson blood covers the sailor's suit, and, filling the frame, suffuses the screen itself. At this moment what was blood becomes mere color, the screen a painted surface. Once again the spectator experiences an oscillation of meanings as realism is replaced with abstraction.

As we have seen, then, it is not only Hitchcock's films of the 1960s that contain such effects. There is the railroad station scene in *North by Northwest* (1959), for example, in which porters called Red Caps dot the scene with vibrant spots of red that are both naturalistic and abstract. And what about realism in *To Catch a Thief* (1955), the film that won the Academy Award for Best Color Cinematography in 1956 – but was considered too gaudy by critics? With respect to its famous "cigarette-in-the-egg" shot – a cigarette is put out in the middle of the bright yellow yolk of a fried egg – Eric Rohmer argues that in this scene color contributes to the film's realism. Color completes certain film objects – the egg, he argues, "*exists fully only in color*," becomes "real" only in color."[8] A similar egg in a still life by Buffet does not function in the same way, he contends. For Rohmer – himself a painterly filmmaker – Hitchcock's egg "only exists through color," whereas Buffet's painted egg "lives only for it." In the one footnote to his essay, however, Rohmer notes the existence of a similar moment in *Rebecca*, a black-and-white film of 1940, during which a cigarette is stubbed out in a jar of cold cream. Surely it is texture, then, that is at issue in such moments. The violated yolk generates momentary revulsion in the spectator, it is true, but it is not its *color* that produces this affect. On the other hand, one might well argue that the yolk is chosen not only for its texture but *also* for its color and shape, for the perfect circle of color that – just for a moment – is visually before us. Don't we – just for a moment – perceive the yellow circle as an abstraction? It is precisely color that enables the slippage between object and outline.

To Catch a Thief does not have a consistent color system; it does not often use color metaphorically. But everywhere there are painterly effects, Côrot-like spots of red: red poppies in the midst of a bank of lavender, red flowers on tables, red-haired women. Yes, of course, this could simply be realism at work – until at another point in the film the camera pulls back from a close-up of clusters of flowers. The red, pink, and white mounds of carnations – like so many blobs of paint – suggest a moment in which color comes first, takes precedence over the things that give it shape. Once the camera tracks back far enough to reveal the blobs of color as carnations in their marketplace setting, that moment is over – but hasn't it registered, nevertheless? First color is perceived as such – only then does it assume the shape of the beautiful, if commonplace, flowers. Here, too, modernism and realism register as alternating effects.

The use of color as paint is imaged literally in the second *Man Who Knew Too Much* (1956), made not long after *To Catch a Thief* and *The Trouble with Harry*, a time of continued experimentation with color. In an establishing shot, the vendors' stalls in a Marrakesh marketplace are signaled by a sea of brown umbrellas, with one pale-blue umbrella in their midst. Prominent and disturbing within the visual field, this blue umbrella will have no narrative function in the film; it will not mark a locale of any significance. Rather, it would seem to constitute Žižek's famous trope of the stain in the visual field, the stain that renders the image discomfiting, uncanny.[9] (Another example of a stain produced by color is that of the red, phallic fire hydrant in the opening credits of *Rope,* the only spot of red in an otherwise dull image. Nevertheless, its relation to the homoerotic narrative is clear.) Although the casual spectator of this film may not recall the solitary blue umbrella later in the film, the spot of blue is linked by way of color to a later incident that – like the presence of the umbrella – will have no narrative significance in the film. In this sequence, the French spy Louis Bernard is chased out of the marketplace and through the narrow alleys that surround it. He is in disguise, arrayed in white Arab garb and in blackface, and as he runs through the streets he knocks over a can of pale blue paint and falls into the puddle it constitutes. His caftan stained with blue paint, from this point on Bernard is a marked man. But there is red in the frame, too: an array of red cloths hangs from a clothesline above Bernard as he falls into the paint. Does this conjunction of this red, white, and blue constitute a patriotic display? That is doubtful, despite the fact that the American identity of the protagonists (played by James Stewart and Doris Day) is repeatedly emphasized. The paint, I would suggest, is simply color as such.

At the end of the chase, Bernard finds himself once again in the marketplace, where he is stabbed in the back. When red blood seeping out of his wound joins the blue-and-white of the caftan, blood is again likened to paint. Does this color combination confirm the concatenation of colors as another reference to the American flag? It is doubtful, although the design does call our attention to color as metaphor. Dying, Bernard makes his way to over to James Stewart's Ben McKenna, to whom he reaches out a blue paint-covered hand – blue in contradistinction to the many bloodied hands one finds in Hitchcock. When McKenna in his turn reaches out to touch Bernard, he discovers that the fugitive is in blackface: McKenna's fingers leave white tracks on the brown makeup. In an interview that is a supplement to the DVD, Patricia Hitchcock confirms the significance of this scene for Hitchcock, who particularly wanted the paint on Bernard's face to come off on Stewart's hands. Although many tests were made, Pat Hitchcock asserts, the makeup would not come off. The problem was finally solved when white powder was applied to Stewart's hand, allowing him to leave fingerprints on Bernard. What about this sequence was so important to Hitchcock? Perhaps that the makeup and its removal recontextualizes the blue paint and the blood on the caftan. While the blue paint is applied color, a blood stain – even if it resembles paint – is of the body; it partakes in the real, hence is of another order entirely. As a simulation of skin color, the brown makeup inhabits an area somewhere between paint and blood – it is artifice, simulating nature. The makeup, too, is applied color, designed to deceive and susceptible to erasure, but, as a signifier of race, its connotations are sometimes a matter of life and death. In *The Man Who Knew Too Much*, the rather contrived conjunction of paint, blood, and makeup in the marketplace scene points toward the unstable border between art and the real so central to Hitchcock's oeuvre.

Bleeding

Interestingly, the movement between the realist and modernist use of color in Hitchcock is part of a more general tendency in his films to oscillate between these two poles. For instance, his films variously feature the modernist, figured movement out of the frame and through a metaphorical fourth wall. Sometimes this occurs as a "color bleed" in which the color red is indirectly motivated by the diegesis. This is color as flashes of light – conveniently the color of blood – rapidly emanating from the center of the frame as though spurting from a wound. In *Rear Window* (1954), flashes of red mark the afterimage experienced by Thorwald as Jeff resorts to a flash device in order to blind his opponent. Here the red suffusion of the film frame suggests the conjunction of body and image produced by the optical imprint the flash leaves on the retina – this is a realist reading. A flash of red figures similarly in *Spellbound* (1945) when a bullet is figuratively shot into the space of the movie theater. Here, too, the red-suffused shot suggests the physical merger of character with spectator at the level of perception – a mixed effect, arguably both realist and modernist at once. When the single flash of red perforates the black-and-white images of the film, in some sense this suggests that the film is bleeding into the space of the spectator, thus briefly figuring the collapse of spectatorial and diegetic reality.

At this point, it may be useful to describe the mediatic trope central to such concerns, the trope defined by William Egginton as "bleeding." For Egginton this term describes an "obsessive concern" of spectacle from the time that it was "organized in such a way as to presuppose an ontological distinction between the space of the viewer and the space of the character."[10] With his focus on the strategies that make representation appear realistic, Egginton distinguishes between a mode that insists on the "reality" of the medium, "presenting the medium (the film image) as if it were the object – [i.e.,] reality itself," (210),[11] and one that suggests to the spectator that the object s/he sees stands in for another object. Whereas the first mode – in which the film image is presented as though it were reality itself – is predicated on the separation of spectatorial space from diegetic space, the second mode often undermines this separation. The collapse of spectator space and diegetic space in the first mode results in a "reality bleed," a term Egginton takes from Cronenberg's *eXistenZ* (1999), where it refers to the phenomenon in virtual reality games wherein the "real world" enters the world of the game. Egginton describes "bleeding" as a collapse of the distinctions between two levels of reality, usually a *sudden* collapse that catches the spectator off guard. As his example, Egginton mentions *Pleasantville* (1998), where the bleeding of one fictional world into another is produced "quite literally as a color bleed."[12]

As a mediatic trope, "bleeding" is useful in describing the collapse of ontological registers in Hitchcock films, including the figured merger of spectatorial reality with film mentioned earlier. The designation of the "color bleed" is especially pertinent for those sequences accompanied by flashes of red just barely motivated by the diegesis. Returning briefly to *Rear Window*, we recall that it is flashes of red that mark the scene in which Thorwald enters Jeff's space. In an alternation of point-of-view shots, the spectator sees more viscerally than usual through the eyes of the characters. In this same sequence, however, Thorwald disturbs Jeff's characteristic position of facing the courtyard and metaphorically enters Jeff's space from the position of the spectator. Thus, these realist color effects take place within the context of a modernist move.

Let's return to the other instance of "color bleeding" in Hitchcock that deserves particular attention, to the gun barrel in close-up, which fires directly out of the frame in *Spellbound* (1945). Here, too, the film penetrates spectatorial space as the gun goes off "in our faces." As the bullet is figuratively shot into the space of the movie theater, a single flash of red perforates the otherwise black-and-white images of the film, as though to suggest that the film frame were indeed bleeding into the space of the spectator, triggering the collapse of representation with reality. Equated with Dr. Murchison as he points a gun simultaneously at himself and at the camera, the spectator figuratively becomes the suicide's (blinded) victim. Once again a flash of red marks the image of the gun at the moment of shooting, suggesting that it is Murchison's retinal image that we see. This is a subjective shot, of course, seen through the eyes of a character at the point of death. But the sequence begins with an extreme close-up from behind of a hand holding a gun. We see the gun from the point of view of the murderer, but the scale and position of the hand suggest that it is an extension of our own bodies. When the gun is slowly turned around to face Murchison – and the spectator – it shoots us both in the eye. More obviously even than in *Rear*

Window, this sequence features a modernist penetration of the fourth wall. And here, too, the red suffusion that follows immediately upon its firing suggests the physical merger of character with spectator at the level of perception. But while this burst of color suggests an afterimage – a real effect of vision – it points equally to its own artifice, an astonishing flash of red amid the black-and-white of the film's other images. Once again a modernist move oscillates with a realist goal; once again the color red is both blood and paint.

NOTES

1 Honoré de Balzac, "The Hidden Masterpiece," *The Works of Balzac*, vol. 28, trans. Katharine Prescott Wormeley (Boston: Little, Brown, 1900), pp. 360, 361.

2 Jean-Luc Godard, "Let's Talk about Pierrot," *in Godard on Godard*, trans. and ed. Tom Milne (New York: Da Capo Press, 1972), p. 217.

3 Gilles Deleuze, *Cinema I: The Movement-Image*, trans. Hugh Tomlinson and Barbara Habberjam (Minneapolis: Minnesota University Press, 1986), p. 118.

4 Stanley Cavell, *The World Viewed: Reflections on the Ontology of Film* (Cambridge, MA: Harvard University Press, 1979).

5 Frieda Grafe, "Verblichen, die Farben der DDR: Hitchcock's Palette und Rohmer als Vermittler," *Filmfarben, Schriften*, Vol. 1 (Berlin: Brinkmann & Bose, 2002), p. 98.

6 Sergei Eisenstein, "Color and Meaning," *The Film Sense* (New York: Harcourt Brace & Co., 1975), pp. 113–156.

7 Richard Allen, "Hitchcock's Color Designs," *Color, The Film Reader*, eds. Angela Dalle Vacche and Brian Price (New York: Routledge, 2006), p. 138.

8 Eric Rohmer, "Of Taste and Colors," *Color, The Film Reader*, eds. Angela Dalle Vacche and Brian Price (New York: Routledge, 2006), p. 124.

9 Slavoj Žižek, "The Hitchcockian Blot," *Looking Awry: An Introduction to Jacques Lacan Through Popular Culture* (Cambridge, MA: MIT Press, 1992), pp. 88–122.

10 William Egginton, "Reality Is Bleeding: A Brief History of Film from the Sixteenth Century," *Configurations* 9 (2001), p. 210.

11 Egginton, 210. Egginton calls the first mode "illusionism" and the second "realism," but since his terms conflict with what is usually referred to as realism in film and confuse distinctions with which we have been working, I will not refer to his categories by name.

12 Ibid.

12

MARK GOBLE

Live Nude Hitchcock: Final Frenzies

I

It is hard to describe the course of Alfred Hitchcock's late career as anything but a story of decline and fall: the numbers at the box office get smaller; the critics get more brutal; longtime colleagues and collaborators leave his side, some exhausted from demanding years of service, some retiring in deteriorating health, and others simply dying – from natural causes of the kind that figure so infrequently in his films. After making two of his most startling masterpieces early in the 1960s, and then following up *Psycho* (1960) and *The Birds* (1963) with *Marnie* (1964), one of his most perverse and complex films, Hitchcock devoted the remainder of the decade to a pair of desultory efforts that revisited the conventions of the espionage thrillers he effectively invented in the 1930s. Both *Torn Curtain* (1966) and *Topaz* (1969) were released to poor reviews, made far less money than expected, and have lived for decades near the bottom of any list of Hitchcock's worst, where they are more than occasionally joined by *Frenzy* (1972) and *Family Plot* (1976), which are judged as relative achievements to the degree that they provide at least some reason to believe that Hitchcock's fifty years of making films ended with something other than a run of abject failures.

This downward trajectory is so familiar from Hitchcock biographies and popular assessments of his work – and the consensus of aesthetic disregard for his last films so strongly held – that rehearsing it might seem like a prelude to some new appraisal of what Hitchcock accomplished after *Marnie*, or at least the setup for some claims about why we have been wrong to overlook and unjustly disparage Hitchcock at the bitter end. Alas, this is no setup. Hitchcock's decline is sad, and it is visible. There are many reasons to think more seriously about his final films – especially for what they say about the historical *finality* of Hitchcock in the late 1960s and early 1970s – but it remains the case that *Torn Curtain* makes a hash of elements from *The 39 Steps* (1935), *Rebecca* (1940), and *North by Northwest* (1959), and that *Frenzy* tries to be an uncensored and more violent *Psycho* only to remind us that repression, for Hitchcock in particular, is where the action really is. Hitchcock, as I will argue shortly, does produce a version of "late style" as Theodor Adorno and Edward Said have conceived it, but unlike the "alternative and unregulated modes of subjectivity" that Said finds in Beethoven or Visconti, Hitchcock has almost nothing new to bring to his last films.[1] Late Hitchcock is self-conscious to the point of pastiche and cites earlier moments and episodes from his own masterpieces so rapaciously that it is tempting to consider them postmodern, as if the flatness of their characters was a stylized reaction to the depths he once explored in films like *Spellbound* (1945) or *Notorious* (1946); as if the conviction in their own devices that they seem to lack is actually a way of working through the aftermath of films so powerfully invested in their formalism, like *Rope* (1948), *Rear Window* (1954), or *Vertigo* (1958), that they constitute closed worlds of cinematic design and visual logic. *The Birds* or *Marnie* certainly invite interpretation along these lines, and the way they show Hitchcock devolving his style into an assembly of horrifying gimmicks and detached effects has inspired various critics to characterize them as almost avant-garde for their contorted narratives and under-motivated spectacles of emotional disturbance, sex, and violence.

In other words, if we look at Hitchcock in the early 1960s – at not just *The Birds* and *Marnie,* but also *Psycho* (1960) – we see a series of films that represent exactly the kind of strange, distorted masterpieces that we associate with the idea of "late style." With these works Hitchcock seems aiming for the auratic intimations of "lateness" that Said so movingly explores as "a kind of self-imposed exile from what is generally acceptable, coming after it, and surviving beyond it."[2] The problem of Hitchcock's last four films is that they come after even all of this. Hitchcock's too-late style?

At the risk of taking Adorno and Said's high seriousness in the direction of the gutter – where Hitchcock was certainly at ease – let me suggest that his last films are not interesting simply because his subjectivity was suddenly "unregulated" sometime in the 1960s and so was able to "[set] free the masses of material that he used to form."[3] In many ways, as we will see, Hitchcock in the last decade of his career experienced limits and constraints that he had not suffered since the 1940s, if not farther back into his years in Britain. I don't think Hitchcock's final works can possibly stand up when reckoned against the kinds of fragmentary, tortuous achievements that Adorno and Said ascribe to Beethoven, Richard Strauss, or Jean Genet. And it is less kind still, however necessary, to judge them in light of Hitchcock's own films from the early 1960s. "In the history of art late works are the catastrophes," according to Adorno.[4] But in Hitchcock's case, it is also fair to use the language of the movie business and admit that some of his catastrophes were merely flops. Which is not to say that Hitchcock's final films are without value for all the ways they strain and suffer to keep up with a changing cinematic culture of the late 1960s, a culture perhaps too permissive to be scandalized by the thrills that Hitchcock promised even at his most depraved and tawdry. Indeed, the significance of Hitchcock's late films comes into sharper focus if we observe that there is only one thing he objectively and graphically accomplishes in movies when his best days were gone, and even his "late style" began to fail him: after a lifetime pushing at the limits of convention, Hitchcock finally gets to put a naked woman's body on the screen.

II

Cinematic nudity predates the invention of cinema. Naked women feature prominently in the serial photography of Eadweard Muybridge, for example, and we know from Linda Williams that Muybridge lecture audiences in the 1880s were treated to animated displays of sequences of highly eroticized "human locomotion" projected with his "zoopraxiscope," a crucial forerunner to modern cinema.[5] By the 1890s, examples of erotic or pornographic cinema were already in wide circulation, and several noteworthy films from the silent era had female nude scenes occasioned by their "artistic" or Biblical subjects, and thus hoping to avoid various regimes of censorship that soon emerged in most European and North American countries. While female – and, to a lesser degree, male – nudity persisted in underground, avant-garde, and ethnographic cinema of the 1920s, most mainstream national cinemas turned increasingly restrictive in the 1930s. Hollywood adopted the Motion Picture Production Code in 1930, and censors working under Will Hays began enforcing a constantly changing set of rules that not only governed nudity and sexual content on screen but rendered all manner of topics, biological realities, and even narrative outcomes forbidden to any movie hoping to enjoy a wide release in the United States. The British Board of Film Classification similarly pursued consistently more conservative and repressive regulations on cinematic content by the 1930s, meaning that some of the relatively racy scenes in Hitchcock's earliest films, like June's bathtub scene in *The Lodger* (1927) or Alice's disrobing in *Blackmail* (1929), remained among the most explicit sequences he had shot before he started work on *Psycho* – all the exertions of "Miss Torso" in *Rear Window* (1954) notwithstanding.

Hitchcock's own exertions in respect to *Psycho*'s shower scene were far more fascinating. Preparations for its filming involved not only Saul Bass's famously elaborate storyboards but feats of considerable ingenuity from camera operators, set designers, and costumers to ensure that Marion Crane's murder would be more visceral and violent than anything audiences had seen before, while technically continuing to uphold the letter, if not the spirit, of the Production Code. As Stephen Rebello observes in his exhaustive account of making *Psycho*, "Hitchcock simultaneously succeeded in titillating and shocking the viewer while concealing the nudity of the victim and the true identity of the attacker."[6] Janet Leigh, who played Crane in the film, was never nude on camera or on set; moleskin was liberally employed by costumer Rita Riggs to cover breasts, buttocks, or other parts as needed during the long shoot. "I began to think of it as sculpture," Riggs remembers, "if we had to see part of a breast, say, under the crook of an elbow, I would sculpt moleskin, then glue, cover, and trim away until just the amount of body that was needed was visible."[7] Leigh insists that "Mr. Hitchcock *never* asked [her] to do the scene in the nude because showing nudity on screen was simply out of the question. Doing the scene actually in the nude would have negated how clever and subtle he was at *suggesting* things."[8] That said, Hitchcock also employed a model and dancer, Marli Renfro, as a body double who regularly worked in the nude and was filmed extensively in the fatal bathroom, though none of this footage was finally used; it is, however, Renfro's naked body that Norman Bates (Anthony Perkins) wraps up in the shower curtain and deposits in the trunk of Marion's car. Renfro further played an important role in the publicity campaign that preceded *Psycho* and powerfully contributed to the promotional mystique that Hitchcock engineered. It was widely reported, after all, that Hitchcock had hired a model to allow for a "rear-view scene of Miss Leigh" that he gave every knowing, calculated indication of intending to include in the completed film.[9] Hitchcock carefully promised some sort of serious transgression in respect to Hollywood norms of censorship in several interviews he gave while filming, replying memorably to one question about what he planned to do about the Production Code by pointing out, "through petulant lips," according to the reporter, that "'men do kill nude women, you know.'"[10]

By the time Hitchcock was ready to submit the shower scene in *Psycho* to the censors, he had already been negotiating over various aspects in the film's script that pushed at the limits of the Production Code. Both passing moments of innuendo in Joseph Stefano's screenplay ("Bed? Only playground that beats Las Vegas.") and deeper insinuations of incest between Norman and his mother were deleted on the orders of Paramount. Which Hitchcock did, at least in part according to Rebello, because he and Stefano had larded the screenplay with obvious transgressions to draw the censors' attention away from the flagrant nudity it was imperative for the shower scene to suggest but not, of course, depict.[11] When the completed sequence was shown to a board of seven censors, three reported that they saw nudity while two did not; and then Hitchcock famously repacked the exact same cut of the film and returned it to the board. The three members of the board who had seen nudity now saw none and were satisfied with Hitchcock's "changes," but two other members of the board, who had not seen any nudity on their first viewing, now insisted that there were shots that unacceptably showed too much of Janet Leigh. In further negotiations, Hitchcock proposed to trade cuts to the shower scene in return for the permission to retain another sequence that censors also identified as a clear Code violation: the opening love scene between John Galvin and Janet Leigh in bed, which was more or less a direct assault on the standing prohibition of anything erotic that took place in a bed, or horizontally, or between partially undressed actors. Here, Hitchcock seems to have prevailed less by way of trickery than by attrition in offering to reshoot the scene but only if the censors would come to the set to supervise what they would eventually have to deem permissible. No such visit ever occurred, according to Rebello, and after several more exchanges about the shower scene – which, again, was never cut – *Psycho* was approved with only minor dialogue changes. And while later fans and film scholars have far outdone the censors in identifying individual frames of nudity in the shower sequence that flash by too quickly for most viewers to perceive, the only taboos that Hitchcock was able to take credit for violating in 1960 were rather circumscribed. He was able to retain the shots of John Galvin and Janet Leigh in bed, and he was permitted to achieve another breakthrough as well: shortly before stepping into the shower, Marion Crane became the first character in a Hollywood film to flush a toilet onscreen.

Over the course of the 1960s, Hollywood filmmakers pushed with increasing vehemence at what many critics, directors, and even studio executives found to be the increasingly anachronistic standards of the Production Code. This is a familiar story whose basic contours are well known, and which I will not rehearse here.[12] Where Hitchcock clearly excelled at the institutional gamesmanship it took to get the censors to sign off on *Psycho* – indeed, he seems to have relished the courtly rituals of transgression and its accommodation – many of the period's most powerful assaults on the Production Code came from outside the studio system entirely, either from abroad, where European filmmakers had been operating with considerably more license since at least the 1950s, or from the margins of the U.S. film industry, where independent distributors allowed for a range of films, experimental, avant-garde, and otherwise, to find their ways to audiences unconcerned with Motion Picture Production Association (MPAA) approval.

In this respect, Russ Meyer's *The Immoral Mr. Teas* (1959) was squarely in the category of "otherwise" and had little in common with Jean-Pierre Melville's *Bob le Flambeur* (1956) or Jack Smith's *Flaming Creatures* (1963) except for on-screen nudity; but as the first "nudie-cutie" filmmaker to enjoy widespread popularity in the United States, Meyer helped establish a viable market for circulating and showing graphic movies in public and not strictly at private screenings in homes or clubs where stag films and other forms of pornography had long been popular. With profits estimated at more than $1.5 million on a budget of $24,000, *The Immoral Mr. Teas* marked an even more impressive return on investment (62.5:1!) than Hitchcock managed with the wildly popular *Psycho* even if Meyer's grindhouse classic could not hope to match the gross profits ($32 million) of a major Hollywood film in national release. With a plot that is little more than a pretense for its main character to see women naked (he is left with X-ray vision after waking up from anesthesia at his dentist's office), *The Immoral Mr. Teas* merely strings together a series of occasions for female bodies to be seen, and ends with Mr. Teas visiting a psychiatrist in hopes of being cured of his hallucinations. He promptly sees through his doctor's clothes and leaves her office as the concluding narration of the voice-over gives a lesson that Hitchcock would certainly have approved: as Mr. Teas returns to a world of women who will be unknowingly exposed to his rapacious gaze, we are told that "some men are happy to be sick." A real psycho, in other words.

The case of Michael Powell's *Peeping Tom* (1960), however, reminds us that not every film that broke new ground in bringing more visceral imagery to the screen met with popular success. Featuring a brief moment of nudity early in its narrative, *Peeping Tom* was savagely attacked by British newspapers when it was shown to critics, and performed dismally when first released. In many ways a perfect counterpart to *Psycho*, with its sexualized violence and scopophilic serial killer – rendered partly sympathetic by childhood traumas that, unlike the relationship between Norman and his mother, we see played out before us – the failure of *Peeping Tom* just months before the scheduled opening of *Psycho* provided Hitchcock with a cautionary example that helped convince him that there should be no press viewings of the film before its theatrical debut. This is certainly not the only reason *Psycho* triumphed where *Peeping Tom* so altogether failed, but it shows how carefully even Hitchcock – with a strong commercial record in the 1950s and singular status as an entertainment "brand" – had to calibrate the affronts to censorship and moral standards he was willing to undertake.[13] And he might especially have sympathized with Powell, as neither *The Birds* nor *Marnie* performed nearly so well as *Psycho*. *The Birds*, with its elaborate use of animation and special effects, as well as complex location shoots, cost more than $3 million to produce, and by earning only $11 million at the box office barely grossed one-third as much as its far cheaper predecessor. *Marnie* fared still worse, bringing in roughly $7 million against a production budget of $3 million.

These reversals left Hitchcock partly at the mercy of his friend and former agent, Lew Wasserman, who became the chief at Universal Pictures after the studio's purchase by MCA in 1962. Although Hitchcock also owned a portion of the company, he lacked the capital – in every sense – to pursue the projects he most wanted to develop in the wake of *Marnie*. So while Hitchcock had already begun preparing for his next film with Hedren, he now was explicitly forbidden by the studio to produce the script, entitled *Mary Rose*, which was an adaptation of a James Barrie ghost story about a young girl who vanishes on her wedding anniversary, only to return as an apparition who first haunts her son and then eventually threatens to kill him decades later. There is little reason to think that *Mary Rose*, imagined as what its screenwriter called "a nightmarish" vehicle for Hedren, would have made Universal happy, and it is hard to see how Hitchcock's intense and likely inappropriate attention to Hedren could have led to anything but another late "catastrophe," to recall Adorno and Said. Wasserman instead steered Hitchcock toward the material that became *Torn Curtain* and *Topaz* – two espionage thrillers that, to diminishing returns, the studio hoped would salvage Hitchcock's reputation by giving him the chance to work within the genre that provided many of his greatest films, including *The 39 Steps*, *Notorious* (1946), and *North by Northwest*. But not even the pairing of Paul Newman and Julie Andrews, two of the most bankable stars of the day, could rescue *Torn Curtain* from feeling like an anachronism for most reviewers. When *Topaz* was released on Christmas, 1969, Hitchcock's latest disappointment made his anachronism appear almost ludicrously complete. For not only was *Topaz* an even more desultory return to plot conventions and motifs from his own earlier works, but the film itself was set in the days surrounding the Cuban Missile Crisis of 1962 – an event that barely figures in the movie even as it perversely reminds us that Hitchcock too was effectively old news. Also in theaters, Christmas, 1969: *Easy Rider*, *Alice's Restaurant*, *Putney Swope*, *Midnight Cowboy*, *Take the Money and Run*, and *Bob and Carol and Ted and Alice*.[14] Some of these films have aged far worse than *Topaz* did, but not one seemed so immediately geriatric in the moment. Hitchcock had hoped his superior, more realistic versions of James Bond movies – he devoutly screened each new film in the series to keep track of how much they stole, or so he argued, from his example – would restore his reputation as a modern master. The particularly disastrous *Topaz* grossed only $6 million, which was exactly what *Rebecca* had earned almost thirty years before. We hardly need to adjust for inflation to know it was a bomb.

Thus Hitchcock was poorly positioned to take advantage of the new terrain that had been opened up by other filmmakers who had further pushed the Production Code into obsolescence while he spent the remainder of the 1960s retracing his own generic steps. In 1964, Sydney Lumet's *The Pawnbroker* became the first mainstream American film to feature female nudity. Developed for MGM, the film was ultimately self-financed by its producer when no major studio would accept it for distribution even after it had debuted to great acclaim at the Berlin Film Festival. In focusing directly on the consequences of the Holocaust for its protagonist, Sol Nazerman (played by Rod Steiger), *The Pawnbroker* sought to introduce a series of subjects that Hollywood had avoided, and more importantly to present them squarely from the perspective of a Jewish survivor. But the controversy that the film just as provocatively courted – and that led to the delay of its release for almost a year – centered on a brief nude scene roughly halfway through the narrative that was harrowing for both its narrative force and racial politics. Hoping to convince Nazerman to help her boyfriend Jesus – who will eventually die in a sacrificial gesture that confirms the symbolism of his name – a black prostitute halfway undresses for Nazerman in a painfully ineffectual gesture of seduction. The film then cuts almost immediately to a flashback sequence in a concentration camp where Nazerman sees his own wife, who we know has not survived the war, similarly rendered as object for the pleasure and debasement of her Nazi captors. Never known for understatement, Lumet intercuts between these moments of abjection at a pace just short of "clatter montage," as Eisenstein would term it, that visually conflates two female bodies whose shared nakedness cannot possibly register the same horrors of exploitation and exchange, even as the film all but merges them in Nazerman's post-traumatic gaze. Despite the horrific context for both instances of nudity, *The Pawnbroker* could not gain a seal of approval from the office of the Production Code, and since neither Lumet nor Ely Landau, the film's producer, would agree to cut the sequence, it remained unseen in the United States. Only after Lumet appealed to the MPAA board was the film deemed "a special and unique case" that could, as such, be released by Allied Artists and American International Pictures (the distributor of Roger Corman's Poe adaptations!) in violation of the Code's absolute ban on nudity.

Hitchcock regularly screened noteworthy films by younger directors, and there is every reason to assume he would have seen *The Pawnbroker* – especially since Lumet was close to Peter Bogdanovich, who had worked closely with Hitchcock during a retrospective of his career that Bogdanovich had organized at the Museum of Modern Art, and which had also featured the premiere of *The Birds* in 1963. We know for certain, however, that Hitchcock paid close attention to another of the period's most important nude scenes in a film that had no interest whatsoever in balancing its *outré* imagery with moral seriousness. Michelangelo Antonioni's *Blow-Up* (1966) became the first mainstream film with full frontal nudity to circulate in wide release in the United States, and, with box office returns of more than $20 million, was among the top grossing movies of the year – and it far surpassed *Torn Curtain*, despite the highly bankable presences of Newman and Andrews. What Antonioni lacked in star power, however, he more than made up in style and affectation, and it is difficult to conceive a film more altogether of its present than *Blow-Up*, with its "Swinging London" locales and fashions, its blank narrative of paranoia and alienation, and its radically inconclusive ending that, like Susan Sontag's famous essay of the same year, is an argument "against interpretation."[15] It was not just that Antonioni's film, even more than some of his existentialist Italian mysteries like *L'Avventura* (1960), borrowed so liberally from Hitchcock's own motifs and preoccupations with visual desire and epistemological uncertainty; *Blow-Up* also took place in Hitchcock's birthplace, and treated London as a site of erotic mystery and perversion that made the expensive locations of *Torn Curtain* seem as lifeless as the on-screen chemistry that so completely failed to make Newman and Andrews into new versions of Cary Grant and Ingrid Bergman.

By July 1966, Hitchcock had begun working on a film to be entitled *Frenzy*. He hired Howard Fast, the author of *Spartacus* and also a pseudonymous series of crime novels, to start on a screenplay. But instead of showing Fast a selection of his own films to establish the stylistic parameters of the collaboration (as Hitchcock had been doing with writers since the 1940s), he screened several films by Antonioni. "My god, Howard!" Fast later remembered Hitchcock saying, "I've just seen Antonioni's *Blow-Up*. These Italian directors are a century ahead of me in terms of technique! What have I been doing all this time?"[16] Throughout the disappointing months spent filming *Topaz*, Hitchcock continued to produce revised scripts and screen tests for what was emerging as the story of a psychotic artist and serial killer whose victims would include a string of nude models, explicitly dispatched on-screen. This was not the *Frenzy* Hitchcock finally released in 1972, but the highly graphic film he does make – about a serial killer of women in a strangely anachronistic yet contemporary London – very much reflects the forms of cinematic modernism, both American and European, that he was determined at last to embody with a vengeance.

III

There are four women whose naked bodies the viewer sees in *Frenzy*. Two are dead already, and appear only as corpses, one very near the film's beginning and the other just before it ends. The other two are characters murdered by the notorious "Necktie Strangler" in the course of the narrative; the first victim whose death we witness is Brenda Blaney (played by Barbara Leigh-Hunt), the ex-wife of the film's protagonist, Richard Blaney (Jon Finch), and the second is Babs Milligan (Anna Massey), who is Blaney's lover. Their killer is Bob Rusk (Barry Foster), a wholesale fruit distributor in Covent Gardens and also Blaney's friend. Any suspense about the Necktie Strangler's true identity is dispelled just twenty-five minutes into the film, when Rusk enters Brenda Blaney's offices (she runs a dating service) and, after closing the door a bit too quickly, is addressed as "Mr. Robinson," the name under which he has been looking for "women of a specific type" who might be willing to "submit" to "certain peculiarities" that Brenda reminds him are quite outside the bounds of what her "very normal clientele" are into. By the time Rusk confesses to Brenda that she is his "type of woman," we know to fear the worst, although the exceedingly graphic scene of rape and strangulation that follows is still almost too much to bear. We are later spared the sight of Babs's murder by way of an elegant tracking shot that is, for good reason, among the film's most famous sequences. Yet we do see her character briefly naked after she has slept with Blaney, and again when Rusk must retrieve an incriminating piece of evidence from her body, which he dumps in a truck of potatoes heading north from London. Here, all the violence that Hitchcock did not show us when Babs was murdered is just as bad when it is rendered the second time as farce: Rusk must struggle mightily to pry a pin loose from fingers that have closed in rigor mortis, and so must be audibly and sickeningly broken, before he can put his diamond-studded "R" back in his lapel. Babs's body eventually thuds out onto the highway, its head covered in a potato sack and almost run over by a police car.

When the police expose her grotesquely molded, dirty face, it, of course, recalls the final image of Brenda Blaney which Hitchcock brutally composes into an almost clownish death mask, a caricature with fixed eyes and sprawling tongue that draws as much on the example of Wile E. Coyote as it does on Marion Crane. Indeed, Hitchcock used the shot of Brenda Blaney's death to correct an error from *Psycho* by making sure that Leigh-Hunt's pupils are visibly contracted, not dilated. And Babs's horrifying rictus is, at least in part, a knowing gesture too, since Anna Massey had played the tortured love interest of the serial killer in Powell's *Peeping Tom*. There she

Figure 12.1. *Frenzy* (1972).

Figure 12.2. *Frenzy.*

survives the carnage when the killer commits suicide in the end and lets her live. Hitchcock was not so kind (Figures 12.1–12.3).

Working on location in London for the first time in more than twenty years, Hitchcock made *Frenzy* on an impressively small budget and saw it earn more profit than did any of his films since *Psycho*, which is, in every way, its predecessor. In the revised edition of François Truffaut's interviews with Hitchcock appearing shortly after their subject's death, he details the joy with which Hitchcock appeared at Cannes after *Frenzy* debuted to great

Figure 12.3. *Frenzy.*

acclaim; the film, he writes, "was impregnated with charm," which might be an unfortunate turn of phrase for a film about a serial killer of women driven by impotence and misogyny, but consistent with a chorus of reviews in 1972 that welcomed *Frenzy* as Hitchcock's return to form, and even controversy.[17] "Does *Frenzy* Degrade Women?" asked Victoria Sullivan in *The New York Times*, responding affirmatively in response to critic Vincent Canby's enthusiastic review, in the same paper, that described the murderer in the film as "a genial London fruit wholesaler" – a telling career choice for a Hitchcock villain, as we will see.[18] The National Organization for Women (NOW) observed the third annual Women's Rights Day by bestowing one of eight "Keep Her in Her Place" awards on *Frenzy*, which, to Hitchcock's disappointment, received no Oscar nominations. Yet feminist critics since Tania Modleski have come to see *Frenzy*'s grotesque and even ostentatious violence toward women as provocatively self-conscious in the way it lets Hitchcock indulge and comment on some of his signature obsessions.[19]

It was not just the film's excruciating violence that made *Frenzy* seem more personal after the rote performances of genre in *Torn Curtain* and *Topaz*. Like the homicidal murderer Barney Rusk, Hitchcock's own father had been in the greengrocery business before later earning his living as a Limehouse fishmonger on Salmon Lane; the decidedly down-market milieu in *Frenzy* hardly marks the first time class had figured in one of Hitchcock's films, but rarely had it seemed so "English" in its character. That said, a central London world of greengrocers, barkeeps, and "matrimonial agencies" like Brenda Blaney's does not exactly feel contemporary, and *Frenzy*'s interest in what, following Raymond Williams, we might call "residual" occupations with marginal, uncertain futures suggests that Hitchcock's return to some familiar territory was, strictly speaking, more archaeological than autobiographical. Hitchcock wanted to film in Covent Garden in part because its fruit and vegetable markets were to be replaced by the much larger markets at New Covent Garden, which were being built while he was in London (and opened in 1974). Hitchcock's London, however, is difficult to modernize. The film starts, after all, with a boosterish politician promising a new era in which the Thames "will soon be clear … of waste products" – just as a naked corpse floats face-down into view. A particularly morbid vision of urban renewal is, so to speak, the butt of this grisly joke. This first scene also invokes the opening sequence of Hitchcock's first thriller, *The Lodger*, which similarly begins with a crowd gathering to gawk at the female victim of a serial killer; but as revivified and rendered graphic for a post-1960s sensibility, now the body is wearing nothing but the necktie the killer has used to strangle her.

All this to say that the surpassing "Englishness" of *Frenzy* also makes it feel like Hitchcock's somewhat belated contribution to the "New American Cinema" of the 1960s with which *Torn Curtain* and especially *Topaz* had been so unfavorably compared. Where each of these films had pursued their plots across a cosmopolitan mix of European countries and American cities – and, in the case of *Topaz*, an imagined Cuba as well – there is almost no perceptible commitment to any sense of place or geographic authenticity, and for every dutifully composed establishing image of Copenhagen, Paris, or Berlin (filmed by second-unit directors while Hitchcock remained in Hollywood), there are just as many examples of the rear projection effects and matte shots that had long distinguished Hitchcock's style. *Frenzy*, on the other hand, wants to register an aesthetic of London particularity that speaks to the extent to which location shooting had become essential to a younger generation of Hollywood filmmakers; while not exactly *McCabe and Mrs. Miller* (1971) or *Mean Streets* (1973), *Frenzy* does manage to maintain the aesthetic of its location from start to finish, and works self-consciously to ground its cinematic world in the particularities of living, urban space.

Yet it is Hitchcock's fascination with dead naked women that perhaps speak better to the exertions he undertakes in *Frenzy* to modernize his own late style. For not only does the graphic nudity in *Frenzy* reflect the more permissive standards of the "new" Hollywood that had emerged in full by the late 1960s; it also represents the culmination of a drive toward more carnal views of bodies in even Hitchcock's major failures of the period. Hitchcock, as we have seen, had with *Psycho* what might be called the effect of nudity in its absence: the self-promotional gusto with which he flirted

Figure 12.4. *Marnie* (1964).

with the prospect of an outright violation of the Production Code helped make the film into a commercial triumph, and confirmed the mythology of Hitchcock's crafty genius. With *The Birds*, Hitchcock had gone in a differently graphic direction by rendering various avian species as so many slashers going after human flesh and blood. In *Marnie*, however, the violence of the film's fixation on its protagonist again led Hitchcock to simulate the appearance of nudity on-screen. When Mark Rutland (Sean Connery) enters Marnie's room and makes clear that he intends to consummate the marriage into which he has coerced her – she has left him in his own room to go to her separate bed, only to have him follow her rejection with the obvious innuendo of "But I do want to go to bed, Marnie, I want very much to go to bed" – it is her striking scream of "No" that prompts Mark to remove her nightgown (Figure 12.4).

Mark then pauses before cloaking Marnie in his own robe, but even as this gesture and his pained expression try to mitigate the aggression of his desire, he proceeds nonetheless to kiss her. This kiss ends, of course, in one of the film's most famous shots as the camera, moving in over Connery's shoulder to frame Hedren in a close-up and following (or pushing?) her toward the bed where her immobile body will be made to satisfy her husband. Marnie's blank expression and unblinking eyes make her visually the very image of a corpse, and narratively mystifies the absence of her will, as if the only way to advance the story of her traumatic past was to subject her to a bit of "rape play," to borrow a term from the world of BDSM, where her consensual non-consent is performatively assumed. We know

Figure 12.5. *Torn Curtain* (1966).

from Hitchcock's biographers that *Marnie*'s screenwriter, Jay Presson Allen, and Connery himself were decidedly uncomfortable with the way this scene suggests that Rutland rapes his wife. For Hitchcock, however, it seems more likely that it is simply the case that Marnie's safeword is not "no."

By any measure, *Torn Curtain* is a far tamer film than *Marnie* is, and the lack of chemistry between Andrews and Newman – and between Hitchcock and his stars on the set – has long been prominent in assessments of why it goes so quickly wrong. From its opening shot of Andrews and Newman provocatively in bed but altogether buried under heavy woolen blankets, we perhaps should know that *Torn Curtain* is not another *Psycho*, and that Hitchcock will be treating Andrews, just one year after *The Sound of Music* (1965), with considerably more propriety than he did Janet Leigh or Tippi Hedren. Still, *Torn Curtain* does have a shower scene (Figure 12.5), in which we see atomic scientist Michael Armstrong (Newman) more or less as Sarah Sherman (Andrews) sees him as she takes a phone call meant to give him more instructions about a defection to East Germany he is supposed to stage as part of an elaborate plot to steal a rival scientist's discoveries in missile defense technology. Like Marion Crane, Armstrong has a lot to come clean about; but we remain as viewers with his increasingly perplexed fiancée, Sarah, and can only wonder about his motives at a distance that is at once erotically charged and yet alienating too. There are several curtains that we breach along the way (the Iron Curtain, of course, but also at the final ballet performance, and metaphorically Sherman at last is brought inside Armstrong's performance as a spy), but this one in particular would not be

Figure 12.6. *Topaz* (1969).

"torn" by Hitchcock in 1966.[20] Nor was he able to film a nude scene he had scripted for *Topaz* that was to feature Karen D'Or and Frederick Stafford. Here, the problem was less an issue of censorship than of circumstance, as Hitchcock learned only after both actors were cast that each had surgical scars on their torsos that were too prominent to mask on-screen. We do see them embrace, but only from the shoulder up, and the film's most carnally arresting scene by far is that of D'Or's death (Figure 12.6), when the pooling folds of her purple dress are captured in a dazzling overhead shot that chastely has her body fall into a symbolic show of blood that would be truly ghastly if it were red. In both *Torn Curtain* and *Topaz*, perversely enough, Hitchcock's style is best displayed at moments when we are kept from seeing something graphic, which is to say that style here functions to displace or sublimate, to provide a language – formal, self-conscious, even, perhaps, old-fashioned – for otherwise divulging what he know is there, but not on-screen.

By this logic, *Frenzy* has practically no style to speak of. Rusk's rape and murder of Brenda Blaney is less an exercise in point of view or camera movement and more a test of sheer duration. The scene, from start to finish, is almost ten minutes long, and only halfway through does Rusk begin his assault on Brenda, which unfolds in more or less real time as he first rapes her, fails to climax, and then strangles her for just over a minute before she dies. When Marion Crane is killed in *Psycho*, the physical attack takes place in roughly sixteen seconds of overwhelming sensory detail; Bernard Hermann's score is syncopated with Leigh's screams and several sound effects, and the editing is frantically accelerated so that the film's own "cuts," as countless critics have observed, try to keep pace with Norman's violence. But no music accompanies the murder of Brenda, who prays while she is being raped (over Rusk's guttural incantations of "lovely"), and her scream is silenced almost immediately when Rusk starts to strangle her. The emphasis on Brenda's slow, immobile suffering does not just represent a different way of manipulating the viewer's aesthetic response to graphic violence than we witness in *Psycho*, but also gives us the time – whether we desire it or not – to observe and calibrate, and even possibly resist the film's manipulations as they do their work. The speed and energetic choreography of *Psycho* wants to shock the viewer, to deliver a sense of trauma that deliberately outpaces narrative and formal expectations (who is attacking Marion Crane? who is the main character?). *Frenzy* proceeds with the opposite of, well, "frenzy." This is why Modleski is right to argue that the film does not "[endorse] all the violence it portrays."[21] In placing this sequence "among the most disturbing scenes cinema has to offer," Modleski does not suggest we should excuse the palpable misogyny of Hitchcock's almost always prurient attention to all the ways that women can be shown to suffer, but rather that *Frenzy* also might do more to alienate us from the thrills and pleasures of watching women suffer than do many of Hitchcock's arguably greater and undeniably less graphic films.

Thus when Babs is later killed in Rusk's apartment, the fact that Hitchcock ostentatiously removes us from the scene of her rape and murder seems very much like a trap to catch us wanting to see something obscene again, as if the lack of censorship on either nudity or violence means that they must necessarily appear before our eyes when they are present in the narrative. The camera follows Babs and Rusk into his building, then halfway up the stairs to his apartment on the second floor, from where we watch as he leads her inside on the fateful line we have already heard him say to Brenda: "I don't know if you know it, Babs, but you're my type of woman." Since it is so obvious that we know what happens next, Hitchcock has no need to show us. But instead of cutting to the next scene (which involves another comic dinner for the Scotland Yard detective who is hunting the Necktie Strangler and must simultaneously have his stomach turned by his wife's appalling "nouvelle cuisine"), Hitchcock employs an extremely long tracking shot that walks us back and out of Rusk's building, taking just over a minute to place us back on the street amid the noise and commerce of Covent Garden, which will – or so it seems – drown out any cries Bab might make upstairs. The shot is tremendously affected and affecting, even though it is hard to say exactly what emotion it is trying to convey: here, a stylized aesthetic at the most Hitchcockian degree of technical proficiency lets us admire the handiwork of a master who, after all, never could resist a complex camera movement, even as the serial compulsions of another, darker expert at his craft are thankfully obscured.

But only for a time, as Rusk will later realize he has lost his most tell-tale accessory (his diamond-studded "R") which occasions, first, a nervous search through his apartment, and then a rapid series of flashbacks to Babs's rape and murder, during which we learn that she had managed to grab the tiepin while struggling, unsuccessfully, for her life. This is why Rusk finds himself in the back of a potato truck once again committing grotesque violence against a woman's body, although this time in a bit of nasty slapstick that revisits the setup of *The Trouble With Harry*, but with considerably more attention to the ugly facts of how dead bodies do and do not behave.

By any measure, *Frenzy* was a more successful film than any Hitchcock had produced since *Marnie*, and its entirely respectable numbers at the box office – and even better profits given its relatively small budget – made it a modest triumph by one of the measures Hitchcock himself took most seriously.[22] *Frenzy* proved that Hitchcock not only could operate within the looser rules of the "new" Hollywood that emerged during the 1960s, but that he would remain a crucial figure as still more graphic styles of cinema – in genres that his own extremes seem practically genteel – gained in notoriety, if not prestige. Wes Craven's *Last House on the Left* (1972) and Tobe Hooper's *Texas Chainsaw Massacre* (1974) helped establish the genre of the slasher film that Hitchcock in part invented, just as *Deep Throat* (1972) and *Behind the Green Door* (1972) were popularizing hard-core pornography with little homage or indebtedness to the avant-garde stylistics that so impressed Hitchcock when he saw them paired with full frontal nudity in *Blow-Up*. Hitchcock made only one film after *Frenzy*, and *Family Plot* might have been notably up-to-date in its casting and milieu – with Karen Black, Bruce Dern, and Barbara Harris playing motley figures caught up in the search for a missing heir who turns out to be a San Francisco kidnapper – but there is nothing graphic, or even lurid, that Hitchcock strains to put before us. His last years were not especially happy, and after his wife, Alma, suffered a debilitating stroke in 1976, Hitchcock was far more isolated, personally and professionally, than he had ever been.

If *Frenzy* stands as perhaps the singular accomplishment of Hitchcock's last years of filmmaking, then it is worth finally being more specific about the character of its accomplishment. I have most often spoken of "nudity" in pointing to a less censored iconography of female bodies that Hitchcock had pursued, in one form or another, across the sweep of his fantastically durable career. Yet as Kenneth Clark reminds us in his classic 1956 study of the art-historical genre of "the nude" – a book whose attitudes toward women are very much of its and Hitchcock's time – "the English language generously distinguishes between the naked and the nude. To be naked is to be deprived of our clothes, and the word implies some of the embarrassment most of us feel in that condition. The word 'nude,' on the other hand, carries, in educated use, no uncomfortable overtone."[23] By this reasoning, there is only a fleeting glimpse of anyone who is truly "nude" in Hitchcock, and we barely have more than seconds to see Babs as a "balanced, prosperous, and confident body." The scene is short and unremarkable, and takes place in the hotel room where she and Blaney have spent the night; the camera shows her sitting on a bed, and then pans to show her walk into the bathroom just as a newspaper is slipped under the door, its headline detailing "Another Necktie Murder" next to Brenda Blaney's picture. Thus even here, we hardly have an expression of what Clark calls "the body reformed" apart from the specter of some merely *naked* body, "huddled and defenseless" as it suffers the predations of a psychopath. Or Alfred Hitchcock, as the case may be.

But Clark's terminology speaks to a distinction between the idea of the nude and the mere reality of being naked that might also be a relic of an older time. Consider the work of another British artist who began depicting nudity in the late 1960s and who, like Hitchcock, knew very well that simply showing someone without clothing was hardly evidence that nothing is repressed (Figure 12.7).

Lucian Freud, of course, was Sigmund Freud's grandson, and had been a prominent member of a group of figurative painters in Britain who had emerged in the 1950s, when their resistance to abstract expressionism signaled their departure from postwar modernism as it developed in the United States. We see here Freud's first full-length nude, "Naked Girl," from 1966. Many of Freud's subsequent paintings would famously become more laden with paint and heavy texturings of impasto, and their subjects' poses often seemed increasingly contorted and uncomfortable as they get crowded onto couches or splayed on beds or wooden floors. It would not be fair to hold up Freud as a comparison to the dead female bodies Hitchcock shows us in *Frenzy*, although the layout of Freud's "naked girl" does resemble the image of the final victim of the Necktie Strangler that Blaney discovers in Rusk's bed (Figure 12.8).

Having been wrongly imprisoned for Rusk's crimes, Blaney escapes to London and apparently hopes to clear his name and avenge himself on Rusk, who comes back to find not only Blaney in his apartment but the Scotland Yard detective as well – ready to arrest the right man for the murders we have witnessed. Freud's "Naked Girl" is not subjected to the indignities Hitchcock inflicts on the last nude of his career; with her bulging

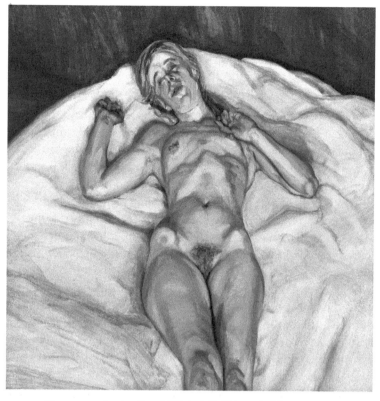

Figure 12.7. Lucian Freud, "Naked Girl" (1966). Oil on canvas.
Courtesy of The Lucian Freud Archive / Bridgeman Images.

Figure 12.8. *Frenzy.*

tongue and rolled-back eyes, she is rendered something less than human, and she is the perfectly gratuitous companion to the dead body that puts *Frenzy*'s plot in motion. Here, in fact, is the frontal view of an anonymous corpse whose backside we have seen already, the "recto" that is coming long after the "verso," which Hitchcock perversely shows us first. Indeed, there is only one unnamed "Victim" in *Frenzy*'s complete credits, so it may very well be the case that this actress, Susan Travers, is rendered naked twice to be a body that the Necktie Strangler has left behind. Her contorted features make for a death mask far more terrible to look at than the face in Freud's similar composition, where we assume the model has survived the framing of her nudity.

More importantly, seeing Hitchcock's *Frenzy* in light of Freud's "Naked Girl" gives us another way of thinking about the impulse to make bodies wholly visible that Hitchcock was not able to indulge until the very end, when it was almost too late for him to get nudity on film. The results are rather ugly and distorted, but they reveal, if nothing else, that Hitchcock's most primal drives and cinematic fantasies – including some that had been impossible to realize for most of his career – belatedly had their moment in a period when it was difficult to tell the difference between gratuitous displays of naked women and stylized affronts to convention that made new intensities of expression visible in a body of work whose time was quickly passing. On April 29, 1980, Alfred Hitchcock went the way of all flesh.

NOTES

1 Edward Said, *On Late Style: Music and Literature Against the Grain* (New York: Pantheon Books, 2006), p. 14.
2 Said, *On Late Style*, p. 16.
3 Theodor W. Adorno, "Late Style in Beethoven," in *Essays on Music*, ed. Richard Leppert, trans. Susan H. Gillespie (Berkeley: University of California Press, 2002), p. 566.
4 Adorno, "Late Style in Beethoven," p. 567.
5 See Linda Williams, *Hard Core: Power, Pleasure, and the "Frenzy of the Visible"* (Berkeley: University of California Press, 1989; expanded ed. 1999), pp. 37–43.
6 Stephen Rebello, *Alfred Hitchcock and the Making of* Psycho (New York: Open Road Integrated Media, 2013), p. 116.
7 Rebello, pp. 103–104.
8 Rebello, p. 103.
9 Rebello, p. 104.
10 James W. Merrick, "Hitchcock Regimen for a 'Psycho,'" *The New York Times*, 27 December 1959.
11 Rebello, p. 86.
12 For more on the history of censorship in Hollywood, see Matthew Bernstein, ed., *Controlling Hollywood: Censorship and Regulation in the Studio Era*

(New Brunswick, NJ: Rutgers University Press, 1999) and Leonard J. Leff and Jerold L. Simmons, *The Dame in the Kimono: Hollywood, Censorship, and the Production Code* (Lexington: The University Press of Kentucky, 2001).

13 For more on Hitchcock's emergence as a "brand," see Jerome Christensen, *America's Corporate Art: The Studio Authorship of Hollywood Motion Pictures* (Palo Alto, CA: Stanford University Press, 2012).

14 Patrick McGilligan, *Alfred Hitchcock: A Life in Darkness and Light* (New York: HarperCollins, 2003), p. 694.

15 "Against Interpretation" appeared in book form in 1966's *Against Interpretation and Other Essays* (New York: Farrar, Straus and Giroux, 1966).

16 McGilligan, p. 681.

17 François Truffaut with Helen G. Scott, *Hitchcock*, revised edition (New York: Simon & Schuster, 1983), p. 339.

18 Victoria Sullivan, "Does *Frenzy* Degrade Women?" *The New York Times*, 30 July 1972; Vincent Canby, "*Frenzy*," *The New York Times*, 22 June 1972.

19 Tania Modleski, *The Women Who Knew Too Much: Hitchcock and Feminist Theory* (New York: Routledge, 1988), p. 102.

20 There was, in fact, brief male nudity in two studio features of 1966, *The Bible* and *Seconds*.

21 Modleski, *Women Who Knew Too Much*, p. 112.

22 *Frenzy* grossed $12.6 million on production costs of $3 million.

23 Kenneth Clark, *The Nude: A Study in Ideal Form* (Princeton, NJ: Princeton University Press, 1984; originally published 1956), p. 3.

PART IV

Hitchcock Beyond Hitchcock

13

JONATHAN FREEDMAN

The School of Hitchcock: Swimming in the Wake of the Master

Where has Hitchcock *not* left his mark? He directed fifty-odd films, as well as introducing some seventy television shows and directing many of them; his work has been the recipient of hommages (e.g., Truffaut's *The Bride Wore Black* [1968]), parodies (e.g., Mel Brooks's *High Anxiety* [1977]), ripoffs (Brian de Palma's *Obsession* [1976] and *Dressed to Kill* [1980]), and creepily faithful remakes (Gus Van Sant's *Psycho* [1998]). An even more compelling legacy can be found in just about every suspense and horror film of the last fifty years, which rely on such demonstrably Hitchcockian techniques as Kuleshov-effect-inflected point-of-view shots, sudden shocks, destabilizing narrative strategies – think how many leading ladies have been killed off since *Psycho*! – and an attitude of cool contempt toward a greedy but guilty audience. The school of Hitchcock is a commodious one: some students may have dropped out, others graduated with honors, but directors, producers, and stars all keep on attending – and so do audiences.

It is telling that, while innumerable filmmakers have spent their time under Hitchcock's sway, many of the most distinguished ones can be listed among them. Any roster of directors registering Hitchcock's influence would have to include François Truffaut and Claude Chabrol (both of whom, in their days as critics, were among the first to take his work seriously before they started making films that grew out of this engagement), Martin Scorsese, Michelangelo Antonioni, Francis Ford Coppola, Atom Egoyan, Jonathan Demme, Henri Cluozot, Chantal Akerman (who brings Hitchcockian sensibilities to a film devoted to the work of another modernist master, Marcel Proust, in *The Captive* [2000]), David Lynch, Pedro Almodovar, and Roman Polanski. And the beat goes on: in 2013, Korean director Park Chan-Wook released *Stoker*, a violence-courting reimagination of *Shadow of a Doubt* (1943).

As they revise his central themes and revisit his preoccupations, these directors – true auteurs all – help us see Hitchcock's own work in a different light, illuminating not only his achievement but also the work done in genres that grew up through and around his work. But the engagement of these directors with Hitchcock's films and their aftermath serves a larger end. As they challenge, contest, update, and transform his central themes and techniques, making them part of their own vocabulary and vision, these directors – and we – better understand the social configurations of power, sexuality, and knowledge with which Hitchcock was so intimate and which his films did so much to articulate.

In what follows, I want to focus on three such encounters sustained over almost twenty years: Demme's *Something Wild* (1986), Egoyan's *Exotica* (1994), and Florian Henckel von Donnersmarck's *The Lives of Others* (2006). I choose these three not only because they are interesting and thoughtful works in their own right but because they represent compelling responses to Hitchcock's oeuvre that extend, in powerful and provocative ways, his concerns and those in the genres emerging from his films. Demme unites the mode in Hitchcock that stresses a freewheeling, improvisational response to a nettlesome world (represented best in *North by Northwest* [1959]) with one that stresses murderously psychotic dimensions of subjectivity (*Strangers on a Train* [1951] or *Psycho* [1960]) as part of a deconstruction of a normative America also undertaken, less generously, by Hitchcock before him. Like the Hitchcock of *Vertigo* (1958) or *Rear Window* (1954), canonized and critiqued by feminist film theorists, Egoyan pursues the male gaze and its relation to fetishistic sexuality; the place he brings us to, however, is not only that of the exercise of male power via ocular experience but one of memory, mourning, and loss linked to a communally shared trauma. Von Donnersmarck translates the Hitchcockian idiom of surveillance into a different key – one in which the act of surveillance redeems the observer and saves the life of the observed, a twist not just on Hitchcock but on a whole series of films inspired by his work, from Francis Ford Coppola's *The Conversation* (1974) through Michael Haneke's *Caché* (2005). In all these cases, the directors not only traverse the terrain massively dominated by Hitchcock, they offer different ways of conceptualizing the landscape Hitchcock made his own: the landscape of our contemporary experience writ large.

Jonathan Demme's engagement with Hitchcock has been career-long. One early film, *The Last Embrace* (1979), features a tricky wrong-man plot and a climactic fight scene at a famous public site – in this case, Niagara Falls. Hitchcockian in a different way are the many bows that Demme's greatest commercial success, *Silence of the Lambs* (1991), makes to *Psycho*, as the eminent Hitchcockian Leslie Brill has observed.[1] The real-life case on which the "Buffalo Bill" subplot of the movie is based – a MacGuffin if there ever was one, since the quest for this predator leads to one for the far more insidious and commanding Hannibal Lecter – is the same as the one that inspired *Psycho*: the case of Ed Gans. The sets (especially the claustrophobic basement), the props (a stuffed bird), many of its shots (the use of point-of-view shots to establish Kuleshov-like identification), the music – all these identify *Silence* as a post-*Psycho Psycho*. Most powerful of all is Demme's mocking invocation of psychiatric authority, an account that enters, however spuriously, at the end of *Psycho* to stabilize the horror of what we have confronted. The pseudo-babble of Hitchcock's psychiatrist is transformed into the seductive patter of Dr. Hannibal Lecter, who uses the insights of psychiatry to inflict crimes even more barbaric than those that Norman – or even Alfred – could have imagined, and who therefore poses exactly the dilemma, the existence of sheer motiveless evil, that Hitchcock's jargon-dispensing shrink seeks to guard against.[2]

There is, however, a different vein in Hitchcock to which Demme connects as well – the comedy of self-reinvention. In *North by Northwest*, a breezy, rootless hero finds himself on the road, fleeing for his life; along the way he meets a beautiful woman with whom he spars and falls in love, not necessarily in that order; he traverses spectacular national landscapes, dodges death, and finds in the end a new commitment and a new identity along with a new successful relationship, all improvised. With this plot, the film has much in common with such great American road movies as Frank Capra's *It Happened One Night* (1934), a notion not lost on American philosopher Stanley Cavell. In his extraordinary reading of *North by Northwest*, Cavell directs our attention to Hitchcock's

> hymning of capacities for adventure and for improvisation. I mean by these capacities the virtues that allow you to become at home in the world, to establish the world as home. The capacities permit, if necessary, living together on the road, as if loving were the finding of a direction, that is, of a directedness, just ... as Hitchcock's title names more than just a given direction.[3]

The final shots of *North by Northwest* enact this evolving, in-motion evocation of "directedness." Roger pulls Eve Kendall, who has seduced and betrayed him yet loved him, and whose life he has saved, into the top bunk of the sleeper on their train, followed by a shot of the train going into the tunnel with the words "The End" projected over it. This is of course an adolescent joke on Hitchcock's part, and a comic reflection of male anxiety – marriage understood as the end of sex, and hence life, freedom, possibilities. Yet the image of continuing movement also invokes the basic comic energies that drive the film. The end of Roger the cad is also the beginning of Roger and the (radiantly named) Eve, and the marriage that traditionally ends comedy is affirmed as part of the forward motion of life, even – especially – sexual life.

Demme, too, is a great believer in movement as a correlative of self-reinvention. His first critical success, *Handle with Care* (1977), portrayed a small community reorganizing its desiring and affectional life around CB-communicating truckers; his first big hit, *Melvin and Howard* (1980), begins as a road movie – a regular Joe named Melvin Dummar picks up a bedraggled Howard Hughes on a Nevada road and so richly entertains him that Hughes leaves a massive fortune to Melvin, with disruptive consequences all around. The mode in these two films is distinctly Capraesque: the road becomes, as in *It Happened One Night*, a place where social differences are leveled as romance is brewed, merging an ideal of social democracy with faith in the making of individual affections. The first half of *Something Wild* invokes the same dynamics, bringing them into seemingly benign contact with a number of familiar light-comic Hitchcockian themes. The movie begins with an impulsive act of petty criminality by an ordinary-seeming citizen, stockbroker Charles Driggs (Jeff Daniels), who, in a moment of impulsive transgression, pockets a check at a Manhattan diner. He is observed by "Lulu" (Melanie Griffith), a beautiful, free-spirited woman who essentially blackmails Charlie into accompanying her, drags him to a nearby motel, ties him to the bed, calls his boss, hands him the phone, and pulls his pants down and begins performing oral sex on him while he is forced to excuse his absence from the office. She then leads him through acts of petty criminality – a liquor-store theft here, a car crash there – all the while keeping his handcuffs on (a sly allusion to Hitchcock's own sly allusion to this particular kink in *The 39 Steps* [1935]), ultimately leading him back to her hometown to accompany her to her high school reunion. Along the way, they improvise a Capraesque relation, making up a kind of a bond on the fly that pleases their need for adventure and their desire for romance.

In this process, Charlie also shows himself to be a Roger Thornhill–like improviser, clearly if facilely handling each of the challenges Lulu poses him with an improvisatory ingenuity that would be creepy if it weren't so brilliantly enacted by Jeff Daniels, who is to goofy charm what Cary Grant was to suave sophistication. Like Thornhill, too, he is shown to be almost comically disconnected from any stable selfhood. Roger points to his cufflinks, which spell ROT, to affirm his identity, famously replying when asked that the "O" in the middle stands for "nothing." Charlie cannot even stand by his name tag, as he demonstrates when he meets Lulu's sultry friend Irene at a dance:

IRENE: I'm Irene; I don't believe in name tags.
CHARLIE DRIGGS: Oh. Hi. Ah... [points at his name tag] Charlie. I never had many concrete convictions about 'em one way or another.

Given this ambiguous, open-ended take on identity, it is appropriate that "Lulu" turns out to be the more drably named Audrey, a woman who has remade herself in the guise of silent-film star Louise Brooks, and that she similarly remakes the dull Charlie by re-dressing him at the local vintage-clothing store as well as by testing him in stressful situations. We learn, too, that Charlie is in need of such a makeover: at the dance, he meets a colleague from work who notes his metamorphosis with an obsequious thumbs-up and observes that Charlie's wife (like Roger's three spouses) has recently left him. Charlie celebrates this new role with a comic dance, followed by a slow, tender one with Audrey, but at precisely the moment of the apotheosis of the new Charlie, the film suddenly changes registers. Sidling into the frame is Ray, Audrey/Lulu's ex-husband newly released from prison, played with menacing creepiness by Ray Liotta. Despite Audrey's demurrals, Ray entices Charlie elsewhere, then stages a robbery, beats and humiliates him, and kidnaps Audrey. But – again like Thornhill, once he has discovered the truth about Eve – Charlie displays a new capacity for commitment. Rather than giving up and slinking back to his humdrum life, he follows Ray and Audrey, bides his time, then improvises a counterattack of his own. Charlie confronts Ray at a diner and threatens to expose him to the police, taking his wallet, then imitating one of Lulu's tricks by walking out and sticking him with the check. Momentarily triumphant, he rescues Audrey and returns her to his own sterile house in the Long Island suburbs. But there is no easy release, no magical lifting to the top bunk of a sleeper car. Instead, Ray comes crashing into Charlie's house and the two fight to the death – in this case, Ray's.

And as they do, the film comes to resemble *North by Northwest* less than other, less-freewheeling moments in the Hitchcock oeuvre, especially double-obsessed films such as *Strangers on a Train*. The association is not random. When Ray follows Charlie and breaks into his house, the two come increasingly to resemble one another, criss-cross fashion. Wearing matching, blood-streaked white T-shirts as they fight, their similarity becomes ever more emphatic, as the hypercivilized Charlie attempts to strangle working-class Ray (Figure 13.1), and further in a sequence of shot/countershot matched images as Ray impales himself on his own knife, held in Charlie's hands (Figures 13.2 and 13.3), then emphasized even further as the camera swings around 90 degrees to place them on the same plane (Figure 13.4).

If Lulu/Audrey helps Charlie experience what she calls "the other side" of himself, we realize that this other side is called Ray; the fight ends, as does the final sequence of *Strangers,* with the psychotic double inseparable from his normative twin.

Demme thus melds the two modes of Hitchcock's films: the ones that hail reinvention and the ones that constrain the self by means of the logic of

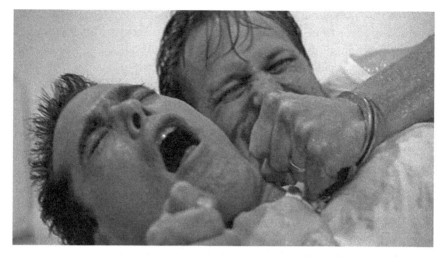

Figure 13.1. Criss-cross – to the death.
Something Wild (1986).

Figure 13.2. Ray impaled on his own knife, held by Charlie.
Something Wild.

shared guilt and the mechanisms of doubling. Lulu and then Ray, we realize, are the means by which Charlie accesses his "wild" side, but they also manifest the out-of-control aspects of that wildness, however justified. Ray's role in the film is to remind us that playing at wildness can slip out of control – that the forces of the libido can be as destructive as they are life-affirming. And more: as Cavell has powerfully argued, there is a national dimension to this story of personal reinvention. Commenting on the comic contrivance of Thornhill proposing marriage to Eve while they are tumbling across the presidents' noses on Mount Rushmore, he writes: "[W]hile America can

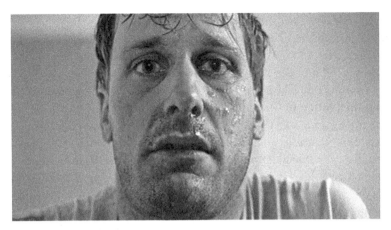

Figure 13.3. Quick cut to Charlie's reaction.
Something Wild.

Figure 13.4. One dies, the other lives, but the shot brings them together one last time.
Something Wild.

no longer ratify marriage ... the achievement of true marriage might ratify something called America as a place in which to seek it." Both the couple in Hitchcock's film – indeed, any couple – and America exist in a state of possibility, not one of static achievement; both seek to become a "more perfect union" that they must continually improvise in order to make real (262). This is the essence, too, of the road movies that Hitchcock and Demme both invoke, where physical movement through space correlates with the making not only of a new relationship but also of democratic America – the classic example of which is the scene in Capra's *It Happened One Night* where the soon-to-be couple, Clark Gable and Claudette Colbert, find themselves on a bus whose passengers break out in a collective singing of "The Daring Young Man on the Flying Trapeze," a scene echoed when, picking up one hitchhiker after another, Charlie and Lulu join their guests in a rolling, rollicking rendition of the Troggs' "Wild Thing."

Yet Demme's film insists on the perdurability of class as a way of undercutting this drama of individual and national concord. Charlie exemplifies the cognitive and social skills of the professional-managerial class (glib, self-assured, factitious); his ability to transform himself is of a piece with the soulless, superficial nature of the workplace that is the only source of his identity. Ray is his lower-class counterpart: physical, aggressive, sardonic, hard-edged, seething with class resentment – indeed, Ray's working-class contempt for soft, malleable, professional Charlie is palpable in the sneer with which Ray pronounces his name ("Charrrrr-leeee") and the brutality with which he abuses him. It also informs the fury he feels at Audrey's dallying with Charlie: he screams at her, when he finds her in Charlie's ranch house, "So you finally made it to the suburbs, bitch!" The fragility of that house – it falls apart like balsa wood when Ray and Charlie start grappling with each other, and even when Ray handcuffs Charlie to a pipe, he is easily able to bust it and break free – suggests the fragility of Charlie's middle-class standing and lifestyle. But in so many other ways, that class position supports him. Indeed, his privilege is related to his sneakiness. He is fine with stealing a check if the waitress is poor and black; his ability to talk himself out of any jam is clearly related to his success in the workplace; he traps Ray in a diner, secure in the knowledge that the police will serve and protect a middle-class person such as he and not working-class Ray, and so on. True, at the end of the film he has to fight Ray on Ray's terms, mano-à-mano, but he does not so much triumph as win accidentally – Ray runs into the knife that kills him. True, too, that he and Audrey/Lulu meet again at the same diner, each dressed in hipster clothes, ready to make a kind of Cavellian romance after the film is over. But the film's insistent reminders of class difference disabuse us in advance of the potential of their union. When Charlie and Ray are locked in their deathly embrace, they are established not only as doubles but as antonyms of a fundamentally divided national narrative that also structures the relation between Audrey and Charlie. Demme's allusions to Hitchcock's two modes, his recognition that they, too, are doubles of each other, only reminds us of the extent of this divide.

Like *Something Wild*, Canadian filmmaker Atom Egoyan's *Exotica* invokes numerous elements of Hitchcockian cinema: the wrong-man plot; the emphasis on doubles and doubling; the mixture of an interrogation and exploitation of scopophilia. But its greatest relevance to the Hitchcock canon is the way it seems, at first blush, to be an illustration of the feminist film theory that took Hitchcock as its central exemplar of cinematic practice and used it to deconstruct male domination via visuality *tout court*. Laura Mulvey's famous essay "Visual Pleasure and Narrative Cinema" (1977), which introduced the now hyperfamiliar term "the male gaze" to critical discourse, based its culture-bending analyses on critical readings of *Rear Window* (which becomes a privileged exemplar of voyeurism) and *Vertigo* (which does the same for fetishism). In this work Mulvey not only uses Hitchcock for her analytic ends but canonizes him as the very essence of cinema, and indeed the cultural practices cinema exemplifies and the social norms it enforces. To be sure, soon after she published "Visual Pleasure," Mulvey began to complicate her analysis.[4] And in the past twenty years, the notion of "the gaze" has extended into queer and race-based criticisms, so much so that we now think of the queer or the white gaze with as much persistence as we did the male one. That being said, the idea of a domi-nant power relation of male over female exercised through the visual faculty remains crucial in criticism and pedagogy in film studies, gender studies, literary studies, and cultural studies, to name just a few.

There may be no better illustration of this gaze and its power dynam-ics than the stripteases and lap dances that form the center of Egoyan's film (and informed the film's publicity campaign, in vivid illustration of the currency of Mulvey's critique). They are undertaken by Christina, a twenty-something woman who works in a strip club, Exotica, in downtown Toronto. When called forth by the DJ, Eric, who lavishes her performance with an obscene pedophilic commentary, and cued by the music of Leonard Cohen – his great song "Everybody Knows" provides an insidiously effec-tive thematic complement to the film's concerns – she first does a striptease in a Catholic school uniform outfit (Figure 13.5), then gives a lap dance to a customer named Francis who is clearly a repeat customer. During the dance her spectator is put in the familiar position of the male gazer at a female body – Christina is to us as Miss Torso is to Jeff in *Rear Window*. This dynamic is further accentuated when Christina gyrates on Francis's lap. His eyes are plaintively fixed on her chest in what we assume to be a frankly sexual gaze. We know – everybody knows – what we are seeing and hearing, and it is just another version of the same old story of voyeurism and objec-tification, male power and female submission.

Or is it? It turns out that everyone in the film knows something we do not, and that something complicates what we have been seeing. Christina, we ultimately learn, was the babysitter for Francis's daughter, who had been killed in some unspecified violent atrocity in which Francis himself had been a suspect. The DJ, Eric, is a former lover of Christina whose relationship with her began when they found the body of the child together; as a flashback

Figure 13.5. Schoolgirl/stripper Christina.
Exotica (1994).

late in the film reveals, as the future owner of the club carries Eric's child, he seems to be engaged in a complicated love relation with Christina as well. Her performance gives off a different charge when we realize, as we do not fully until the end of the film, that she is dressed in the same schoolgirl outfit as was the dead girl. The odd, repetitive striptease and lap dance then come to seem less like a sexual performance and more like an attempt to master trauma through reenacting it, using the occasion of sexual display to restage the shock, terror, and sheer awfulness of the loss and to deny the death that has transfixed them all. By dressing as the dead child, Christina both assumes her identity and stages for Francis and herself the fantasy that the girl is still alive. And his gaze at Christina hence seems less a sexualized leer and more a desperate attempt to believe this could be true.

The dynamics here complicate not only Mulvey's analysis of voyeurism in *Rear Window* but also her account of fetishization with reference to *Vertigo*. The establishment of a fetish, Mulvey's psychoanalytic account insists, is made by the traumatic recoiling from the female genitalia by the male subject, whose castration anxiety (if she doesn't have a penis, then maybe his might be taken away) is resolved by displacing that recognition onto another part of the body, or onto clothing (underwear, shoes, etc.) metonymically related to the first. Egoyan's representation of fetishism is more expansive. True, like Judy/Madeleine in *Vertigo*, Christina allows herself to be remade in a fetishistic guise to serve the purposes of male fantasies. But the fetishistic self-remaking of Christina turns out to be not part of a heterosexual dyad, but rather part of a complex social web in which re-clothing herself as the dead child speaks simultaneously to her own and Eric's trauma as well

Figure 13.6. Seeing what musn't be seen.
Exotica.

as to Francis's. It is not really a resolution for a putative castration anxiety; rather, it is part of a relation in which she sets out to "soothe" Francis (her words), and it harkens back to a preexisting relationship in which Francis has been a genial, encouraging presence in the teenage Christina's life, which is shadowed, in ways the film does not specify, by other abuses. Moreover, it speaks to, as it reenacts, the trauma of discovery of the body for Eric, who attempted to shield the (younger) Christina's eyes from it – another tribute to the vicissitudes of vision under the sign of loss, not desire (Figure 13.6).

It is clear that Eric's odd, obsessive-compulsive behavior – he launches a plot to get Francis to touch her, the one forbidden act in the club, and the one that gets Francis thrown out of it – is linked both to his jealousy of and to his sense of affinity with Francis. Eric ratifies this at the end of the film by embracing Francis, the two of them conjoined by losses – of the daughter, of Christina – that have merged. That this embrace is followed by a series of flashbacks – to Francis as a happy father proudly enumerating his daughter's accomplishments, to Chistina as an unhappy adolescent walking back into her abusive household after talking with him – suggests that, tumultuous and disturbing as they may be, the events in the strip club have led to a collective loosening of the mechanisms of compulsive reenactment through the events these characters have witnessed and the explosions they have generated.

I have only begun to anatomize the tangled array of relations that structures the film, but by now the point should be clear. Egoyan complicates feminist film theory analysis without negating it. He suggests that the complexities of loss, the inevitability of trauma, the desire or need to

FREEDMAN

repeat the past all inflect behavior in ways that may push into voyeurism and fetishization but also move beyond them, touching on equally deep responses to trauma and death. In so doing he engages with Hitchcock in two quite specific ways. The same entanglement of fetishization, trauma, and death is at the center of *Vertigo*: Scottie's attempts to master his own trauma, born of repeated acts of witnessing (the death of the policeman at the beginning of the film; the vision of the real Madeleine falling to her death), by re-clothing Judy have the terrible effect of repeating the past again, not annulling it. When Judy falls to her death as Madeleine had done before her, and as Scottie ends the film in a crouch that indicates his own final descent into despair and madness, we recognize that there can, in Hitchcock's world, be no respite, no cure – only ceaseless repetition of the trauma, until the death that shadows each of the characters overcomes them. (Scottie's crouch recapitulates his dream, earlier in the movie, of following Madeleine into the grave, suggesting that what he will find henceforth is nothing short of death in life.)

Egoyan's movie is thus far more optimistic because it sees in music, dance, and by extension art itself – even the degraded art of striptease, the dance that Christina is forced to perform and the music that accompanies it – a means of mastering trauma by reenacting it in symbolic form. He also understands the stew of passions generated in and around such reenactment as suggesting an aesthetic resolution to seemingly insoluble problems. The end of the film is, to be sure, not overly optimistic: the flashback concludes with teenage Christina trudging back into a house we sense to be a place of abuse and degradation. And we know, too, all the tragedies that are about to unfold for her and Francis. But in its own sinuous, tail-swallowing way, the film suggests what neither Hitchcock nor Mulvey can allow for: that the repetition of the traumatizing narrative in artistic form ultimately provides a release from trauma because it offers a symbolic working-through of its insidious power.

Oddly optimistic, too, is *The Lives of Others*. This film, like *Exotica*, participates in a genre that can be traced to Hitchcock's work: the "surveillance film."[5] Such films, growing out of *Rear Window*, take the technological monitoring of other people, add a good dose of post-1960s paranoia, and create scenarios of increasing use of technologies to scope, spy on, control, order, and arrange human fates. From *The Conversation* (1974) through the surveillance videotape that serves as the centerpiece of *Caché* (2005) to the total surveillance that is the subject of *The Truman Show* (1998) – in which the entire environment in which its protagonist lives turns out to be one gigantic set on which every detail of his life is stage-managed and beamed to the masses – surveillance becomes crucial to the manner as well as the

242

matter of films. Writers on the genre tend therefore to begin their accounts of it with Coppola's movie *The Conversation*, in which the decoding of an ambiguous piece of audiotape by an eavesdropping expert, Harry Caul, becomes key to his (ultimately mistaken) understanding of a murder plot he seeks to forestall. And the influence of Hitchcock is commensurately downplayed: in one of the leading surveys of surveillance films, for example, his name does not even appear; in another, *Rear Window* is mentioned only in the notes.[6] But this is a mistake, because what Hitchcock contributes to the genre is a dynamic by which the psychology of the surveillant is as much a subject of the film as that of those observed.

Thus the peculiar psychic life of L. B. Jeffries is the real subject of *Rear Window* – and not only as it is revealed by his scoping, or even by his shifting fascination with his fashion-plate girlfriend Lisa Fremont, who cannot win his affection until she enters and helps further the narrative he spins about the goings-on across the way. Even more powerfully, the mini-dramas he views in the windows across from his own room, to which he is confined by a broken leg sustained while photographing a race-car accident, are projections of his innermost thoughts, fears, and desires.[7] But these vary considerably. They range from the alluring dancer he calls "Miss Torso" (desire) to the spinster he dubs "Miss Lonelyhearts" (what Jeff might become if he persists in his bachelorhood); from the composer who shaves while listening to an ad reminding men of the loss of their physical powers after forty (no comment needed) to the newlywed couple who start out with bursts of nonstop sex (it is the woman, tellingly, who seems most energetic) and end with impending domestic conflict; from the couple who sleep outside and whose dog is killed by Thorwald to a female artist making a sculpture in a vaguely female form. It is important to note the profusion of relations on display in the windows into which he gazes. While many of these suggest that a committed sexual life is a disaster, there are others that suggest that it is not: the married couple who sleep together on the fire escape, for example, or even "Miss Torso," who greets with delight her short, pudgy GI boyfriend, Stanley, at the end of the movie. (True, he is more interested in visiting the refrigerator than in embracing her, but this is perhaps the point of a certain kind of domesticity.) And several of the mini-narratives turn on creativity – not only that of the musician in the upper-right corner of the set, who successfully completes his song over the course of the film (its last haunting word is "Lisa," a tribute to Lisa Fremont), but that of the sculptor in the lower left, who seems to be putting the finishing touches on her own artwork.[8] These narratives hum with possibilities left unexplored by Jeff as he fixates more and more on the narrative of Thorwald and his dismembered wife, and this tells us something about Jeff – that he cuts himself off from a world of creativity that would otherwise be available to him, a world largely female, or at least full of a feminizing vulnerability he tries to deny. This is more than a film about Jeff's reaction to his sense of being effectively castrated by his accident – which, crudely put, is the essence of one influential feminist-inflected reading of the text; it's about his relation to relation itself. It shows us all the things he has to deny himself in his quest to avoid the feminization that his macho profession –photographing race cars and atom bombs – has paradoxically inflicted on him.

This concern with the surveillant as well as the subject seems somewhat old-fashioned in the face of the rising techno-determinism at the center of the surveillance genre. Then again, so does the insistence on human vision as a means of surveillance, which pales into insignificance in the face of the next stage of surveillance, the one in which the NSA, Google, and Facebook all engage: data surveillance, in which every keystroke in every e-mail we write, no matter how intimate, or every website we visit is processed somewhere, somehow, for either commercial or national-security purposes or both. At least in old-fashioned surveillance films, there is someone or something human to be watched, and something human in the response – even in Michael Haneke's *Caché*, where, while the source of the surveillance tapes that arrive to disrupt the lives of a bourgeois French couple remains mysterious, the effects those tapes have can still be registered. Both are features, it seems to me, that grow out of Hitchcock's founding contribution to the genre, like the ones that grow out of *The Conversation*. In its own way a thoroughly magnificent film, *The Conversation* is similar to *Rear Window* in that it focuses on a commitment-phobic man, Harry Caul; it deviates from the *Rear Window* path by making the act of surveillance epistemologically problematic. Jeff may be all kinds of things, but he is not making up what he sees; in the end he is validated by the discovery of Thorwald's murder and dismemberment of his wife. In Coppola's film, Harry misconstrues the nature of the ambiguous dialogue his bugs have overheard, and he involves himself in the lives of those on whom he has been eavesdropping, with disastrous consequences for all concerned. Thinking that the two lovers he is listening to are in danger, he misunderstands their desire to kill the person he thinks is out to murder them. In the end, Harry learns that he himself is under the same kind of surveillance to which he has subjected others; he can respond to his predicament only by retreating into the narrowest version of his life, playing long, mournful solos on his saxophone while he waits for his fate to be decided elsewhere.

The Lives of Others returns from these farther shores of surveillance to an essentially Hitchcockian take – that the narratives about surveillance not only turn on the life of the surveyer but effectuate some important cathartic

Figure 13.7. The observed ...
The Lives of Others (2006).

change in that figure. Set in the late days of East Germany, the film has at its center Stasi agent Gerd Weisler, who is assigned to monitor playwright Georg Dreyman, an acceptable luminary in the officially sanctioned East German cultural sphere. Setting up a Harry Caul–like audio surveillance operation, Weisler wonders why, all of a sudden, Dreyman has become an object of interest; Weisler learns that his boss has ordered the surveillance to curry favor with the Minister of Culture, who covets Dreyman's girlfriend/ actress/muse, Christa-Maria.

Weisler is frequently presented in the film in the position of privileged observer, hearing and knowing all. But the more he hears and the more he knows, the less certain he becomes of his own authority. Not only does he become aware of the abuse of power that has caused his surveillance; he identifies increasingly with the couple he is observing, opening up a world unavailable to him in his dreary existence as a secret policeman whose emotional life essentially comes down to copulating with prostitutes once a week. He listens in on an emotionally vibrant relationship; he begins to read Brecht and listen to the same music as the cultured playwright Dreyman. In one of its most moving episodes, the film, which has been cutting back and forth between Dreyman's and Christa-Maria's lives and Weisler's eavesdropping, turns to the couple for a protracted sequence: Christa-Maria has been molested in the car, returns home, showers, takes the illegal drugs she uses to mask her pain, then crawls into bed with Dreyman, asking him to hold her. They both turn sideways, spooning, comforting each other (Figure 13.7).

The film cuts to an image of Weisler, who has fallen asleep in exactly the same position as the couple: his role as an external authority observing with godlike impassiveness collapses, and he becomes one with them (Figure 13.8).

Figure 13.8. ... and the observer.
The Lives of Others.

The logic here extends but reverses that of *Rear Window*. As has often been observed, the reciprocal nature of the relation between the detached, if voyeuristic, observer Jeff is at its most problematic in his relation to Lars Thorwald. All of Jeff's anxieties about marriage are reflected in Thorwald's encounter with his wife – a seeming invalid who argues from her bed with her frustrated husband. Jeff's visual construction of the world is also highly Thorwaldian: when Jeff dubs the dancer across the way "Miss Torso," he visually dices her supple body as effectively as Thorwald does his wife's. Here the dynamics are not dissimilar – it is as if Weisler's unconscious has been shaped by the couple about whom he is dreaming – but the spin is completely different; rather than reifying his worst impulses, Dreyman and Crista-Maria point him to his best.

Which is not to say that the film is a happy, utopian parable of the jailer redeemed by his prisoner. The system within which Weisler operates is one that constrains him, in all senses of the word. Although the state puts him in the position of distanced observer, thereby enabling the transformation that undoes his service to it, that same position imprisons him. He repeatedly attempts to break out of the spectatorial role: he adopts the guise of a fan to warn Christa-Maria that she is being watched; then, after she is interrogated and reveals the presence of a contraband typewriter, he swoops in before the Stasi can arrive to discover it, removing the offending object. But while his efforts may save Dreyman, Weisler cannot do the same for Christa-Maria. Her failure to meet her lover's gaze tells all, and she rushes out into the street and kills herself rather than face the consequences of her betrayal. Weisler is the first to reach her body; beginning to tell her that the typewriter is safe, he is forced to give way to Dreyman, who holds her as she dies. All attempts at intervention, all attempts at substitution, fail: in the end Weisler is consigned to the very role of spectator that fuels his desire to be something much more.

So far, then, the film holds oddly but persistently to the *Rear Window* paradigm. Jeff, the unseen seer-wannabe, similarly fails when he attempts to intervene in the drama taking place in front of him. The conditions that mandate his detachment – his broken leg, and more generally his disposition to be an observer – mean that he cannot intervene in the Thorwald investigation that he initiates, which he has to delegate to his ineffectual policeman friend Duffy, and ultimately to Lisa, who carries out his operations. And just as Weisler is unable to rescue Christa-Maria, so Jeff is left to quiver impotently as Thorwald assaults Lisa; only the intervention of another surrogate, insurance nurse Stella, whom he sends to the police, saves her. And like Jeff, who shows himself to Thorwald and then is targeted by him, Weisler undertakes actions that cause him to be revealed to his corrupt superiors, who send him off to a provincial post office as punishment.

But here Von Donnersmarck's film diverges from the pattern of Hitchcock's and from the surveillance genre he spawned. The turning of the tables on the observer is followed by a further plot twist that moves in a benign direction. After reading his own file, Dreyman realizes than an unknown Stasi agent has been protecting him and, after failing to discover that watcher's identity, writes a book about his experiences, unveiling Weisler's activities and praising him, however anonymous he must remain. The observer becomes the observed, the observed the observer, and the result (as in *Exotica*) is the creation of a work of art that transforms both. The film ends with Weisler purchasing the book, saying triumphantly, "This book is for me!"

Here, the Hitchcockian form that the film invokes and departs from is fully replaced by a different mode, signified by a different gesture of closure than is typical in Hitchcock's films. Von Donnersmarck's ending is unabashedly affirmative. Closure, by contrast, is frequently problematic in Hitchcock: sometimes the plots are resolved by chance or happenstance (as with the pseudo-miraculous conclusions of *The Lodger* and *I Confess* [1953]) or by gestures that undercut the conclusion (such as Lisa, having promised to go on an adventure with Jeff, picking up her copy of *Vogue* while he dozes at the end of *Rear Window*). And there were alternate endings proposed for *Suspicion* (1941), *Vertigo*, and *The Birds* (1963). Even when there are happy endings in Hitchcock, there is nothing in Hitchcock's films I can think of as affirmative in the way of this conclusion, at least nothing affirmative that is so richly motivated by the rest of the film (with the possible exception of *North by Northwest*). It is somewhat perverse for me to end on this note, then, since it is an un-Hitchcockian one: certainly the direction of Hitchcock-inspired films at large inclines away from the affirmative place that all three of the films I have mentioned lean toward. (I could have ended with a triptych of *Taxi Driver* [1976], *Body Double* [1984], and *Silence of the Lambs* and emerged with a radically different conclusion.) But if I had to defend the choice, I would say that it illustrates what excellent filmmakers, like any excellent artists, do: they enter into crucial dialogue with their predecessors and seek to change the configuration of the works with which they are in dialogue.

So as this essay concludes, and with it this volume, we might want to follow the example of the artists I have mentioned and wonder at the ways in which Hitchcock's vision might offer us opportunities for critical dialogue with, as well as greater awareness of, the psychic and social configurations that construct our understanding of the world and of ourselves. These filmmakers all propose not a passive but a creative response to that world. They point to the making of alternate identities, of dance, of art, of fiction, of nonfiction, as a way of negotiating with it. For all the extremity of Hitchcock's later work, and for all the deliberate cultivation of perversity throughout his career, isn't that finally one lesson of Hitchcock as well, the reason we go back again and again to his films: that they articulate, give shape to, and help us master the most disturbing aspects of our experience? In any event, these directors suggest that the Hitchcockian thematics of voyeurism, suspicion, doubling, and death can be engaged with to yield a different outcome: that in bringing us into close contact with our nightmares, his films can also inspire us to dream otherwise.

NOTES

1 Leslie Brill, "Hitchcockian Silence: *Psycho* and Jonathan Demme's *Silence of the Lambs*," in David Boyd and R. Burton Palmer, eds., *After Hitchcock: Influence, Imitation, Intertextuality* (Austin: University of Texas Press, 2006), p. 32.
2 For a different response to the end of *Psycho*, see Stephen Tifft's contribution to this volume (Chapter 8).
3 Stanley Cavell, "North-by-Northwest," in Marshall Deutelbaum and Leland Pougue, eds., *A Hitchcock Reader*, 2nd ed. (London: Wiley, 2009), p. 260.
4 Laura Mulvey, "Afterthoughts on 'Visual Pleasure and Narrative Cinema' inspired by King Vidor's *Duel in the Sun* (1946)," in *Visual and Other Pleasures* (Bloomington: Indiana University Press, 1989), pp. 31–40.
5 I am grateful to Heather Poole for bringing this context to my attention.
6 David Lyon, *Surveillance Studies: An Overview* (London: Polity, 2007), makes no mention of *Rear Window* in its treatment of surveillance films; the chapter on film inaugurates the genre with *The Conversation*. In Sébastian Lefait, *Surveillance on Screen: Monitoring Contemporary Films and Television Programs* (Lanham, MD: Scarecrow Press, 2013), it's Hitchcock's *Rope* that is briefly treated, not *Rear Window*.

7 For an extensive reading of these mini-narratives across the courtyard from Jeff, see John Fawell, *Rear Window: The Well-Made Film* (Carbondale: Southern Illinois University Press, 2001), pp. 72–109.

8 In the artwork, titled "Hunger," we learn, the body has a hole where the stomach should be: as such, it is at once an expression and a sublimation of the various hungers that Lisa, Miss Lonelyhearts, and even perhaps "Miss Torso" share throughout the film. John Fawell reads this hunger as women's sexual hunger for men, another example of the voracious lonely females Jeff encounters. Brigitte Peucker goes even further, seeing it as resonant of a form of cannibalism, and a negative counter to the composer's more positive creativity. See her book *The Material Image: Art and the Real in Film* (Stanford, CA: Stanford University Press, 2007), pp. 165ff. My own view is that in making art out of desire, both the composer and the sculptor suggest a road not taken by Jeff.

INDEX